The Rice Trade in Asia

This book analyses the development of the rice trade in Asia since 1945.

This book focuses on the three historically important exporters Myanmar, Thailand and Vietnam as well as the two key importers Indonesia and the Philippines. The book addresses the impacts of several major transitions during this period on the rice trade in these nations, namely their initial recovery post-war, the political turbulence during and following the independence struggles of these nations and the impact of the Vietnam War. It also tracks the fluctuating impact of the various *El Nino*/Southern Oscillation (*EN*SO) climatic events across the period on harvest and exports, for example, in events such as the rice crisis of 1973–1975.

Using data from the London Rice Brokers' Association Circular to create a detailed narrative of the rice trade, this book will be of interest to students and scholars of Asian history, economic history and economic development in post-war Asia.

A.J.H. Latham was Lecturer and Senior Lecturer in International Economic History at Swansea University and is now in active retirement.

Routledge Studies in the Modern History of Asia

187. **Coalition Navies during the Korean War**
Understanding Combined Naval Operations
*Edited by **Ian Bowers***

188. **Japanese Diplomacy and East Asian International Politics, 1918–1931**
Ryuji Hattori, Translated by Graham B. Leonard

189. **Nation Building in Japan, 1945–1952**
The Allied Occupation and the US-Japan Alliance
Peter K. Frost

190. **The European Discovery of Confucian Revolution**
The Classic Roots of Modern Regime Change in China, Japan, Korea and Vietnam
David Williams

191. **Cultures of Modernity and the U.S.-Japan Cold War Alliance**
Masami Kimura

192. **Sino-Muslims, Networks, and Identity in Late Imperial China**
Longstanding Natives and Dispersed Minorities
Shaodan Zhang

193. **Traditional Malay Monarchy**
Asbol bin Haji Mail

194. **Comfort Women of the Japanese Empire**
Colonial Rule and the Battle over Memory
Park Yu-Ha

194. **The Rice Trade in Asia**
A. J. H. Latham

For a full list of available titles please visit: https://www.routledge.com/Routledge-Studies-in-the-Modern-History-of-Asia/book-series/MODHISTASIA

The Rice Trade in Asia

A.J.H. Latham

Routledge
Taylor & Francis Group
LONDON AND NEW YORK

First published 2025
by Routledge
4 Park Square, Milton Park, Abingdon, Oxon OX14 4RN

and by Routledge
605 Third Avenue, New York, NY 10158

Routledge is an imprint of the Taylor & Francis Group, an informa business

British Library Cataloguing-in-Publication Data
A catalogue record for this book is available from the British Library

ISBN: 978-1-032-79596-6 (hbk)
ISBN: 978-1-032-79601-7 (pbk)
ISBN: 978-1-003-49291-7 (ebk)

DOI: 10.4324/9781003492917

Typeset in Times New Roman
by KnowledgeWorks Global Ltd.

To the Warden, Fellows and Staff of Merton College, Oxford

Contents

List of Tables

Acknowledgement

It would not have been possible to write this book without the goodwill of the London Rice Brokers' Association, who, many years ago, allowed me to copy and use the back copies of their monthly *Circular* for my research. I also subscribed for over 30 years.

Preface

I must thank everyone who has helped me in the course of writing this book, especially as always my wife, Dawn, and son, George, who have had to cope with the many hours over the years that I have been in my study not participating in family activities. I must also thank Heita Kawakatsu, Governor of Shizuoka Prefecture, and all the other members of the "Nichibunken" group at the International Research Centre for Japanese Studies in Kyoto for their discussions and encouragement when I visited over many years. I must also thank Larry Neal and his seminar group at the University of Illinois, Champaign-Urbana, where I was visiting Professor of Economics in 1979 and 1988. Similarly, I would like to thank Jeffrey Williamson and his seminar at Harvard, where I presented a paper and for his continuing interest in my research at many conferences. At Oxford, my thanks are to the late Peter Mathias, who invited me to give a paper at All Souls College, and who was also a regular visitor to the Nichibunken group. There are many others to whom I also owe a debt of gratitude and I must thank them all, including the anonymous reader for Routledge, whose suggestions have been included in the final text.

Glossary

A1 and 2	Burma broken rice grades
B1, 2 and 3	Burma broken rice grades
Basmati	Indian high grade rice
Bonlai	Taiwan variety of rice
Calrose	U.S. Californian variety of rice
cargo rice	80 per cent milled rice with the bran remaining mixed with 20 per cent paddy
ENSO	*El Nino*/Southern Oscillation
Emata	Burma variety of rice
faq	fair average quality
Food for Peace	See P.L.480
Gulf	U.S. Gulf of Mexico variety of rice
IRRI-6, IRRI-8	Special varieties of high yielding rice developed by the International Rice Research Institute, Los Banos, Philippines.
Joshi	Pakistan variety of rice
Khao Dok Mali 105	Thai variety of fragrant rice
Loonzain	The Burma name for cargo rice
Medoung* or *Meedone	Burma variety of rice
Milchar	Burma variety of rice
Ngatsaing* or *Ngatsein	The largest group of Burmese varieties, with short, bold, medium grain, fairly translucent and hard with good milling outcome
non-faq	*faq* means fair average quality, so *non-faq* means low quality.
parboiled rice	Paddy which has been steamed and dried prior to milling
paddy	Rice in the husk
Pathumthani 1	Thai variety of fragrant rice
P.L.480	U.S.A. Public Law 480 (Food for Peace)
rough rice	Paddy (occasionally cargo rice)
Small Mills Specials or SMS	Burma rice milled at small mills

Sughandi	Burma variety of rice
Ton	Tons here are metric tons (1,000 kilos) unless otherwise stated. In the early post-war period Burma (and India and Pakistan) often gave its figures in the *Circular* in the long ton, which measures 1,016 kilos or 2240 lbs and it is sometimes difficult to decide which ton specification is being used. Note that the difference between the metric ton and the long ton is very small, some 16 kilos.
urea	A fertiliser
U.S.D.A	United States Department of Agriculture
whole rice	Husked, milled or hand-pounded rice not containing broken grains smaller than three quarters of the whole grain. Sometimes just husked rice.
Yawg Yaw	Burma variety of rice of low quality
Zeera	Burma variety of rice

Note: 100% means 100% unbroken rice, which is the finest milling quality. But other percentage figures such as 5%, 10%, 15% and 25% give the percentage of brokens in the quantity. The higher the percentage of brokens, the lower the milling quality.

Introduction

This book is about the rice trade in Asia since 1945. It can be seen as a sequel to my book *Rice and Industrialisation in Asia* (Latham 2022), although it is not necessary to have read that book to understand this. From 1945, the intra-Asian rice trade was very different from that of the free market of the interwar years and was now largely controlled by the participating governments, both as exporters and importers. The move to government control had taken place in the 1930s in response to the depression and now continues. The focus is on the three historically most important rice-exporting countries: Myanmar (Burma), Vietnam (French Indo-China) and Thailand (Siam). Of these, Myanmar never recovered its pre-war dominance of the trade and moved into a protracted decline. By 1956, the mills there were not capable of producing high-quality grades, and the only European mill that still existed had not been working for two years, and there was no intention of re-opening it (*London Rice Brokers' Association Circular (LR-BAC)* 28th March 1956 3). For many years, Vietnam, too, was a minor participant due to political issues. Thailand, however, emerged as the major exporter. However, at the end of the 1980s, Vietnam suddenly re-appeared as a major exporter, although not as great as Thailand. Myanmar, however, remained a minor participant. Of the importing countries in Asia, the focus is on Indonesia (Dutch East Indies), which was a major purchaser, as was the Philippines, particularly when the region was hit by occurrences of the climatic fluctuation *El Nino*/Southern Oscillation (*EN*SO) as it was repeatedly (Latham 2009). These climatic fluctuations are a key feature of this study.

The book uses as its major source the *LRBAC*, which was published monthly from 16th July 1869 to 4th March 2014, and to which I have had privileged access. As far as I am aware, it has never previously been extensively used for academic research. However, I used it in my paper, "The International Trade in Rice and Wheat since 1868: A Study in Market Integration" (Latham 1986). I also used it for my book *Rice: The Primary Commodity* (Latham, 1998) and for my recent book *Rice and Industrialisation in Asia* (2022).

DOI: 10.4324/9781003492917-1

References

Fischer, W., McInnis, R.M., and Schneider, J. (Eds) (1986) *The Emergence of a World Economy, 1500-1914*, Wiesbaden, GmbH: Franz Steiner Verlag, *Part II, 1850-1914*. (Papers of the IXth International Congress of Economic History, Berne). Reprinted in N.F.R. Crafts (Ed.) (1996), *The Growth of the World Economy*, Vol 3. C. Knick Harley (Ed.) (1996), *The Integration of the World Economy, 1850-1914*, Vol 1, Cheltenham: Edward Elgar, 341–59. Reprinted in Latham and Kawakatsu (2011), *The Evolving Structure of the East Asian Economic System since 1700*, 44–61.

Latham, A.J.H. (1986) The International Trade in Rice and Wheat since 1868: A Study in Market Integration, in Fischer, McInnis and Schneider (1986), 645–663.

Latham, A.J.H. (1998) *Rice: The Primary Commodity*, London and New York: Routledge. In Japanese (1999) Tokyo: Norin Tokei Kyotai.

Latham, A.J.H. (2009a) Climatic Fluctuations and the International Rice Trade: A Preliminary Investigation, in Latham and Kawakatsu (2009), 221–33.

Latham, A.J.H. (2009b) *Intra-Asian Trade and Industrialisation. Essays in memory of Yasukichi Yasuba* (Ed. with Heita Kawakatsu), Abingdon and New York. Routledge. Paperback (2014).

Latham, A.J.H. (2022) *Rice and Industrialisation in Asia*, Abingdon and New York: Routledge.

Latham, A.J.H. and Kawakatsu, H. (2011), *The Evolving Structure of the East Asian Economic System since 1700: A Comparative Analysis*, Abingdon and New York: Routledge. Paperback (2016) Routledge.

1 The Asian rice trade 1945–1949

Up until the 1930s, there was a relatively free market for rice in Asia, but this declined abruptly as governments took control of the trade during the depression to ensure food supplies (Latham 2022 159–160). After the war, government control continued. At first, Burma (Myanmar), Siam (Thailand) and French Indo-China (Vietnam) resumed as major exporters. Later, in 1948, Burma became independent, and though it sustained its exporting activities for a while, it soon began to decline from which it never recovered. In French Indo-China, there was political turbulence, leading to the Vietnam War, and it soon ceased to be a major exporter, although it was to return to prominence in the 1990s.

The war years saw disruption and despair. Probably the best example of this was the Bengal Famine of 1943, which saw a possible doubling of the normal death rate and a much disputed loss of life of between 1.5 and 3 million. Burma was an important supplier of rice to Bengal, so when Rangoon fell to the invading Japanese army on 10th March 1942, there were inevitably serious repercussions in Bengal. Fear of an attack on the coastal districts of Bengal led to a "Denial Policy" in May 1942, in which 30,719 tons of surplus rice was purchased by government agents so that it could not be used by the Japanese if they invaded. Similarly, the military authorities commandeered boats capable of carrying more than ten passengers to prevent their use by the Japanese, some 46,146 boats out of a total of 66,563, crucial to transport and the distribution of rice in a vast area of river-based Bengal. These actions caused great disruption but were justified when there were five Japanese air raids on Calcutta itself between 20th and 28th December 1942. Traders left the city, shopkeepers closed up and the government requisitioned the rice stock of wholesale dealers to feed the city. The crisis had begun.

The causes of the subsequent famine have been a source of much debate. Bhatia argues that the stoppage of rice imports resulting from the fall of Burma should have been a warning to the authorities in India that the food situation in India had become critical. He accuses the provincial administration of incompetence and the central government of a callous disregard for its duties. Prices of rice rose rapidly and became beyond the reach of the poor, who began to starve. Eventually, large quantities of food grains did arrive in the last quarter of 1943, but for lack of storage facilities, they were stocked in the open covered

DOI: 10.4324/9781003492917-2

by tarpaulins in the Royal Botanical Gardens, where they rotted whilst people starved. It was not until the visit of the newly appointed Viceroy, Lord Wavell, at the end of October 1943 that the army came to help the civil authorities. Several thousand troops arrived in Calcutta between 11th and 27th November, and took on the work of moving foodstuffs and organising relief to bring the famine under control.

Sen, however, takes a novel approach. Amongst other things, he derides the need for the denial policy against the "possibly arriving Japanese", also referred to as the "elusive Japanese", arguing that the seizure of boats in particular interfered with river transport and fishing. In a closely argued paper, he shows that there was ample rice and foodstuffs, including wheat, in the province. Food availability was higher in 1943 than in 1941, when there was no famine. He argues that the real problem was that rapid inflation, caused by government emergency expenditures on defence measures, meant that rice prices rose sharply. People in rural areas, in particular, were unable to secure enough money from the exchange of the goods they produced or their labour to enable them to buy rice. In Sen's terms, rice exchange entitlements had shifted. Essentially, there was a distortion of the normal market relationships which ensured all could buy food, and food distribution was skewed in favour of those who could obtain sufficient inflated money to buy food. These were, in particular, those employed by government and in defence and industrial activities. It was a priority to keep Calcutta functioning to maintain the war effort. Deaths were concentrated not amongst the dwellers of Calcutta but among the rural poor, particularly those not actively involved in growing rice. So famine took place even though there was enough rice to feed everyone (Bhatia 1963 309–339. Sen 1981 52–85, 195–216) Mukerjee castigates the British authorities for the famine, and Churchill in particular, but fails to note the essential point that if there had been no war, there would have been no famine (Mukerjee 2010).

After the war, competition and the free market did not return. To begin with, the big three – Burma, Siam (Thailand from 1939) and French Indo-China – resumed their positions as major exporters. But after Burma (Myanmar from 1989) became independent from Britain in 1948, the government maintained such low prices for farmers that much of the incentive to grow rice was lost, exports declined, and the country ceased to be one of the great rice exporters. In French Indo-China (Vietnam from 1954), long-standing political turbulence continued through the 1970s, including the Vietnam War (Gunn 2014, Huff 2019). The turbulence, combined with government intervention, turned this major exporter into a major importer. However, by the 1990s, a substantial recovery had taken place. So for much of this period, only Thailand of the big three remained a major exporter, and even there, the government maintained control. But China, once a deficit country, emerged as an exporter, using the foreign currency thus obtained to buy greater quantities of wheat. Pakistan also became an exporter, but the big surprise of the post-war world was the emergence of the United States as a key exporter as a result of subsidised production and aided sales. Vietnam was, for a while, a major recipient! (Barker and Herdt 1985 188–189).

Table 1.1 Rice exports (selected countries) 1934–2010 (metric tons 000)

	Annual average							
	1934–1948	*1948–1952*	*1960*	*1970*	*1980*	*1990*	*2000*	*2010*
Myanmar	3070	1231	1721	640	653	213	251	592
Vietnam	1320	381	340	–	33	1624	3477	6892
Thailand	1388	1293	1220	1063	2791	4017	6141	8905
China	16	–	1173	1829	1376	405	3070	598
India	277	19	–	27	472	505	1532	2225
Pakistan	393	73	68	482	1086	743	2016	4178
USA	71	536	997	1740	3054	2473	2736	3747

Source: FAO *Trade Yearbooks*.

Table 1.2 Rice imports (selected countries) 1934–2010 (metric tons 000)

	Annual average							
	1934–1948	*1948–1952*	*1960*	*1970*	*1980*	*1990*	*2000*	*2010*
India	2,094	779[a]	698	582	19	66	13	–
Bangladesh	–	–	323[b]	510	548	380	260[e]	679
Sri Lanka	530	425	528	544	168	131	14	150
Malay/Sgpr	718	511	641[c]	366	167	330	595	930
Singapore	–	–	–	293	188	220	355	310
Indonesia	280	383	962	956	2011	49	1355	685
Philippines	37	92	–	–	–	592	642	2,378
Vietnam[d]	–	–	14	891	451	1	–	–
China	704	127	27	5	130	62	244	363
Hong Kong	522	163	369	344	359	374	309	340
Japan	1757	525	174	18	13	18	655	663

Source: FAO *Trade Yearbooks*.

[a] Excludes Pakistan and Bangladesh from 1948.
[b] Figure is for Pakistan which included Bangladesh.
[c] Includes Sabah and Sarawak from 1960.
[d] Includes Cambodia (Kampuchea).
[e] FAO estimate.

Only about 5 per cent of rice produced now reached international trade, and this after individual countries had supplied their own needs. Deals between countries were now done on a government-to-government basis, as they controlled rice supplies within their own domestic markets. Whether this was done efficiently is open to question. The application of modern technology advanced faster in wheat production than in rice, so wheat prices dropped relative to rice. In consequence, consumption of imported wheat rose in many rice-producing countries, including Vietnam, Indonesia, the Philippines, China and even Japan. If the constraint of government control led to rice-eating countries coming to depend on cheap imported wheat, one may reflect upon the ultimate benefit of the elimination of competition and the free market in rice! (Barker and Herdt 1985 185–201. Siamwalla and Haykin 1983 9–35). The discovery of a process using wheat to make noodles suitable for inclusion in Asian diets was a key feature in facilitating wheat imports in Asia (Kaneko 2009, also cited in Latham and Kawakatsu, 2009).

Table 1.3 Rice exports (selected countries) 1945–1950 (metric tons 000)

	Annual average						
	1934–1938	*1945*	*1946*	*1947*	*1948*	*1949*	*1950*
Myanmar	3070	–	424	807	1235	1193	1197
Vietnam	1320	44	100	67	190	104	115
Thailand	1388	194	455	385	811	1215	1508
China	12	–	–	–	–	–	20
India	254	–	–	–	–	–	–
Pakistan	393	–	300	331	145	–	–
U.S.A.	71	330	374	436	394	515	492

Source: FAO *Trade Yearbooks*.

Table 1.4 Rice imports (selected countries) 1945–1950 (metric tons 000)

	Annual average						
	1934–1938	*1945*	*1946*	*1947*	*1948*	*1949*	*1950*
India	1701	–	362	485	867	767	358
Bangladesh	–	–	–	–	–	–	–
Sri Lanka	530	181	257	263	416	403	498
Malay/Sgpr	718	–	284	271	458	526	464
China	704	–	205	360	580	410	90
Hong Kong	522	–	105	143	124	75	196
Indonesia	280	–	98	116	139	276	331
Philippines	37	–	222	70	120	145	3
Vietnam	3	–	6	–	–	–	–
Japan	1,757	–	16	2	56	130	671

Source: FAO *Trade Yearbooks*.

If the government controlled international rice trade from 1945 lacks the individual detail of the rice trade of earlier years, it is not without its own drama. The London Rice Brokers' Association did not publish their circular from the 24th March 1942 until 30th April 1947. This edition begins with the words "It is to be hoped opportunities will present themselves to enable this Association to recommence publication of reports though the information available is so far restricted" (*London Rice Brokers' Association Circular* (*LRBAC)* 30th April 1947 1). But the next edition was not until 10th June! (*LRBAC* 19th June 1947). The August edition carried an extract from *The Economist* of 19th July headed "RICE SITUATION", which stated that the rice-producing countries had been seriously affected by the war and rehabilitation had been slow. The weather had been unfavourable over the last two seasons in the major exporting areas, and acreage in Burma, French Indo-China and Siam was little more than half pre-war levels. There was little labour available to clear paddy fields, and farmers had fled outlying areas due to military activities. Political and financial instability had discouraged production. Transport facilities had been destroyed or worn out during the war and needed replacement, and a shortage of consumer goods, particularly textiles, was aggravating inflation. World output of rough rice (i.e. paddy) in 1946–1947 was 5 per cent below the pre-war level of 106 million tons, but in the main exporting countries, Burma, French Indo-China and Siam, production was only about 60 per cent of the 1935–1939 figure. Exports in 1946–1947 were very small, and prospects for 1947–1948 were also poor. The pre-war level of output would not be enough to feed the people in these areas, as the population was estimated to have risen by 10–15 per cent (*LR-BAC* 22nd August 1947 1).

Of the three great exporters, Burma, Siam and French Indo-China, Burma was initially alone in reporting a steady gain in acreage after the war (*LRBAC* 24th October 1947 1). A State Agricultural Marketing Board was set up to replace the Agricultural Projects Board set up two years previously and would handle the processing and marketing of agricultural produce in Burma, including the procurement and export of rice (*LRBAC* 20th November 1947 1). On 5th January 1948, the Siamese government announced the abolition of the Government Rice Purchasing Bureau and the transfer of its functions to the government-operated Thai Rice Company in order to protect Siam's rice trade and prevent low-quality rice being exported. It would also build up stocks for local consumption and handle the country's entire distribution of paddy to the mills, nine of which it already operated itself (*LRBAC* 14th January 1948 2). Recovery continued in the big three, with favourable weather and harvest in the three countries estimated at 28 per cent up on the previous year and 46 per cent up on the year before that. Acreage was expanding rapidly in Burma but needed to expand considerably to match pre-war output, and there were acreage increases also in Siam, though exports were only running at 45–60 per cent of pre-war figures. Exports were recovering in French Indo-China but were hampered by political conditions in the country (*LRBAC* 10th August 1948 2).

The political situation then began to deteriorate in Burma, causing an almost complete suspension of rice exports (*LRBAC* 13th September 1948 1). There were disturbances in some of the rice-growing districts, which threatened expected export growth, and although the exportable surplus continued to grow in Siam, the political situation in French Indo-China remained unstable, limiting export expansion (*LRBAC* 15th October 1948 1). In the end, Burma's 1948 exports were only 41 per cent of the pre-war average because of the political situation, and 1949 exports were expected to be worse, with Siam now the leading exporter. Similarly, the political situation in French Indo-China ensured that exports in 1948 were only 12 per cent of the pre-war level (*LRBAC* 25th January 1949 1). The Burma Government planned in 1949 for a cultivated area similar to that in 1948, but this depended on clearing the Irrawaddy Delta of insurgents (*LRBAC* 17th June 1949 1). Meanwhile, in India, Premier Pandit Nehru launched a drive to increase food production, as India needed to import about 10 per cent of its food, mainly wheat and rice. Other foods were to be consumed as much as possible (presumably sorghums and millets), and wheat was substituted for rice wherever it could be, as it was half the price of rice, keeping the import bill down (*LRBAC* 26th July 1949 1). Back in Burma U Ba Gyan, the Minister of Agriculture announced that rice production would be down for 1950 because continuing disturbances were preventing rice planting (*LRBAC* 23 November 1949 1). The United States Department of Agriculture (USDA) later reported that rough rice production in Asia's traditional surplus areas, Thailand, Burma and Indo-China, was down to 14,965,000 tons for the period 1949–1950, a reduction of 816,000 tons from the preceding year and 3,174,000 tons less than the pre-war average. Burma's acreage was 21 per cent or 2,070,000 acres, below that of 1948–1949, and production was 16 per cent less. The crop was estimated at only 57 per cent of the pre-war average. Conditions were similar in Indo-China, and production had been declining since 1947–1948. But in Thailand, production had continued to increase since the war, and official estimates for 1949–1950 stood at 5,414,000 tons of rough rice (*LRBAC* 28th June 1950 1).

USDA also reported that production had also increased steadily in the Philippines since the war, with the 1949–1950 crop considerably above that of 1948–1949, despite infestation by army worms in the seed beds and plantings delayed by insufficient rainfall. The harvest of 1949–1950 was estimated at 2,585,000 tons of rough rice, compared with 2,494,000 tons in 1948–1949 and 1,623,000 tons in 1945–1946. Pre-war 1935–1936 to 1939–1940 production averaged 2,131,000 tons (*LRBAC* 29th June 1950 2).

References

Barker, Randolph and Herdt, Robert W., with Beth Rose (1985) *The Rice Economy of Asia*, Washington, DC.: Resources for the Future.

Bhatia, B.M. (1963) *Famines in India: A Study in Some Aspects of the Economic History of India (1860–1945)* London: Asia Publishing House.

FAO Trade Yearbooks. See also faostat.fao.org

Gunn, Geoffrey C. (2014) *Rice Wars in Colonial Vietnam. The Great Famine and the Viet Minh Road to Power*, Lanham, MD: Rowman & Littlefield.

Huff, Greg (2019) Causes and consequences of the Great Vietnam Famine 1944–5, *Economic History Review* 72 (1) 286–316.

Kaneko, Shinsuke (2009) *The Global Wheat Trade and the Industrialisation of Monsoon Asia, 1951–2001*, in Latham and Kawakatsu (2009) 234–248.

Latham, A.J.H. (2022) *Rice and Industrialisation in Asia*, Abingdon and New York: Routledge.

Latham, A.J.H. and Kawakatsu, Heita (Eds) (2009) *Intra-Asian Trade and Industrialisation, Essays in Memory of Yasukichi Yasuba*, Abingdon and New York: Routledge. Routledge Paperback (2014).

Mukerjee, Madhusree (2010) *Churchill's Secret War: The British Empire and the Ravaging of India during World War II*, New York: Basic Books.

Sen, Amartya (1981) *Poverty and Famines: An Essay on Entitlement and Deprivation*, Oxford and New York: Oxford University Press.

Siamwalla, A. and Haykin, Stephen (1983) *The World Rice Market: Structure, Conduct and Performance*, Washington, DC: International Food Policy Research Institute.

2 The Asian rice trade 1950–1959

The narrative of the rice trade in Asia in the troubled post-war years is continued, particularly focussing on the situation in Burma as it deteriorated. Before the war, Burma had been the leading Asian rice exporter, but now exports were only a third of pre-war levels and Thailand vied with Burma as an exporter. Vietnam was suffering from its own political problems and is rarely mentioned. In pre-war days, rice and wheat were sold at similar prices, but now wheat was five times the pre-war level, and rice eight times, and Asian countries were importing wheat rather than rice.

Table 2.1 Rice exports (selected countries) 1950–1960 (metric tons 000)

	1950	*1951*	*1952*	*1953*	*1954*	*1955*	*1956*	*1957*	*1958*	*1959*	*1960*
Myanmar	1197	1268	1261	969	1460	1640	1863	1753	1410	1692	1721
Vietnam	115	332	230	196	354	96	–	183	112	245	340
Thailand	1508	1612	1413	1342	1001	1236	1263	1570	1143	1091	1220
China	20	120	192	268	293	623	976	485	1265	1661	1173
India	–	–	–	–	5	104	43	–	–	–	–
Pakistan	–	206	14	89	139	223	59	–	1	69	68
U.S.A.	492	491	790	696	555	516	819	734	568	685	997

Source: FAO *Trade Yearbooks*.

Table 2.2 Rice imports (selected countries) 1950–1960 (metric tons 000)

	1950	*1951*	*1952*	*1953*	*1954*	*1955*	*1956*	*1957*	*1958*	*1959*	*1960*
India	358	761	733	192	612	269	325	745	396	295	698
Bangladesh	–	–	–	–	–	–	–	–	–	–	–
Sri Lanka	498	402	405	410	402	385	491	522	482	583	528
Malay/Sgpr	464	581	527	546	321	547	591	527	640	535	641
Singapore	–	–	–	–	–	–	–	–	–	–	–
Indonesia	331	408	759	358	258	126	763	563	681	604	962
Philippines	3	129	63	–	42	63	42	120	220	6	–
Vietnam	–	–	–	–	–	–	27	17	1	4	14
China	90	20	15	4	–	157	86	111	11	–	27
Hong Kong	196	185	236	311	107	263	282	313	381	353	369
Japan	671	792	978	1079	1432	1246	759	347	505	277	174

Source: FAO *Trade Yearbooks*.

DOI: 10.4324/9781003492917-3

In 1951, Burma formed four syndicates or companies to deal with rice exports, under the direction of the State Agricultural Marketing Board, one for Europe, one for Africa, one for the Red Sea and Persian Gulf and one for the Far east, but prices were prohibitively high (*London Rice Brokers' Association Circular* (*LRBAC*) 27th April 1951, 1). Political problems remained and bandits continued to disrupt production, leaving 2,600,000 acres of rice land idle. Factors preventing the recovery of the land included banditry, the condition of the abandoned fields, a shortage of livestock for draught, land nationalisation, the lack of an efficient credit system and a shortage of labour (*LRBAC* 10th October 1951 1). At the end of the year, insurgents damaged railway bridges and railway lines, including the Prome line, which was likely to affect supplies of *Sughandi* qualities of rice-reaching Rangoon (*LRBAC* 4th January 1952 1). Then in 1952, the four syndicates were abolished, with the Authorities reserving about two-thirds of the export surplus for government-to-government transactions under their control, the rest for private trade (*LRBA*C 30th January 1952 2).

There was a great need for rice in Southeast Asia, because in pre-war days, Burma exported about 3,250,000 tons, but this had fallen to 1,250,000 tons owing to the Japanese invasion during the war, and the continuing political unrest which followed. What rice was available for export in the region, particularly from Burma, Siam and French Indo China, went mostly to Japan, which had access to the U.S. Dollar, now the key currency for purchasing rice (*LRBAC* 22nd April 1952 1). Before the war, India had imported annually about 1,500,000 tons of rice, mainly from Burma. But in 1951, it took only 545,000 tons of rice from Burma and Thailand out of a total of grain imports of 4,700,000 tons, importing wheat and flour, maize, barley and rye to fill the gap. Rice was at an abnormally high price, but the other grains were half the price of rice (*LRBAC* 13th May 1952 3–4). By August 1952, rice, which before the war had cost £5 to £6 per ton, was costing over £75 per ton, driving India and other countries to substitute wheat and other cheaper cereals (*LRBAC* 20th August 1952 1).

In June 1952, Saigon temporarily banned rice exports from French Indo-China to try and stop speculation in rice, because the price of rice had risen enormously (*LRBAC* 6th June 1952 1). Meanwhile Thailand, quite apart from government-to-government deals, was exporting in normal private commercial trade to Indonesia, which could pay the high prices currently obtained for rice. Total Thai exports were expected in 1952 to return to pre-war levels of 1,500,000 to 1,600,000 tons (*LRBAC* Supplement June 1952 1–2). Thai exports to the Philippines were also substantial as the 1951–1952 rice crop there had been reduced by dry weather and infestation of the rice stem borer (*LRBAC* 1st April 1952 2).

The FAO reported that per capita food production was still well below pre-war levels, and rice production had failed to expand in 1951–1952. Exports from Burma were hardly a third of pre-war days, and the situation in French Indo-China was similar (*LRBAC* 18th November 1952 1). Those in the rice trade believed the scarcity in Southeast Asia was because exports from the region were only half what they had been before the war. In Burma's case, this was because of continuing unrest, and the very high prices which were far from being an incentive were actually a disincentive to production, because of the enormous profit which could be achieved without extra effort or output (*LRBAC* 1st December 1952 1).

In April 1953 an Indian trade delegation to Rangoon failed to agree to a barter deal for 500,000 tons of Burma rice worth Rs 400,000,000, because Burma only needed Indian commodities worth Rs 240,000,000 (*LRBAC* 30th April 1953 1). Then Burma announced it was withdrawing from the Ottawa Trade Agreement of the British Empire of 1932 as from 30th September (*LRBAC* 26th May 1953 1). Burma was gradually disengaging from the outside world. In June 400,000 tons of milled rice lay in the ports of Burma, as buyers would not buy at the prices on offer. Before the war, buyers and sellers dealt with the bulk of the rice crop in the early months of the year to ship it before the monsoon set in, so it arrived at its destination in good condition. However, although it was now a month into the monsoon season, these large quantities had still not been sold (*LRBAC* 30th June 1953 3). But in July, Burma sold 400,000 tons of rice in government-to-government deals at £60 per ton, and another 200,000 tons in private trade at £9–15 per ton higher. Of this, Indonesia bought 120,000 tons in government-to-government deals and 60,000 tons in private deals, Japan 107,000 tons, plus 43,000 tons and Ceylon 90,000 tons and 45,000 tons (*LRBAC* 28th July 1953 1). It was then reported that Burma was abandoning the tender system for private non-government-to-government sales, and bids from overseas buyers would be considered by the State Agricultural Marketing Board (*LRBAC* 28th August 1953 2). Yet Burma still had large unsold stocks and was desperate to sell them before they deteriorated. Despite prices being reduced, buyers were reluctant to buy because they too feared the rice would be damaged, even if it was re-milled and re-bagged before shipment (*LRBAC* 30th October 1953 1). Now the Japanese government announced the rice harvest could be the worst for 40 years due to floods and a typhoon (*LRBAC* 30th October 1953 3). It was in fact the worst since 1934, and the government would import at least 1,600,000 tons of rice (*LRBAC* 25th November 1953 2). Of this, 300,000 tons were to come from Burma of poor-quality *Ngatsein* Small Mills Specials (SMS) 42 per cent broken (*LRBAC* 15th December 1953 1). Later, figures indicated that in 1953, Japan imported 1,057,000 metric tons, of which Burma supplied 189,000 tons, Thailand 418,000 tons and the United States 160,000 tons (*LRBAC* 21st May 1954 2). In February 1954, Burma sold 700,000 tons of old crop rice Small Mills Specials to India, and was negotiating to sell India a further 600,000 tons of new crop (*LRBAC* 25th February 1954 1).

But Burma still had a carryover from the previous season together with Siam of about 1,000,000 tons. Before the war, this did not happen and only happened now because the exporting countries were selling government to government as much rice as they could at the highest prices, and not offering any reductions. So consumers were turning to wheat and other cereals, and private buying had declined (*LRBAC* 22nd April 1954 1). The situation was made worse by buyers for governments which imported rice insisting they also had a price reduction if an exporting government subsequently sold rice to another government at a lower price. This forced the governments of exporting countries to maintain the high prices of their main deals, and let rice stay in store and deteriorate. This was leading to a situation where even larger stocks of unsold and spoiled rice would be carried over into 1955. It would probably end up as animal feed (*LRBAC* 21st May 1954 1. *LRBAC* 25th August 1954 1).

In pre-war days, rice and wheat sold at roughly the same price, but by 1954, sterling prices were five times the pre-war level, and rice prices were eight times higher. So in 1953 Asian countries together imported 6,500,000 tons of wheat, but only 3,000,000 tons of rice. Burma and Siam were left with over 1,750,000 tons of unsold rice (*LRBAC* 22nd June 1954 1). By now, European buyers had lost interest in Burma rice. Before the war, Europe was the second-largest buyer of Burma rice in 1938, taking 800,000 tons of rice including byproducts and 300,000 tons of bran. But pre-war qualities like *Ngatsein* Super Cleaned 5 per cent brokens, *Sughandi* Super Cleaned 5 per cent brokens, and *Sughandi* and Bassein *Loonzain* were no longer available at reasonable prices. The authorities were prepared to sell to commercial buyers at the same price as government contracts, but this would mean high prices for Small Mills Specials 42 per cent brokens new crop 1953/54 and European buyers were not interested. (Ed. with a milling rate of 42 per cent brokens, this was poor-quality rice). Undefined quantities of Small Mills Specials 42 per cent brokens from 1952 and 1953 crops were also on offer at considerable discounts (*LRBAC* 25th August 1954 2).

The situation in Burma and Siam continued to deteriorate. Rice exports from Burma between January and August 1954 were 1,025,643 tons out of the new crop export surplus of 1,400,000 tons, not counting the carryover from the previous year of 700,000 tons, and unspecified quantities left from the 1952/53 crop (*LRBAC* 29th October 1954 2). In Siam, by the end of September, only 750,000 tons had been sold out of an exportable surplus of 1,800,000 tons (*LRBAC* 29th October 1954 3). Then the Singapore government announced it was removing all restrictions on the import and sale of rice. In pre-war days, Singapore had been a major re-distribution centre in the intra-Asian rice trade (*LRBAC* 29th October 1954 1). So the first post-war imports of open market Burma rice, some several thousand tons, were expected to arrive in early 1955 (*LRBAC* 28th January 1955 1). China too agreed to buy 150,000 long tons of Burma rice in a pact by which China would buy Burma Small Mills Specials rice, and Burma would buy Chinese exports such as cotton and silk yarns, piece goods and fruit (*LRBAC* 30th November 1954 2). This agreement was extended so that China would import annually from Burma 150,000 to 200,000 tons of rice from 1955 to 1957. In 1955, China was to pay for Small Mills Specials rice from the 1954 crop (*LRBAC* 30th December 1954 1). Japan also bought 220,000 tons of new crop Burma *Ngatsein* Small Mills Specials (*LRBAC* 30th December 1954 2).

Echoing the return to free market conditions which had just taken place in Singapore, it was rumoured in Bangkok that the rice trade there was to be returned to private hands as from lst January 1955. But shippers would have to sell about 50 per cent of their foreign currency earnings to the government at the official rate of exchange (*LRBAC* 30th December 1954 3). This turned out to be true (*LRBAC* 28th January 1955 3). Burma followed suit, and private firms of any nationality were to be allowed to export any of the 1955 crop to any country except those with which the State Marketing Board had a contract. However, the rice would have to be obtained from the State Marketing Board, which fixed the prices, and these were too high to attract Western purchasers (*LRBAC* 29th January 1955 2). But old Burma hands Steel Brothers & Co. were soon quoting new crop 1954–1955 *Ngatsein* SMS, No.2 Rice, *Ngatsein Loonzein*, *Medoung Loonzein*, and *Sughandi Loonzein* (*LRBAC* 25th February 1955 2). It was also announced in Rangoon that 200,000 tons of rice had been sold in government-to-government contracts to Poland, Czechoslovakia, Hungary and East Germany. The Czech government were taking £3,000,000 worth of rice, the East German government 50,000 tons of rice that year and £3,000,000 worth each year for the next three years and Hungary was taking 20,000 tons. All these transactions were essentially "barter" transactions in exchange for engineering goods. Negotiations were continuing with the Polish government (*LRBAC* 30th March 1955 1). But buyers in Western Europe continued to show little interest at the prices on offer (*LRBAC* 26th May 1955 1).

If Burma and Siam were making news, French Indo-China (Vietnam) was now rarely mentioned. Japanese occupation followed by the war for independence from the French had reduced the rice exports to a trickle. But after the French were defeated at Dien Bien Fu in May 1954, Vietnam was partitioned into North and South, and later that year, the French withdrew from the South. Now a Franco-Vietnamese trade agreement was announced by which Vietnam would supply France with 115,000 tons of rice at a preferential tariff 30 per cent below normal export duty (*LRBAC* 30th March 1955 2).

In London, *The Times*, on 2nd June 1955, discussed the current glut of rice and described it as Burma's major economic problem. Rice traders argued the glut was due to the high price of rice relative to wheat, but Burmese sources said the problem was the disappearance of the traditional markets of India, China and Japan. The *Circular* agreed, pointing out that the average pre-war imports of rice to India were 1,500,000 metric tons and no wheat, but by 1952 rice imports were down to 704,000 metric tons, and wheat imports were running at 2,251,100 metric tons. In 1953, rice imports were 221,000 metric tons and wheat 1,578,000 metric tons, and in 1954, 560,000 metric tons for rice and 345,000 metric tons for wheat. As for Japan, pre-war imports of rice ran at 1,732,000 metric tons on average, and no wheat, but by 1952, rice imports were down to 856,000 metric tons, but wheat imports were now 1,640,000 metric tons. In 1953, the figures for rice were 1,003,000 metric tons, and wheat 1,867,000 metric tons and in 1954, the figures were 1,006,000 metric tons for rice and 2,088,000 metric tons for wheat. Clearly, large quantities of wheat were now being imported to both India and Japan, which before the war had taken almost none. These wheat imports substantially replaced rice imports and also augmented them. To make matters worse for Burma, Europe had previously imported from Burma about 500,000 tons of rice and broken rice yearly, but this market was now practically lost. In 1937, European imports of rice from Burma had been 432,174 tons and in 1938, 459,148 tons, but by 1953, the figure was down to 17,600 tons and in 1954 (11 months), 38,900 tons (*LRBAC* 21st June 1955 1).

In an attempt to re-introduce Burma qualities to Europe, the State Agricultural Marketing Board (S.A.M.B) shipped some 12–15,000 tons of *Ngatsein*, *Medoung* and Koykyee *Loonzain* for the main Continental European ports, but at prices unlike to attract any interest (*LRBAC* 21st June 1955 1). However, an agreement was made with Russia, by which Burma would supply 150,000–200,000 tons of rice in a barter exchange for machinery, paper, medicines, chemicals, etc. A further agreement was made for Burma to supply East Germany with 42,000 tons of rice from the 1953, 1954 and 1955 crops (*LRBAC* 27th July 1955 2). Around 30,000 tons were to be shipped in August 1955 under the Russian barter agreement (*LRBAC* 25th August 1955 1). Then it was announced that the Soviet government had offered to co-operate with Burma in programmes of agricultural development, major irrigation works and the establishment of industrial plants, taking rice in payment (*LRBAC* 29th December 1955 1).

The Burma State Marketing Board now announced that they had signed contracts to supply Japan with 250,000 tons of rice and 30,000 tons for Okinawa, and negotiations were in progress to sell 50,000 tons to the Philippines. A three-year agreement had also been made with Romania, by which in the first year Burma would supply 20,000 tons of rice in exchange for machinery. A Yugoslav delegation was in Burma discussing a similar deal, by which 50,000 tons of rice was to be supplied annually for the next five years in exchange for capital goods and consumer goods (*LRBAC* 29th February 1956 1). The Marketing Board also announced that they would allow private traders to buy selected qualities, well milled and with a small percentage of brokens. But they then turned down sales of high-grade *Ngatsein* to the United Kingdom as not being of suitable quality. The quality of *Sughandi* Super 5 per cent was also said to be unsatisfactory. In addition to other defects, the rice contained "white bellies". By this time, the mills in Burma were not capable of producing high-quality grades, and the only European mill that still existed had not been working for two years, and there was no intention of reopening it (*LRBAC* 28th March 1956 3). In general, European buyers had no interest in Burma rice at current prices (*LRBAC* 28th March 1956 3).

The Burmese and Soviet governments signed a trade agreement on 1st April 1956, extending the three-year trade pact between the two countries. Under the new agreement, the Soviet Union would take 400,000 tons yearly for the following four years in exchange for Soviet machinery and other goods (*LRBAC* 30th April 1956 1). But then the Burmese Prime Minister announced that in future, Burma wanted cash for its rice, rather than the recent barter agreements it had been doing with Communist countries (*LRBAC* 31st May 1956 1). This was followed by an announcement from New Delhi that India had agreed to purchase 2,000,000 tons of Burma rice spread over the next five years, at below current prices (*LRBAC* 31st May 1956 3. *LRBAC* 25th June 1956 3). This was followed by news from Bonn that West Germany had signed a three-year agreement with Burma for rice in exchange for investment goods and expertise for the development of the Burmese industry (*LRBAC* 26th July 1956 1).

Rice exports from Burma for the first half of 1956 were estimated at about 940,000 tons, the highest level since the war (*LRBAC* 29th Aug 1956 1). It was reported from Rangoon that the United States was to buy $US 1,100,000 worth of Burma rice to be sent to Pakistan (*LRBAC* 26th July 1956 1). Clearly, there were problems in Pakistan, as it had recently bought 60,000 tons of rice from China, which had also given Pakistan 4,000 tons as a present (*LRBAC* 26th July 1956 4). These 60,000 tons turned out to be Burma rice from a previous triangular agreement between Ceylon, Burma and China (*LRBAC* 29th August 1956 4). But by December, the situation in Pakistan was easing and the free market price of rice in East Pakistan was falling. Pakistan was negotiating with Burma and Thailand for another 100,000 tons of rice (*LRBAC* 19th December 1956 2).

In the autumn, a delegation from the Burma State Marketing Board toured Europe, examining milling, dock and storage facilities, with a view to improving these facilities in Burma. They also made it known that they did not find the barter agreements they had been entering into entirely satisfactory and wanted to operate normal commercial trade in future. 300,000 tons from the next season's crop were to be set aside for ordinary commercial sales (*LRBAC* 24th October 1956 1).

Meanwhile, in Siam, the Bangkok millers petitioned the government to reduce export premiums on all commercial sales of rice due to lack of business (*LRBAC* 26th September 1956 1). In January 1957, it was estimated that Thailand had an export surplus of 1,500,000 tons, of which 200,000 tons had been put into emergency stocks, leaving 1,300,000 tons for shipping. But the upcountry farmers were holding back paddy in the hope of further price raises, and rice millers who had committed themselves to large sales were finding it difficult to find the paddy for milling except at higher prices (*LRBAC* 29th January 1957 2). The crop harvested in December 1956 was possibly one of the largest on record, with the export surplus expected to be 1,500,000 metric tons, about 250,000 metric tons more than the previous year (*LRBAC* 26th February 1957 1).

Now it was the turn of Indonesia to experience problems, and it announced it was to import 700,000 tons of rice from Burma, Siam and other countries (*LRBAC* 29th January 1957 3).

In Burma, plans were being made to speed up rice exports by loading directly from mill to ship, rather than mill to lighter to ship. This would require the dredging of channels and the construction of pontoons. A start was to be made at Bassein, with improvements costing £45,000 and similar improvements were to follow at Rangoon at about double the cost (*LRBAC* 26th February 1957 2). The forecast for the rice crop was 6,361,000 long tons of paddy from 10,032,300 acres, some 600,000 tons more than the previous year, allowing exports of some 400,000–450,000 tons. This forecast took into account possible weather conditions, but not the activities of insurgents, which could be more destructive than the weather. Clearly, Burma's internal political problems remained. Because of government-to-government transactions and barter deals with Communist states, Burma was in a strong position as regards exports, and would not have enough left for all her potential cash customers. Pakistan had bought 50,000 tons and wanted another 50,000 tons later if stocks were available. Malaya too had bought 30,000 tons (*LRBAC* 29th March 1957 1). Government-to-government sales from the new crop, which came on the market in February 1957, were soon over 1,200,000 tons of whole rice, and Burma had outstanding barter agreements of about 1,000,000 tons, although these would not be entirely fulfilled as the authorities wanted to increase government-to-government sales and reduce the quantities for the barter agreements and for the private trade (*LRBAC* 30th April 1957 1). Nonetheless, a few thousand tons of *Loonzain* afloat and shipping were sold to West Germany, which included *Medoung* and *Ngatsein* in what seems to have been a barter agreement. Some small sales had been made to Trinidad and Barbados under a government-to-government agreement (*LRBAC* 29th May 1957). Further, government-to-government deals were done with China for 50,000 tons, Yugoslavia for 30,000 tons and Pakistan for 25,000 tons (*LRBAC* 28th June 1957 1).

In Indonesia, problems continued and the U.S. Department of Agriculture estimated 800,000 tons would be required, but the Indonesian authorities thought it would only be 300,000 tons (*LRBAC* 28th June 1957 3). It was reported from Saigon that South Vietnam was negotiating a sale of salt and rice to Indonesia in exchange for petrol. Pakistan had bought 20,000 tons of Vietnam rice No. 1 40 per cent brokens for July shipment and wanted more, and the Philippines were also seeking 40,000 tons (*LRBAC* 31st July 1957 2). This was the first news from Saigon for some considerable time.

Another country with problems was Ceylon. Ceylon needed 700,000 tons of rice a year to meet its internal rationing supply needs. With 200,000 of rice from a barter deal with China for rubber, and about 200,000 tons from Burma, plus its own domestic production, it should have had enough. But drought had cut internal production to no more than 200,000 tons, and the final outcome would not be clear until the second crop was harvested in January or February (*LRBAC* 30th August 1957 1. *LRBAC* 27th September 2. *LRBAC* 25th October 1957 1).

In Siam, the government imposed restrictions on exports to conserve supplies. The monsoon had come late, and the new crop would be a month late, and smaller than the current crop. Export licences for the private trade in the second half of the year were to be limited to 30 per cent of the amount actually exported in the first half of the year, but government-to-government contracts would not be affected (*LRBAC* 30th August 1957 2). By the end of October, 1,370,000 tons had already been exported, and it was expected that by the end of the year, the declared exportable surplus of 1,400,000 tons would have been exceeded. Fortunately, however, despite the lateness of the monsoon, conditions had improved, and the predicted exportable surplus was now 1,200,000 tons, although trade circles thought this was conservative. However, due to floods, the new crop was going to be late, and the export quotas remained in place, so sellers were reluctant to commit themselves to new crop sales (*LRBAC* 29th November 1957 3).

The problems continued in Indonesia, which was one of the few countries which still bought rice from Vietnam. It now bought 100,000 tons of rice for delivery by 31st December, of which 25,000 tons came from North Vietnam, 25,000 tons from Burma and 50,000 tons from Italy (*LRBAC* 27th September 1957 3). The old crop surplus in South Vietnam was now very small, but the Vietnamese authorities expected to export 250,000 tons of rice and byproducts in 1958 (*LRBAC* 29th November 1957 2). However, in December, the South Vietnam government suspended all exports for Franc and Sterling payments, and only sales in U.S. Dollars were to be continued (*LRBAC* 21st December 1957 2).

Things seem to have taken a turn for the worse in Burma politically, and no accurate forecast could be made for the crops owing to the disturbed state of the country. In 1958, owing to low rainfall, the exportable surplus was not expected to exceed 1,400,000 tons, and perhaps not even that, compared with average exports of 1,500,000 tons or more in good years. Burma had been shipping over 2,000,000 tons in the last two financial years ending 30th September, 1956 and 1957, not because crops had been increasing but because shipments included carryovers from previous years. It was still possible to tender for surpluses from 1953, 1954, 1955 and 1956 crops (*LRBAC* 29th November 1957 1). This reveals how ineptly Burma's export programme had been handled. Then it was announced that Burma was to use US$5,400,000 of U.S. Aid to restore cultivation in 1,200,000 acres of rice land in the Irrawaddy Delta, which had been lying idle since the end of the war in 1945 (*LRBAC* 23rd December 1957 1). But the total crop for the year was only expected to be 5,200,000 tons of paddy, compared to 6,360,000 tons the previous year. There would only be 950,000 tons of rice and byproducts, including a small carryover from previous crops for export in 1958. Because of the disturbed state of the country, it was difficult to get proper estimates, but private sources thought the surplus would actually be closer to 1,300,000 tons of rice and byproducts, including a small carryover from previous crops. It was thought that by setting exports at 950,000 tons, the Burma government was keeping a reserve in case there were shortages later in the year, particularly in Central and Upper Burma. These regions were normally self-supporting but had suffered badly from shortage of rain. Existing long-term commitments to countries, mainly in Asia, would easily take up 950,000 tons, and further requests which the government had received would bring total requirements to 1,300,000 tons. So Burma would have little whole rice for private sale in the coming year (*LRBAC* 30th January 1958 1).

In Siam, the estimated export surplus for 1958 was expected to be 1,200,000 tons, including a small carryover from 1957. This was well down on the 1,560,000 tons shipped in 1957. The new government, as an interim measure, decided to free the export of rice and brokens during January and leave the export premia unchanged. The Thai Minister of Economic Affairs said he would not raise the current export premia unless his hand was forced by the Treasury, but he did want to regulate the issue of export licences to about 100,000 tons each month. However, 120,000 tons had already been licensed for export during January (*LRBAC* 30th January 1958 2).

It was now becoming clear that the quantity of rice available from the two great exporting countries in the Far East, Burma and Siam, would be lower than for several years, down probably in the region of 500,000–1,000,000 tons compared with 1957. Vietnam was clearly no longer considered one of the great rice exporters. This was at a time when many of the big Eastern importing countries had smaller crops, and needed increased exports. Fortunately, the price of alternative food grains was falling (*LRBAC* 28th February 1958 1). In Ceylon, unfavourable conditions and floods had reduced the local crop by 275,000 tons from an expected 500,000 tons to 225,000 tons, and import requirements would be considerably larger than in recent years (*LRBAC* 30th January 1958 3). The shortage was later revised down from 275,000 tons to 70,000 tons (*LRBAC* 28th February 1958 2).

Meanwhile, the Philippine authorities approved a barter of copra (dried coconut) against 50,000 metric tons of rice from Hong Kong to meet an anticipated shortage in 1958 of 120,000 metric tons (*LRBAC* 30th January 1958 3).

In Burma, the situation remained confused. Apart from fulfilling barter commitments to Iron Curtain countries, Burma could only supply its larger customers such as India, Pakistan and Ceylon, leaving little for the smaller countries who were regular importers. But the situation could change as the Burmese authorities were not able to estimate what they might have. Private sales were unlikely (*LRBAC* 28th February 1958 1). In Siam, unseasonable rains were likely to cause damaged grains in shipments of rice later in the year, particularly in the lower qualities, and milling outturns would be reduced. Crop yields were likely to be down, and the predicted 1,200,000 tons for export might not be reached. Exports during January were 181,261 metric tons and the export quota for February was fixed at 125,000 tons of which 65,000 tons were for private business and 60,000 tons for government-to-government business (*LRBAC* 28th February 1958 2). Shipments from Siam did fall, but this was because demand from Singapore was reduced as the re-distribution market there was overstocked as shipments could not be made onward to Sumatra due to hostilities (*LRBAC* 28th March 1958 1).

Imports to Indonesia where problems were continuing were thought likely to range from 500,000 to 700,000 tons, and notably a purchase had already been made of 26,000 tons from South Vietnam, showing South Vietnam was still active though at a reduced level. There were also 30,000 tons from Burma, 60,000 tons from Siam, 20,000 tons from Italy, and surprisingly 165,000 tons from Egypt (*LRBAC* 28th February 1958 3). The Trade Minister confirmed Indonesia would indeed import 700,000 tons of rice in 1958 due to the domestic shortage. The U.S. Department of Agriculture amended an agreement with Indonesia in March 1956, permitting Indonesia to purchase rice instead of cotton. Under this, Indonesia was to buy about 35,000 tons of U.S. rice (*LRBAC* 30th May 1958 2). By August, 450,000 tons of the 700,000 had been contracted for, but because of the exchange situation and problems in the world market, there were difficulties in securing more (*LRBAC* 29th August 1958 2). Now it appeared that the forthcoming Indonesian crop would be the same as in the current year, and it would be necessary to import 600,000 tons of rice (*LRBAC* 30th October 1958 2). An Indonesian Mission left for Burma to negotiate the purchase of 250,000 tons of rice (*LRBAC* 28th November 1958 3).

In South Vietnam, the harvest was estimated at 3,175,000 tons of paddy, down from 3,514,000 tons the previous year, but the export licences for rice and rice products were not being issued and remained suspended (*LRBAC* 20th June 1958 1). However, exports of rice and rice byproducts from Saigon during the five months ending 30th June 1958 totalled 118,487 tons, compared with 65,906 tons the previous year, with the main buyers being Indonesia, the Philippines and Singapore (*LRBAC* 30th July 1958 2).

Siam now had little to offer and Burma was mainly interested in clearing out remnants of previous crops. Both countries had smaller harvests than the previous season, and Far Eastern countries had to turn to countries like Egypt, Italy and Spain for their needs. China now became a keen seller of rice and broken rice, and as it was reported that China had a record harvest, these sales seemed likely to continue (*LRBAC* 30th September 1958 1). In the event, they ceased in December, probably due to difficulties in coping with the number of contracts which had been made (*LRBAC* 23rd December 1958 1). In Rangoon, labour disputes were seriously interfering with the loading of vessels, and it was unlikely these would be settled quickly (*LRBAC* 30th September 1958 1). Meanwhile, attempts by the Burma State Agricultural Marketing Board to dispose of 160,000 tons of various quantities from crops from 1952 to 1957 had failed. The rice was now to be put in three lots for tender in November, 50,000 tons of rice and brokens from the 1952 to 1955 crops, 46,000 tons of rice and brokens from the 1956 crop and 62,000 tons of rice and brokens from the 1957 crop (*LRBAC* 30th October 1958 1).

In the United States, under Public Law No. 480, the sale of 25,000 tons of U.S. milled rice worth US$4,100,000 was authorised to the Philippines, and a further quantity to the value of US$4,200,000 to Ceylon (*LRBAC* 30th June 1958 2). Ceylon indeed had arrangements in place to receive 35,000 tons of rice from the United States, of which 20,000 tons under special arrangements were for local payments in rupees, and 15,000 tons as a gift as assistance after recent flooding. But from Colombo, it was announced that Ceylon's purchases from China would total 300,000 metric tons in the current year (*LRBAC* 30th July 1958 2). But all was not well in Ceylon, and on 20th August 1958 16 ships with 110,000 tons of rice were waiting to discharge at Colombo, some having been there for a month, as port operations had been nationalised and handling had not returned to normal (*LRBAC* 29th August 1958 1). In the Philippines, imports to make up their domestic shortage totalled 117,000 tons by September, but they would probably import no more that year (*LRBAC* 30th September 1958 3).

In Burma, the tender system appeared to have come to an end, and new arrangements for disposing of the exportable surplus were made by the State Agricultural Marketing Board (*LRBAC* 30th April 1959 1). Burma made an agreement with Ceylon for 110,000 tons of rice to be shipped in the current year, these being Small Mills Specials (*LRBA*C 29th May 1959 1). By the end of June, Burma's overall commitments were up to 1,120,000 tons (*LRBAC* 30th June 1959 1). This soon increased to 1,300,000 tons out of an exportable surplus of 1,800,000 tons (*LRBAC* 31st July 1959 1).

Meanwhile, in Siam, rice prices were holding steady as those holding paddy were keeping supplies back from the market. Japan had purchased 80,000 tons consisting of 15,000 tons 10 per cent white rice, 45,000 A1 special and 20,000 tons of 10 per cent glutinous rice. This last sale led to sales of glutinous rice being prohibited (*LRBAC* 26th March 1959 2). There was a slight dip in the market in April but prices recovered sharply due to purchase by South Africa for immediate shipment (*LRBAC* 30th April 1959 2).

In South Vietnam, the 1958–1959 crop had been expected to be good, with an exportable surplus of 250,000 tons for 1959 (*LRBAC* 23rd December 1958 1). Later, the crop was estimated at 3,824,775 tons, and shipments during the first nine months of 1959 amounted to 181,000 tons, an increase of 64,000 tons over the same period in 1958 (*LRBAC* 30th October 1959 4). Things appeared to be looking up.

3 The Asian rice trade 1960–1969

In the early 1960s, Burma continued to be a substantial rice exporter, with 1,500,000 –1,700,000 metric tons annually, rather more than Thailand. But from 1963, exports began to fall, and by 1967, were down to 540,000 tons from which they did not recover.

Thailand's exports, however, increased and in 1964 exceeded those from Burma as they did in subsequent years. Vietnam was in a worse situation, with exports at the low level of 340,000 tons, and by 1964, they had effectively disappeared. For the leading importers such as Indonesia, these were difficult years, with Vietnam, one of their major sources of imports ceasing to export. At a time of shortage in the early sixties, they had, like Vietnam itself, to look elsewhere for supplies. The Philippines faced similar problems.

Table 3.1 Rice exports (selected countries) 1960–1970 (metric tons 000)

	1960	*1961*	*1962*	*1963*	*1964*	*1965*	*1966*	*1967*	*1968*	*1969*	*1970*
Myanmar	1721	1591	1743	1712	1413	1335	1127	540	351	540	640
Vietnam	340	154	83	222	48	–	–	–	–	–	–
Thailand	1220	1573	1271	1417	1896	1895	1507	1482	1077	2054	1063
China	1173	508	619	759	912	1009	1393	1265	952	884	967
India	–	–	–	2	2	2	2	4	2	15	27
Pakistan	68	174	126	365	256	197	429	360	253	312	482
U.S.A.	997	835	1050	1197	1329	1549	1352	1847	1897	1917	1740

Source: FAO *Trade Yearbooks*.

Table 3.2 Rice imports (selected countries) 1960–1970 (metric tons 000)

	1960	*1961*	*1962*	*1963*	*1964*	*1965*	*1966*	*1967*	*1968*	*1969*	*1970*
India	698	607	685	620	720	1012	971	743	757	782	582
Bangladesh	–	491	229	418	283	81	330	371	283	239	510
Sri Lanka	528	469	410	402	658	642	693	354	369	264	544
Malay/Sgpr	641	423	392	477	506	388	336	393	316	316	366
Singapore	–	335	349	439	270	291	261	256	286	237	293

(*Continued*)

DOI: 10.4324/9781003492917-4

Table 3.2 (Continued)

	1960	*1961*	*1962*	*1963*	*1964*	*1965*	*1966*	*1967*	*1968*	*1969*	*1970*
Indonesia	962	1063	1096	1075	1024	193	306	346	707	604	956
Philippines	–	187	–	256	298	559	108	290	–	–	–
Vietnam	14	2	41	–	–	129	434	750	677	341	580
China	27	118	17	99	104	122	53	28	33	10	5
Hong Kong	369	393	426	411	411	370	366	420	313	346	344
Japan	174	135	177	222	415	967	811	509	270	56	18

Source: FAO *Trade Yearbooks*.

So what was happening in Burma? The exportable surplus for 1960 was estimated at 2,000,000 tons of rice and rice products, of which 1,800,000 tons would be rice. Of this 1,600,000 tons were committed in advance in government-to-government arrangements, showing how the Burma rice trade was effectively under government control, and private commercial sale limited (*London Rice Brokers' Association Circular* (*LRBAC*) 24th December 1959 1). More government-to-government deals were pending, leaving little for private trade (*LRBAC* 29th February 1960 1). In April, the State Agricultural Marketing Board (S.A.M.B.) suspended all sales of 1960 crop whole rice pending clarification of their stock position because of their heavy government-to-government commitments. Sales of broken rice were still permitted (*LRBAC* 30th April 1960 1). Problems were still continuing in Indonesia and by June there had been government-to-government sales from Burma of 540,000 tons from the 1959 crop, compared with 400,690 tons the previous year (*LRBAC* 30th June 1960 1). Of the new crop 1960–1961, Pakistan bought 300,000 tons and China had agreed to buy another 350,000 tons (*LRBAC* 28th October 1960 1). By November, 900,000 tons of new crop Small Mills Specials had been committed to Indonesia, Pakistan and China, government to government (*LRBAC* 25th November 1960 1). By January 1961, government-to-government sales from new crop were up to 1,340,000 tons, with an additional 100,000 tons earmarked for Ceylon (*LRBAC* 27th January 1961 1). In March, the State Agricultural Marketing Board's commitments had reached 1,400,000 tons out of an estimated surplus of 1,600,000 tons, again leaving little for private trade (*LRBAC* 26th April 1961 1). Turning to the new crop, by September 1961, government-to-government sales amounted to 1,750,000 tons including bran (*LRBAC* 29th September 1961 1). Then there were floods causing damage which was expected to reduce the amount available for export and little was likely to be available for private trade (*LRBAC* 28th November 1961 1). But by January, deals on the 1961–1962 crop included Indonesia with 465,000 tons, Pakistan 250,000 tons, Ceylon 250,000 tons, China 200,000 tons and Mauritius 50,000 tons although the rice for China was probably for onward shipment to Ceylon in barter for rubber (*LRBAC* 30th January 1962 1). In 1962, General Ne Win launched a military coup (Andrews 1997 118). Since the end of the Second World War, rice sales to international buyers had come from the State Agricultural Board, or from Burma merchants who themselves bought from the Board. But in May 1962, a fair amount of business was done by shippers direct from the Burma mills. This was to be allowed from 1963 but clearly, the authorities were permitting it already (*LRBAC* 29th May 1962 1). In December, India was negotiating for 250,000 tons of Burma rice, and Pakistan had finalised a deal for the same amount from government to government (*LRBAC* 21st December 1962 1). The new crop was estimated to give an exportable surplus of rice and rice products of 2,125,000 tons, of which 1,223,000 tons would be sold from government to government, with further deals pending. These sales included sales to Indonesia of 275,000 tons, Ceylon 225,000 tons, Pakistan 225,000 tons, India 150,000 tons, China 100,000 tons, the U.S.S.R. 65,000 tons and Mauritius 50,000 tons. Of the 100,000 tons sold to China, 60,000 tons consisted of *Ngatsein* and *Emata* rice, with 15 per cent brokens, which it thought would eventually be sold to Cuba. There had been no offers of new crops on a normal commercial basis (*LRBAC* 29th January 1963 1).

Then came the news of the nationalisation of Burma's import, export and distribution trade and that private exports of rice were to be stopped in 1963, except for deals that were already authorised. From 1964, the Burma government alone would be responsible for the domestic distribution of rice, and the State Agricultural Marketing Board would handle all exports of rice and rice products from Burma. It was not clear how the new system would operate, but in any case, there had been no offers of rice or brokens for the private trade for some time (*LRBAC* 28th February 1963 1). In May, a quantity of 2, 3 and 4 brokens became available at Akyab, but no freight was available until after the monsoon, and there were limited quantities at Rangoon (*LRBAC* 31st May 1963 1). With the new crop pending at the end of the year, it was reported that government-to-government business from Burma included 320,000 to Indonesia, 250,000 tons to Ceylon, 100,000 tons to the Philippines, 100,000 tons to China, 50,000 tons to Malaysia, 15,000 tons to Singapore and 4000 tons to the Seychelles. Negotiations were continuing with India and Pakistan (*LRBAC* 29th November 1963 1). Further sales were then made of 200,000 tons to Pakistan, 150,000 tons to India, 130,000 tons to Russia, 55,000 tons to Mauritius, 35,000 tons to Japan, 10,000 tons to the Ryukyu Islands and 5000 tons to the Maldives Islands (*LRBAC* 31st January 1964 1). A further 100,000 tons were then sold to the Philippines, 35,000 tons to Czechoslovakia and 25,000 tons to Poland (*LRBAC* 28th February 1964 1). This all apparently resulted in total government-to-government sales of new crop 1963–1964 of 1,584,000 tons, with an adjusted total reported of 1,472,000 tons (*LRBAC* 3rd April 1964 1). In May, Burma invited bids for new crop *Ngatsein* Burma 15 per cent, *Meedone* Burma 15 per cent and *Emata* Burma 15 per cent, but buyers showed no interest (*LRBAC* 29th May 1964 1). In November, Burma was offering 2, 3 and 4 rice from the 1964 crop and business was done. Boiled rice was also sold and so was B1 1963 crop, re-cleaned and re-bagged. The Government of Burma was asking for an increased price for new crops over the previous year's price on government-to-government contracts, but buyers were resisting (*LRBAC* 27th November 1964 1). In December, broken rice 2, 3 and 4 1964 crops were being offered. The Government of Burma had revised its prices for government-to-government contracts, but most buyers were still unwilling to pay more than the previous year (*LRBAC* 22nd December 1964 1). As a result of Russia paying in advance, it appeared that the basic price had been fixed at slightly more than the previous year (*LRBAC* 29th January 1965 1). More

Government-to-government deals were announced, including 300,000 tons to the Philippines, subject to a court decision in the Philippines (*LRBAC* 26th February 1965 1). This was later confirmed, and there was also government-to-government business with Pakistan (*LRBAC* 30th March 1965 1). More business was done in June in white rice including a government-to-government deal of 30,000 tons to Pakistan (*LRBAC* 25th June 1965 1). By December, new crop rice was being sold on government-to-government terms, including 150,000 tons to India at the same price as the previous year (*LRBAC* 23rd December 1965 1). This was followed by a massive 700,000 tons purchased by Indonesia on government-to-government terms, and 200,000 tons to Ceylon (*LRBAC* 28th January 1966 1). In May, Burma sold India 50,000 tons *Ngatsein* Small Mill Specials 42 per cent for rather more than the price India had paid on its previous 300,000 tons purchase on government-to-government terms (*LRBAC* 27th May 1966 1). The Philippines bought 70,000 tons of Burma *Ngatsein* Small Mills Specials 35 per cent, and another 80,000 tons were sold to India. Abidjan purchased 10,000 tons of *Ngatsein* or *Emata* 15 per cent (*LRBAC* 30th June 1966 1). Long-boiled rice (10 per cent) was quoted but the quality as delivered was not satisfactory. The extraordinary feature this year was the lack of Burma-broken rice (*LRBAC* 28th October 1966 1).

In November, floods were reported in some districts, but a good average crop was expected (*LRBAC* 25th November 1966 1. Then came the news that due to insurgent activities rice production would be less than anticipated, and exports in 1967 would be considerably reduced. Government-to-government allocations were cut back, and prices were raised (*LRBAC* 30th December 1966 1). The news about the fall in exports proved to be true, and in 1967 exports were down by half from 1,127,000 metric tons to 540,000 metric tons, a situation from which they never really recovered (See *Table 3.1* above). Worse was to come. This was a turning point for Burma's rice export trade, and from this time on reports from Burma were more infrequent, and much less informative. In February, damage to the crop was reported, although it is not clear whether this was from floods or insurgents (*LRBAC* 24th February 1967 1). In March, there were no offers for whole or broken rice, a situation which carried through to July. Burma's decline as a rice exporter continued. In August 1967, government-to-government contracts were being reduced by up to 20 per cent due to a shortage of supply (*LRBAC* 25th August 1967 1). The authorities planned to cultivate 12,780,000 acres in the coming year to produce 7,500,000 tons of rice. This compared with the 13,600,000 acres cultivated the previous year, which had only produced 6,300,000 tons as floods had destroyed about 1,000,000 tons. However, the rains were late and sowing in many parts of Burma may have been difficult (*LRBAC* 29th September 1967 1). But by October, it was clear that the exportable surplus from the new crop was again unlikely to be more than 500,000 tons (*LRBAC* 27th October 1967 1). In November, official estimates were of a crop of 8,100,000 long tons, some 1,600,000 tons more than the previous year, although this was thought to be rather optimistic (*LRBAC* 30th November 1967 1). By February 1968, negotiations were in progress or complete on government-to-government contracts, with Indonesia taking 80,000 tons, India 100,000 tons, Pakistan 50,000 tons and Ceylon 80,000 tons of *Ngatsein* Small Mills Specials (*LRBAC* 29th February 1968 1). These were very small quantities compared with previous years! Then further government-to-government sales were reported totalling nearly 450,000 tons (actually 448,900 tons), including India 100,000 tons, Indonesia 80,000 tons, Ceylon 80,000 tons Russia 50,000 tons, Mauritius 50,000 tons, Pakistan 50,000 tons and smaller amounts to Japan, Czechoslovakia, Gambia, Maldives Islands and Seychelles (*LRBAC* 29th March 1968 1). But news came of heavy damage by rains to the crop in the Arracan area, affecting the recently planted crop, and making re-planting difficult due to damage to dams and embankments in the paddy fields (*LRBAC* 31st May 1968 1). At this point, it was reported somewhat cryptically from the United States that it had "sold a major quantity of long grain rice unsubsidised and without special payment conditions to a country bordering on Siam which for many years was the cheapest exporter of long grain Patna type rice" (*LRBAC* 31st May 1968 2). This was surely Burma and suggests real problems there if this great historic rice exporter was having to import rice from the United States. But why the news was "disguised" in this way is unclear. Ominously, there seems to have been no further news from Burma until November when it was reported that Burma rice *Emata* 5 per cent brokens had been offered during October without buying interest and that heavy rains and flooding were reported in the Northern rice growing areas (*LRBAC* 1st November 1968 1). But in December, negotiations had started for government-to-government exports of the 1968–1969 crop. *Ngatsein* Small Mills Specials were being offered (*LRBAC* 23rd December 1968 1). In January, a basic price was stated for government-to-government contracts of *Ngatsein* Small Mills Specials and negotiations were proceeding with the governments who usually bought on this basis (*LRBAC* 31st January 1969 1). In June, sales were reported of *Emata* Super to Hong Kong (*LRBAC* 27th June 1969 2). There were unconfirmed reports that Sierra Leone had bought its annual requirements of full boiled rice (*LRBAC* 31st July 1969 1). Sales of about 60,000 tons of *Ngatsein* Small Mills Specials were reported to Indonesia (*LRBAC* 29th September 1969 1). There was no further news from Burma until 1970, and details of government-to-government sales were not reported.

In French Indo-China or Vietnam, the situation in these years was grave. After the French withdrew from the South in 1954, Prime Minister Ngo Dinh Diem proclaimed himself President of the Republic of Vietnam in 1955. He refused to hold elections and guerrilla activities worsened in 1961 during the Kennedy administration American "advisors" arrived to help Diem against the National Front for the liberation of Vietnam. By the end of the year there were 18,000 of them authorised for combat (Andrews 1997 201).

In these years news of the rice trade was sparse, and levels were low. In February 1961 the market was excited but export licences were difficult to obtain, with prices rising after the Chinese New Year (*LRBAC* 24th February 1961 2). Licences then became more available, but the Government proposed to increase minimum prices substantially (*LRBAC* 28th March 1961 2).

Then trade became impossible as licences were unobtainable (*LRBAC* 26th April 1961 2). In October, it was reported from Saigon that floods from the Mekong River had caused heavy damage to the growing rice crop (*LRBAC* 27th October 1961 2). This clearly had severe consequences, as the following month it was reported from Thailand that Saigon was looking for rice for early shipment, and had already bought 7500 tons from Thailand and was seeking more. This seemed like the first time in living memory that Saigon had purchased rice from overseas and was thought to be due to local conditions preventing the movement of paddy from up-country (*LRBAC* 28th November 1961 2). From November 1961, there was no news from Saigon for many months, so it was a surprise when offers were made from South Vietnam in December 1962, with the business done to both the United Kingdom and Continent for No. 1 long grain current crop 10 per cent brokens (*LRBAC* 21st December 1962 3). However, early shipments from Saigon proved difficult to obtain, despite enquiries from Hong Kong and Singapore (*LRBAC* 29th January 1963 3). By February, No.1 long grain (10 per cent) from the current crop was being quoted (*LRBAC* 28th February 1963 3). 12,000 tons were sold to Portugal and 16,000 tons to Reunion in the Indian Ocean. Sellers were now quoting No. 1 current crop (10 per cent) at a slightly increased price. The business was reported in cargo rice, and for Nos 1 and 2 mixed broken rice to Dakar in Senegal (*LRBAC* 29th March 1963 1). Neighbouring Cambodia was also in the market with 3500 tons of Cambodian No.1 35 per cent brokens being sold to the Ivory Coast (*LRBAC* 30th April 1963 3). In May, South Vietnam was quoting No. 1 long 10 per cent from the current crop (*LRBAC* 31st May 1963 1). Later in the year, Cambodia sold another cargo of 10,500 tons 1 and 2 mixed brokens to Dakar (*LRBAC* 29th October 1963 2). In January 1964, South Vietnam sold No. 1 long current (15 per cent) to the Continent (*LRBAC* 31st January 1964 2). But in February, quotations ceased as export licences were being refused (*LRBAC* 28th February 1964 2).

1965 was the year Vietnam ceased to become an exporter of rice and became an importer (see Tables 3.1 and 3.2 above). In December 1965, 75,000 tons of white rice (25 per cent) brokens were purchased from Thailand with American funds for shipment to South Vietnam at the rate of 15,000 tons a month from January 1966 through to May (*LRBAC* 23rd December 1965 2). In April 1966 South Vietnam also bought 50,000 tons of Gulf medium rice 20 per cent from the United States through its "Food for Peace" activity, and was then granted authorisation to purchase a further 50,000 tons, shipment by the end of June (*LRBAC* 29th April 1966 2). In September, South Vietnam bought about 40,000 tons old crop Californian rice, and 10,000 tons new-crop medium grain from the Gulf of Mexico, also under the "Food for Peace" scheme, and this was followed by a further 50,000 tons of shipments to be completed by 30th November (*LRBAC* 30th September 1966 3). In November, further authorisation was given under the "Peace" programme, for 50,000 tons of U.S. Rice No. 5 or better (*LRBAC* 25th November 1966 3). This was fulfilled with 50,000 tons of Gulf No.5 Medium Grain 20 per cent brokens, and a further agreement was signed by which South Vietnam would later obtain about 200,000 tons of U.S. rice. (*LRBAC* 30th December 1966 3). So in January 1967, South Vietnam bought 75,000 tons as part of this later authorisation (*LRBAC* 27th January 1967 3). In February, there was further authorisation for 75,000 tons, and 55,000 tons of Gulf medium grain rice and 20,000 tons of *Calrose* were purchased, followed by authorisation for another 46,500 tons (*LRBAC* 24th February 1967 2). This was purchased in March, and an agreement was made for another 300,000 tons, of which authority was granted for 100,000 tons (*LRBAC* 30th March 1967 3). Purchases were made of 53,000 tons of medium grain, and 42,000 tons long grain, and against a further allocation, 136,000 tons medium grain and 14,000 tons long grain (*LRBAC* 28th April 1967 3). In August 1967, South Vietnam was granted under the Food for Peace scheme what was known as P.L. 480 authorisation to purchase 50,000 tons of U.S. rice No.5 or better, well milled and no more than 20 per cent broken, the purchase to be completed by 30th September. The U.S. authorities intended to grant P.L.480 allocations to South Vietnam for up to 1,000,000 tons in the current crop year (*LRBAC* 25th August 1967 3). Another 42,000 tons medium grain rice 20 per cent brokens and 10,000 long grain rice 20 per cent brokens were also bought under the scheme in September (*LRBAC* 29th September 1967 3). This was followed by 38,000 tons Gulf medium grain rice, and 10,000 tons long grain rice in October, and South Vietnam was again in the market for another 50,000 tons (*LRBAC* 27th October 3). Then came 70,000 tons No. 5 medium grain rice 20 per cent brokens under P.L.480 in November at a slightly increased price (*LRBAC* 30th November 1967 3). Paradoxically a tender was held in Phnom-Penh in neighbouring Cambodia in the last week of November for 2,000 tons of broken rice, Nos. 1 and 2 mixed, 200 tons of brokens Nos. 3 and 4 mixed, 500 tons No.1 current type white rice 25 per cent brokens, and 292 tons of No. 1 current type white rice 15 per cent brokens for December shipment (*LRBAC* 30th November 1967 1). Further P.L.480 authorisation was granted in December for South Vietnam to purchase 100,000 tons, and under this sales were made of about 70,000 tons medium grain rice No. 5 20 per cent brokens Gulf ports and 30,000 tons long grain rice No. 5 20 per cent Gulf ports (*LRBAC* 29th December 1967 2). Interestingly, in January 1968, it was reported that the current rice crop in the United States was the biggest ever, and estimated at 3,994,100 long tons. This was nearly 7 per cent more than was harvested in the previous season, although the acreage was virtually the same. In view of the continued world shortage of rice, the U.S. authorities had decided to increase the permitted acreage in the next season to 2,400,000 acres as against 2,000,000 tons in the last two seasons. South Vietnam was authorised under P.L.480 to purchase a further 100,000 tons, and was expected to buy a proportion of long grain against this allocation (*LRBAC* 26th January 1968 3). Indeed 60,000 tons of No.5. medium grain 20 per cent and 40,000 tons No. 5 long grain 20 per cent brokens were purchased, and authorisation was granted to purchase another 100,000 tons (*LRBAC* 29th February 1968 3). But in March it was reported that against its previous allocation of 100,000 tons, South Vietnam had only bought about 35,000 tons No. 5 long grain 20 per cent brokens and 10,500 tons No. 5. medium grain 20 per cent brokens. It was understood that Vietnam would still buy 130,000 tons from the present U.S. crop and an appeal for further authorisation was expected for 200,000 tons during the first three months of the new crop (*LRBAC* 29th March 1968 3). In April, South Vietnam bought 51,500 tons No. 5 medium grain 20 per cent brokens during the week before Easter, which completed purchases against P.L.480 allocations from the present crop. But they intended to purchase a further 100,000 tons from the current crop for cash on ordinary commercial terms, and were negotiating for 40,000 tons of this quality. This would absorb virtually the entire carryover from the current U.S. crop (*LRBAC* 30th April 1968 3). It seemed unlikely that there would be any other major P.L.480 transactions this season. But the largest beneficiary under the scheme, South Vietnam, had also bought on normal commercial terms 14,500 metric tons medium grain rice 20 per cent brokens, and 35,000 metric tons long grain 20 per cent brokens for shipment from 10th May to 10th June. They were interested in a further 50,000 tons (*LRBAC* 31st May 1968 2). There were no more P.L.480 allocations in June, although the United States seemed morally committed to supplying South Vietnam under P.L.480 early in the season (*LRBAC* 28th June 1968 3). Then South Vietnam was granted authorisation to buy about 53,000 tons for shipment in September, as part of an outstanding promise to supply them with 200,000 tons in the new season (*LRBAC* 30th July 1968 2). Rather bizarrely it was reported in August that India had bought 60,000 tons of Siam white rice from neighbouring Cambodia (*LRBAC* 30th August 1968 1). The Longshoremen at Gulf and East Coast ports went on strike about the threat to their jobs from containerisation on 1st October but were ordered back to work by an injunction under the Taft Hartley Act for a "cooling off" period, due to expire on 20th December (*LRBAC* 1st November 1968 3). As soon as the injunction expired on 20th December, work at all Eastern Seaboard and Gulf Ports ceased (*LRBAC* 23rd December 1968 3). Nonetheless, the U.S. authorities agreed to make available another 100,000 tons of rice to South Vietnam during 1969, and authorisation was given for the purchase of 50,000 tons for shipment by the end of April (*LRBAC* 31st January 1969 3). New York dockers returned to work on 15th February and New Orleans dockers on 22nd February. The largest rice crop in the history of the United States had now to be moved in less than ten shipping months (*LRBAC* 28th February 1969 3). But the strike dragged on at the other main Gulf rice shipping ports, Huston and Lake Charles (*LRBAC* 28th March 1969 3). In April, P.L.480 authorisation was granted to South Vietnam for 60,000 tons from Gulf ports, which was likely to contain a proportion of long-grain rice. The strike at Houston and Lake Charles finally ended in the week before Easter, but there was still much congestion (*LRBAC* 28th April 1969 3). The permitted planted acreage in the United States was 10 per cent less than the previous year (*LRBAC* 30th May 1969 2). Later in the year, South Vietnam was granted two P.L.480 purchase authorities under existing arrangements, one for about 50,000 tons for shipment by 31st October and the other for about 57,000 tons for shipment by 13th November (*LRBAC* 29th September 1969 3). During September, South Vietnam did indeed buy 57,000 tons of medium grain, having purchased 50,000 tons of medium grain at the end of August (*LRBAC* 29th September 1969 3). Again, under P.L.480, agreement was made to make available 150,000 tons to South Vietnam during 1969/70, and against this agreement authorisation was granted to South Vietnam to purchase about 50,000 tons for shipment by the end of January 1970 (*LRBAC* 28th November 1969 3). During December, further authorisation was granted for South Vietnam to purchase 25,000 tons medium grain rice, and 25,000 tons long grain rice, for shipment by the end of February. Against these authorisations, sales were reported of 25,000 tons to South Vietnam, and enquiries were being made in the market for the remainder (*LRBAC* 2nd January 1970 3).

Meanwhile, Thailand remained a major rice exporter, and would continue to be so, although at this stage it was still exporting rather less than Burma. The exportable surplus for the 1959–1960 crop was estimated at 1,400,000 tons (*LRBAC* 24th December 1959 2). This is compared with the 2,000,000 tons for Burma. In June, prices advanced due to low levels of water in the navigation canals which impeded the supply of rice to Bangkok by boat, and demand from Indonesia and Pakistan (*LRBAC* 30th June 1960 2). Owing to the low rainfall, the new crop was expected to be a month or six weeks late and the Thai government imposed restrictions on the export of rice for the month commencing 20th August. Only 80,000 tons could be exported of which 35,000 were government-to-government contracts (*LRBAC* 31st August 1960 2). As in Burma, the rice trade was effectively under government control. But by October, the restrictions had been lifted and new crops would be obtainable from the second half of December (*LRBAC* 28th November 1960 2). 90,000 tons were quickly sold to Indonesia (*LRBAC* 25th November 1960 2). At the end of the year, there was a decrease in the export premium, and prices were lower for *Loonzain*. *Loonzain* suitable for producing 100 per cent white rice varied in quality and price (*LRBAC* 3rd January 1961 2). Then the government increased the premium on low grade rice and "A" brokens, in order to cover government contracts to Indonesia, as due to lack of supplies the government was finding it difficult to cover their government-to-government commitments. Up to the end of March 1961, 495,000 tons had been exported January/March compared with 300,992 tons in the same period in the previous year (*LRBAC* 26th April 1961 1). The Philippines bought 80,000 ton lower quality white rice 45 per cent (*LRBAC* 30th June 1961 2). They were clearly in need as they also bought 12,000 tons of low quality from Spain (*LRBAC* 30th June 1961 3). By the end of June shipments from Thailand from 1st January were 910,000 tons, considerably more than the same period in recent years (*LRBAC* 31st July 1961 2). But when the government commitments to Indonesia and the Philippines were covered, interest declined (*LRBAC* 31st August 1961 2). Then the Philippines bought another 75,000 tons (*LRBAC* 29th September 1961 2).

Also Indonesia bought 300,000 tons white rice 45 per cent for spread shipment from November to April. Interestingly Saigon was reported to have bought 7500 tons and was seeking more, thought to be due to local conditions preventing free movement of paddy from up-country. As noted under Vietnam above, this felt like the first time in living memory that Saigon had bought rice from overseas (*LRBAC* 28th November 1961 2). In March 1962, regulations were introduced by which for every 100 tons exported, 15 had to be set aside for the government stockpile and government permission had to be obtained for any quantity over 300 tons to Europe. Around 60,000 tons of A1 Brokens were sold to Japan. Subsequently, a special permit was required for sales of A1 brokens (*LRBAC* 30th March 1962 1). The regulations were soon changed so that for 1 ton exported, 1 ton had to be put in the government stockpile, but the other regulations remained as they were (*LRBAC* 30th April 1962 2). The market continued firm through May 1962, and the government made a further sale of 25,000 tons to Indonesia, even though they were having difficulty meeting their existing requirements (*LRBAC* 29th May 1962 2). Restrictions remained on exports (*LRBAC* 29th June 1962 2). Shipments up to the end of June amounted to almost exactly two-thirds of the estimated 1,400,000 tons export surplus for the year, but there was little new business (*LRBAC* 31st July 1962 2). Yet another sale was made to Indonesia of 50,000 tons government-to-government (*LRBAC* 31st August 1962 2). Clearly, the difficulties in Indonesia were continuing. The new crop then started to come in (*LRBAC* 30th November 1963 2). In February, 150,000 tons were sold to Indonesia (*LRBAC* 28th February 1963 2). In May, there were sales to the Philippines and the Far East (*LRBAC* 31st May 1963 2). Around 200,000 tons of current crop were sold government to government to Indonesia, but fears were expressed about the new crop unless rain fell imminently (*LRBAC* 30th July 1961 3). Fortunately, the rains did come in August (*LRBAC* 30th August 1963 2). Then in November, 40,000 tons were sold to the Ceylon government to government, and 100,000 tons remained to be shipped from government contracts to Indonesia. The new crop surplus was forecast at between 1,350,000 and 1,400,000 tons, which was more than had appeared likely (*LRBAC* 29th November 1963 2). In January, 80,000 tons "A" quality broken rice was sold to Japan (*LRBAC* 31st January 1964 2). There were heavy shipments in April and enquiries from the Philippines for 100,000 tons (*LRBAC* 28th April 1964 1). This resulted in sales to the Philippines of 115,000 tons (*LRBAC* 29th May 1964 2). In August business was done in parboiled rice, 10,000 tons for India, 10,000 tons for the Middle East, and 8000 tons to Mauritius (*LRBAC* 28th August 1964 2). There were expectations of a good crop and an increased surplus for export (*LRBAC* 30th October 1964 2). But in November flooding was preventing the free movement of rice down to Bangkok, although there were no reports of damage to the actual crop (*LRBAC* 27th November 1964 2). Parboiled rice was sold to India for January/March shipment and 100,000 tons of parboiled to Ceylon. There were also sales of white rice to Madagascar and enquiries from Mauritius (*LRBAC* 22nd December 1964 2). In January, sales were reported to India of 130,000 tons of white rice for shipment later in the year and there were enquiries from the Philippines, but as with a similar sale from Burma, it was subject to a court decision. 50,000 tons of whole rice and 80,000 tons of A1 brokens were sold to Japan, and 10,000 tons low-quality whole rice to Madagascar (*LRBAC* 26th February 1965 2). As with Burma, the white rice deal with the Philippines was subsequently confirmed (*LRBAC* 30th March 1965 2). A further 40,000 tons of low-quality white rice was sold to Ceylon, and 10,000 tons of parboiled to Mauritius government to government (*LRBAC* 30th April 1965 2). In June, it was announced that an agreement had been made with Ceylon for 100,000 tons of rice each year for the next three years, and 9000 tons of Thai *Loonzain* 15 per cent brokens had been sold to Madagascar (*LRBAC* 25th June 1965 2). The rains were later than expected (*LRBAC* 27th August 1965 2). There were fears that the new crop might be delayed, and to prevent excessive price rises, the government introduced a quota system for exports (*LRBAC* 20th September 1965 2). In November, it was reported the exportable surplus from the new crop was estimated at about 1,800,000 tons, but the crop was a month late and not expected until January. India had agreed on a contract for 100,000 tons of Thai rice for the next three years (*LRBAC* 28th November 1965 2).

Indicating the problems which were now arising in Vietnam, 75,000 tons of white rice containing 25 per cent brokens were purchased from Thailand with

American funds for shipment to South Vietnam at 15,000 tons a month from January to May, and 48,000 tons of A1 broken rice was sold for early shipment to Dakar in Senegal (*LRBAC* 23rd December 1965 2). Around 150,000 tons of rice were sold to India on government-to-government terms and 100,000 tons to Indonesia, but the exportable surplus was now expected to be much less than the 1,800,000 tons forecast (*LRBAC* 31st March 1966 1). Shipments on government-to-government contracts continued at a rapid rate (*LRBAC* 31st March 1966 1). Around 80,000–100,000 tons of A1 brokens were sold to Japan, but restrictions were placed on exports, by which no quantity over 1,000 tons of any quality could be sold without special authority, including white rice 25 per cent brokens or higher (*LRBAC* 29th April 1966 2). Exports reached over 1,000,000 tons in the first six months of the season, and the government now insisted exports could only take place with prior approval of the authorities, which took four or five days to obtain (*LRBAC* 30th June 1966 2). Pakistan bought 5000 tons for immediate shipment, India 75,000 tons for November shipment and Japan a quantity of A1 brokens for December shipment (*LRBAC* 30th September 1966 2). There was almost no carryover from the old crop, and considerable internal demand in Bangkok from northern parts of the country where the rice crop was badly affected by flooding (*LRBAC* 28th October 1966 2). At the beginning of November, the Thai authorities banned all exports to reduce prices in the local market, originally until 21st November, but the ban was then extended indefinitely, possibly until February (*LRBAC* 23rd November 1966 2). Notwithstanding, Ceylon purchased 100,000 tons of parboiled rice 25 per cent brokens on government-to-government terms, delivery to be made in the first half of 1967, and an agreement was made with Indonesia for 100,000 tons white rice 35 per cent brokens. Shipments were taking place on certain government-to-government sales, and parboiled rice was being shipped to the Persian Gulf, and white rice and brokens to Hong Kong, which were traditional market. But as far as Europe was concerned shippers were still quoting subject to export licences (*LRBAC* 30th December 1966 2). Then export taxes were raised to 30 per cent on whole rice, down to 20 per cent or less on brokens, 25 per cent on other whole rice and 20 per cent on broken rice. Licences were granted for traditional Far East markets. But the situation for Europe was unclear, except for broken rice where licences were limited to 100 tons per vessel for any one buyer (*LRBAC* 27th January 1967 2). In March, export taxes were amended again and only limited export quotas were given for April shipment, 45,000 tons for traditional markets and 9000 tons for non-traditional markets (*LRBAC* 30th March 1967 1). Export duties were then increased on white rice and brokens (*LRBAC* 28th April 1967 2). They were increased again slightly, and in order to limit exports to 1,500,000 tons per year, monthly export quotas from July shipments onwards were limited to 100,000 tons, including government-to-government business (*LRBAC* 28th May 1967 2). Export duties were raised again in June for broken rice. July shipment quotas had already been limited to 36,000 tons for private trade most of which was already committed (*LRBAC* 30th June 1967 2). As a result of the diversion of vessels via the Cape, the basic freight rate to Europe from Thailand was increased. Export duties were raised for August shipments, but the policy of the Thai authorities was beginning to reduce prices, and quotations for August shipments were lower subject to export licences (*LRBAC* 28th July 1967 2). In August, it was reported that the rains were late, and many areas were still suffering from drought. As a result field work for the new crop was delayed, and it was feared that the new crop would be late. Quotas for September were increased to 75,000 tons to release substantial quantities urgently required by India. India bought 30,000–50,000 tons of rice, partly parboiled and partly A1 Super. Indonesia also bought 20,000 tons of A1 brokens (*LRBAC* 28th August 1967 2). Some rain fell in the rice-growing areas about the middle of September, well over two months later than normal. But the government reported that about 53 per cent of the normal rice growing areas had been planted before August, presumably on irrigated land. However, the new crop was bound to be late, and there were fears for its outturn. The government reduced its export target for the year from 1,500,000 tons to 1,300,000 tons and gave no crop export quotas for October, although unused quotas for September could be carried forward until October (*LRBAC* 29th September 1967 2). Some new crop was expected to be available for December shipment, but the bulk of the crop was not expected to be harvested before January, and it appeared that the export quota system would remain in force during 1968. It was thought that the government would not set next year's export target above 1,300,000 tons (*LRBAC* 1967 2). Prices in £Sterling advanced about 14 per cent as a result of a recent devaluation of Sterling, and the Conference Freight rate from Thailand to United Kingdom/Continent was increased by 12½ per cent (*LRBAC* 30th November 1967 2). There were conflicting reports from the Thai government authorities of how much rice would be available for export in 1968. Figures ranged from 1,200,000 tons to 1,400,000 tons, the latter including 100,000 tons of glutinous rice and brokens. Quotas for December/January were announced totalling 60,000 tons subject to export licence (*LRBAC* 29th December 1967 2). As the authorities were unable to estimate the amount available for export, they decided to allot monthly export quotas. The quota for January was 45,000 tons of which 65 per cent was reserved for traditional markets. Export licences were required (*LRBAC* 26th January 1968 2). The export tax was increased substantially, and so were price quotations which were subject to export licences (*LRBAC* 29th February 1968 2). During the first three months of the year, export authorisation only amounted to 225,000 tons, including government-to-government sales, however, due to good arrivals in the market, prices were lower (*LRBAC* 29th March 1968 2). Of the 100,000 tons export quota for March, only 80,000 tons were actually shipped. For the two months April/May, an export quota of 250,000 tons was fixed, including 180,000 tons on a private account. Apart from 35,000 tons of A1 brokens reported as sold to Japan, Eastern buyers were holding off and consequently, prices were falling (*LRBAC* 30th April 1968 2). The export quota for April/May of 250,000 tons was extended into June, but because export demand was dwindling, the authorities reduced the export premium, and prices dropped considerably (*LRBAC* 31st May 1968 2).

In June, the authorities abolished the quota system for the time being, and it would not be re-imposed until exports for the year had reached 650,000 tons when the situation would be reviewed. This made little difference as the quotas had never been fully used. Prices continued to decline until government-to-Government sales were made to India, some 50,000 tons white rice 60 per cent brokens, and 30,000 tons parboiled rice 30 per cent brokens. Government-to-government negotiations were in process with Malaysia and Indonesia (*LRBAC* 28th June 1968 2). This led to sales to Indonesia of 35,000 tons, and 40,000 tons to India, government to government (*LRBAC* 30th July 1968 2). Export demand remained poor except for India (*LRBAC* August 1968 2). The Thai government reduced export taxes for shipments from lst November as there were ample supplies of old crop, and a good new crop was expected. Prices fell accordingly (*LRBAC* 1st November 1968 2). There were reports that the new crop might be slightly smaller than expected, which prompted buying from South East Asian countries, leading to higher prices (*LRBAC* 29th November 1968 2). Shipments during 1968 amounted to 1,102,425 tons. The government estimated that 1,200,000 tons would be available in 1969, but traders in Bangkok thought it would only be about 1,000,000 tons. This was partly due to the poor milling quality of the new crop where the milling yield of whole rice was 4 per cent to 5 per cent below normal. Recent government sales included 22,000 tons to Ceylon, 20,000 tons to Mauritius and 14,000 tons to Brunei. On private account, 20,000 tons were sold to Senegal, and 10,000 tons to India (*LRBAC* 31st January 1969 2). There was demand from Singapore and Hong Kong for white rice. Broken rice prices were lower because of the poor milling quality of the rice this season (*LRBAC* 28th February 1969 2). Demand continued from Hong Kong for white rice. Parboiled rice prices were also cheaper, also due to the poor milling quality of the rice, resulting in more being parboiled (*LRBAC* 28th March 1969 2). There was some business in parboiled to Mauritius, and moderate trade to Singapore, whilst India was negotiating for 50,000 tons of white rice. As far as the European and U.K. markets were concerned, Thai rice prices were well out of line with other long grain rice (*LRBAC* 28th April 1969 2). Around 75,000 tons of parboiled rice were sold to India, and demand continued for white rice from Hong Kong and Singapore (*LRBAC* 30th May 1969 2). Thailand exported 408,000 tons from January to May 1969, compared with 783,000 tons in the same period in 1968, and 857,000 tons in 1967. Despite pressure from local merchants, the government stated that the export tax would not be reduced (*LRBAC* 27th June 1969 2). But in August/September, there was indeed a special reduction in the export tax, and prices quoted were lower (*LRBAC* 29th August 1969 2). In September, there were government-to-government sales of 30,000 tons of white rice to Indonesia, and 30,000 tons of parboiled rice to India. The special reduction in the export tax was continued for shipments up to the end of the year (*LRBAC* 29th September 1969 2). In October, business was confined to sales to Far Eastern countries, including 24,000 tons purchased by Japan and then given to Indonesia under an Aid programme. Prices were still out of line for Europe and the United Kingdom (*LRBAC* 31st October 1969 2). Prices even in regular markets seemed uncompetitive with rice from Burma and China (*LRBAC* 28th November 1969 2). It was then reported that exports during 1969 would probably exceed 1,000,000 tons due to fairly heavy loadings for government-to-government contracts late in December (*LRBAC* 2nd January 1970 2).

The major importers in this period are shown on Table 3.2 above. In many respects, the most interesting importer was Indonesia, where imports showed considerable volatility year by year, ranging from 1,096,000 tons in 1962 to 193,000 tons in 1965. The years 1960–1964 were the years of particularly heavy imports of about 1,000,000 tons each year. In January 1960, Indonesia made substantial purchases from Thailand, which appeared to complete their immediate requirements (*LRBAC* 29th January 1960 1). But they then purchased 40,000 tons of 1959 crop from Burma, bringing total government-to-government purchases from Burma by June to 540,000 tons. This compared with 400,690 tons the previous year and indicated continuing problems in Indonesia (*LRBAC* 30th June 1960 1). In October, quotations were available in Thailand for the 1960–1961 crop, shipment in the second half of December (*LRBAC* 28th October 1960 2). Indonesia bought 90,000 tons (*LRBAC* 25th November 1960 2). Indonesia also made substantial government-to-government purchases of new crop from Burma, details not given (*LRBAC* 25th November 1960 1). Indonesia's needs were so great that in April 1961, the Thai government increased the premium on low-grade rice and "A" brokens so as to have enough to cover government-to-government contracts to Indonesia, as there was a shortage of supplies (*LRBAC* 30th May 1961 1). In May, Indonesia was negotiating another 100,000 tons from Burma (*LRBAC* 30th May 1961 1). Thailand continued to cover its commitments to Indonesia through to August (*LRBAC* 31st August 1961 2). This was a period of heavy purchases by Indonesia, and in November, they bought from Thailand 300,000 tons of white rice 45 per cent brokens for shipment from November to April (*LRBAC* 28th November 1961 2).

Indonesia then went on to make Government to Government purchases of 465,000 tons from Burma of new crop rice for shipment during 1962 (*LRBAC* 30th January 1962 1). In May Indonesia made a further government purchase of 25,000 tons from Thailand, even though the authorities were having difficulties meeting their existing commitments (*LRBAC* 29th May 1962 2). In August another 50,000 tons were purchased from Thailand government to government (*LRBAC* 31st August 1962 2). In January 1963 when the new crop came in, Indonesia was reported to have bought 275,000 tons from Burma government to government (*LRBAC* 29th January 1963 1). This was followed by a purchase of 150,000 tons from Thailand (*LRBAC* 28th February 1963 2). In July, a further government-to-government purchase of 200,000 tons current crop was also made from Thailand (*LRBAC* 30th July 1963 2). More undisclosed amounts were purchased from Thailand in August (*LRBAC* 30th August 1963 2). But Burma's continued importance as a supplier was emphasised when Indonesia made a government-to-government purchase of 320,000 tons of new crop rice in November (*LRBAC* 29th November 1963 1). Meanwhile, 100,000 tons remained to be shipped from Thailand to complete government-to-government contracts to Indonesia (*LRBAC* 29th November 1963 2). *Table 3.2* shows imports to Indonesia remained heavy at over 1,000,000 tons annually through to 1965 when they fell to the decennial low of 193,000 tons, although the *Circular* does not give details. This coincided with the disappearance of Vietnam as a major rice exporter, causing a severe shortage in world rice supplies. The last year that Vietnam made exports of any size was 1964 when exports were already down to 48,000 tons. Indonesia had traditionally bought heavily from Vietnam and therefore needed to find a new supplier. But as in Vietnam, these were years of political turmoil in Indonesia, and in September 1965 there was an abortive coup, apparently involving PKI, the Indonesian communist party. The role of President Sukarno, the founder of modern Indonesia was not clear. However, the military, led by its chief of staff, General Suharto, crushed the coup with extreme ruthlessness, killing at least 500,000 people. In March 1966, Sukarno was forced to transfer emergency powers to Suharto, and in February 1967 full powers. Finally, in March 1968 Suharto was inaugurated as Indonesia's President (Andrews 1997 83). So understandably 1966 was a year of low rice imports. However, in January 1966, 700,000 tons of rice was purchased from Burma on government-to-government terms, presumably for delivery that year (*LRBAC* 28th January 1966 1). But this rice may never have arrived as the sum contradicts the FAO figures for the year, which were 306,000 metric tons. Another 100,000 tons were purchased in March government to government from Thailand (*LRBAC* 25th February 1966 1). Clearly, the situation was grave, as the United States gave Indonesia authorisation under the Food for Peace scheme to purchase in the region of 50,000 tons of U.S. Gulf medium grain 20 per cent brokens, shipment to be completed by the end of June (*LRBAC* 29th April 1966 2). Later in the year, Indonesia purchased another 50,000 tons of U.S. rice under Food for Peace (*LRBAC* 25th November 1966 3). Indonesia then agreed government-to-government terms to buy from Thailand 100,000 tons of white rice 35 per cent brokens (*LRBAC* 30th December 1966 2). Nothing more is recorded in the *Circular* until August 1967 when Indonesia bought 20,000 tons of A1 brokens from Thailand (*LRBAC* 25th August 1967 2). The agreement was reached the following month for the United States to provide Indonesia with P.L.480 authorisation for 100,000 tons of rice (*LRBAC* 29th September 1967 3). In October Indonesia bought 50,000 tons of US Gulf medium grain rice 20 per cent brokens under P.L.480 authorisation, and was expected to be in the market again shortly (*LRBAC* 27th October 1967 3). But there seems to have been some desperation in Indonesia over its sources of supply, and in November, Indonesia bought from Egypt 150,000 tons of white rice containing 20 per cent to 40 per cent brokens (*LRBAC* 30th November 1967 1). The Ministry of Information in Djakarta then announced it expected Indonesia would need to import 600,000 tons of rice in 1968 from various sources, compared to the 300,000 tons imported in 1967 (*LRBAC* 30th November 1967 1). This turned out to be true, and as can be seen in *Table 3.2* above, in 1968 imports were at the 707,000 tons level. That month Indonesia was in the market again in the United States for about 50,000 tons under the P.L.480 scheme (*LRBAC* 30th November 1967 3). However, the purchases from Egypt in November reported above were cancelled in December (*LRBAC* 29th December 1967 1). But emphasising the predicament that Indonesia found itself in, in December it bought about 75,000 tons from the Philippines, which was itself usually an importer. Although some purchases they had made from Taiwan were in doubt, and they were reluctant to buy from Italy, Indonesia still required an extremely large quantity of rice for early shipment (*LRBAC* 29th December 1967 1). That month they purchased from the United States under P.L. 480 about 50,000 tons medium grain rice No.5 20 per cent brokens Gulf ports (*LRBAC* 29th December 1967 2). This was a difficult time for any country buying rice, as there was a world shortage connected to the fact that Vietnam was now buying rice rather than exporting it. The United States was increasing production in view of this shortage (*LRBAC* 26th January 1968 3). At the end of February Indonesia bought from the United States. under the P.L.480 arrangements about 48,000 tons No.5. long grain rice 20 per cent brokens Gulf ports (*LRBAC* 29th March 1968 3). They also purchased 80,000 tons from Burma (*LRBAC* 29th March 1968 1). Nevertheless, world sales to Indonesia for shipment over the first six months of 1968 totalled over 400,000 tons covering their full requirements for this period (*LRBAC* 29th March 1968 2). In June, they opened government to government talks with Thailand (*LRBAC* 28th June 1968 2). In July, they bought 35,000 tons from Thailand (*LRBAC* 30th July 1968 2). More unusually, in September they bought 20,000 tons from Venezuela (*LRBAC* 27th September 1968 2). That month the U.S authorities agreed to make available a further 100,000 tons in the current crop year to Indonesia under the Food for Peace scheme P.L.480 (*LRBAC* 27th September 1968 2). This was followed by another Food for Peace authorisation for Indonesia to purchase 25,000 tons of medium grain rice and 25,000 tons of long grain rice for shipment before 15th December (*LRBAC* 1st November 1968 3). Indonesia duly purchased these two lots of 25,000 tons, and further authorisation was given for them to purchase another 50,000 tons for shipment by the end of February 1969 (*LRBAC* 29th November 1968 3). In May 1969, Indonesia purchased 25,000 tons medium grain rice and 75,000 tons long grain rice under the Food for Peace allocations (*LRBAC* 30th May 1969 2). In what seemed like a return to normality, it was reported in September that Indonesia had bought 30,000 tons of white rice from Thailand government to government (*LRBAC* 29th September 1969 2). But it was followed by 75,000 tons of medium grain rice from the United States under P.L.480 (*LRBAC* 29th September 1969 3). Then came a strange purchase by Indonesia of some 50,000 tons of Italian/French rice, 30,000 tons of which came from Italy, which presumably being round grain rice, was not the kind of rice they usually consumed. On 24th October, the export subsidy from Italy for Indonesia was increased (*LRBAC* 31st October 1969 1). Thailand was now confining its sales to Far Eastern countries, and these included a sale of 24,000 tons to Japan which was then given by Japan to Indonesia under an Aid programme (*LRBAC* 31st October 1969 2). Around the middle of October, Indonesia bought 41,452 tons of long grain milled rice from the United States under P.L.480 (*LRBAC* 31st October 1969 3). Agreements were subsequently made under P.L.480 to make available about 150,000 tons to Indonesia during the close of 1969–1970 with authorisation granted for Indonesia to purchase 40,000 tons for shipment by the end of 1969 (*LRBAC* 28th November 1969 3).

The situation in Indonesia may be compared with that of the neighbouring Philippines, although the level of their imports was much less. The period began with the administration of Carlos Gracias (1957–1961) (Andrews 1997 149). 1960 was a year of low imports to the Philippines but in August the Burma State Agricultural Marketing Board sent a mission to try to sell new crop rice to the Philippines (and Indonesia) (*LRBAC* 30th September 1960 1). Diosdado Macapagal (1961–1965) became President in 1961 (Andrews 1997 149). This was a year of imports of 187,000 metric tons, and in June the Philippines purchased from Thailand 80,000 tons of white rice 45 per cent (*LRBAC* 30th June 1961 2). They then purchased from Spain (they were a Spanish colony until 1898) a further 12,000 tons of low-quality white rice (*LRBAC*

30th June 1961 3). This was followed in September by 75,000 tons from Thailand (*LRBAC* 29th September 1961 2). 1962 was another quiet year for imports, but 1963 saw substantial imports at 256,000 tons, and in May, the Philippines bought an undisclosed amount from Thailand (*LRBAC* 31st May 1963 2). In November, they bought 100,000 tons of new crop from Burma (*LRBAC* 29th November 1963 1). *Table 3.2* above shows 1964 was a year of imports of 298,000 tons, which included a further 100,000 tons bought from Burma in February (*LRBAC* 28th February 1964 1). In May they bought 115,000 tons from Thailand (*LRBAC* 29th May 1964 2). Ferdinand Marcos was elected President in 1965 (Andrews 1997 149). This year saw the largest imports of the decade, some 559,000 tons. Government-to-government business was done with Burma for 300,000 tons in February, but the deal was delayed pending a court decision in the Philippines (*LRBAC* 26th February 1965 1). A similar deal was done with Thailand for 130,000 tons of low-quality white rice, but this too was subject to a court decision (*LRBAC* 26th February 1965 2). Both deals were subsequently confirmed (*LRBAC* 30th March 1965 1, 2). 1966 was a year of lower imports at 108,000 metric tons, and the Philippines bought 70,000 tons from Burma, comprising *Ngatsein* Small Mills Specials 35 per cent (*LRBAC* 30th June 1966 1). 1967 saw slightly heavier imports at 290,000 metric tons, and in April the Philippines bought large quantities of rice of unspecified quality and tonnage from the United States on commercial terms (*LRBAC* 28th April 1967 3). Later that year it was reported that the Philippines were taking serious steps to alleviate its chronic rice deficiency. A new strain of rice had been developed known as "IR8" or miracle rice (Ed. From IRRI, the International Rice Research Institute in Los Banos in the Philippines). This was a short-stalked rice (Ed. which prevented "lodging" or stem flattening by the weather) and it was claimed that it yielded up to eight times as much per acre as varieties previously planted in the Philippines. Whilst these claims were to be treated with reserve, even a 25 per cent increase would enable the Philippines to achieve self-sufficiency. Annual production in recent years had been rather more than 2,500,000 tons of paddy (*LRBAC* 29th September 1967 3). Following this, Philippines' purchases of rice for the rest of the decade were minimal, and indeed in 1968 the Philippines announced a tender for the sale of 10,000 tons of rice and it was thought that more was available (*LRBAC* 29th March 1968 2). In September 1968, India bought at tender 25,000 tons of Philippine white rice, 10,000 tons for shipment at the latest by 15TH October and 15,000 tons for shipment at latest by 15th November (*LRBAC* 27th September 1968 1). But if it was thought that the Philippines was now to emerge as a rice exporter, news came in November that year that drought had seriously affected crop prospects and an export ban was imposed, although existing contracts would be fulfilled. There were also reports that the rice bought by India mentioned above had been found to be unsatisfactory (*LRBAC* 29th November 1968 2). Ferdinand Marcos was re-elected in 1969, at a time of demonstrations and strikes against accusations of corruption and police brutality which were to have further repercussions in the 1970s (Andrews 1997 149). No imports of significance seem to have taken place during the year.

Reference

Andrews, John (1997) *Pocket Asia*, London: The Economist-Profile Books Ltd.

4 The Asian rice trade 1970–1979

The story of the 1970s is the virtual absence of Vietnam as an exporter and the low level of exports from Burma by historical standards. These shortfalls were to some extent offset by the continued expansion of exports from Thailand. These years also saw the "forgotten" *El Nino*/Southern Oscillation (*EN*SO) of 1972/73, possibly the most severe since 1891, followed by the lesser 1976/77 event (Cushing 1982 290, Glantz 1996 68–69. See also Latham 2009). However, despite the considerable disruption and chaos of these years, *EN*SO events were not recognised as such at the time, and the *Circular* does not comment upon them in these terms. So the big "event" of the 1970s was the rice crisis of 1973–**19**75 when both Burma and Thailand, historically two of the three leading Asian exporters other than Vietnam, experienced poor harvests and low exports at a time when Indonesia and the Philippines were seeking increased imports as their harvests had also failed.

Table 4.1 Rice exports (selected countries) 1970–1980 (metric tons 000)

	1970	*1971*	*1972*	*1973*	*1974*	*1975*	*1976*	*1977*	*1978*	*1979*	*1980*
Myanmar	640	810	511	132	208	286	628	668	350	590	653
Vietnam	–	–	–	–	2	22	5	1	1	14	33
Thailand	1063	1576	2118	848	1046	951	1925	2931	1606	2796	2791
China	1829	2158	2316	3448	3015	2740	1446	1149	1677	1459	1376
India	27	15	14	17	41	18	37	19	143	375	472
Pakistan	482	182	197	788	597	477	794	960	776	1015	1086
U.S.A.	1740	1477	2035	1630	1725	2138	2106	2287	2278	2300	3054

Source: FAO *Trade Yearbooks*.

Table 4.2 Rice imports (selected countries) 1970–1980 (metric tons 000)

	1970	*1971*	*1972*	*1973*	*1974*	*1975*	*1976*	*1977*	*1978*	*1979*	*1980*
India	582	539	325	264	109	233	414	113	93	110	19
Bangladesh	510	347	658	484	87	268	417	104	304	58	548
Sri Lanka	544	339	266	343	297	465	377	538	186	211	168
Malaysia	366	250	229	308	353	164	183	283	408	239	167
Singapore	293	305	376	238	164	146	225	226	194	214	188

(*Continued*)

DOI: 10.4324/9781003492917-5

Table 4.2 (Continued)

	1970	*1971*	*1972*	*1973*	*1974*	*1975*	*1976*	*1977*	*1978*	*1979*	*1980*
Indonesia	956	508	734	1657	1132	692	1301	1973	1841	1922	2011
Philippines	–	370	455	336	166	134	55	30	–	–	–
Vietnam	580	137	272	270	1336	1310	650	300	35	250	134
China	5	5	–	–	127	18	126	8	171	120	130
Hong Kong	344	370	457	425	314	343	361	340	343	361	359
Japan	18	12	3	24	62	36	22	43	62	14	13

Source: FAO *Trade Yearbooks*.

Burma exports during the 1970s varied between 132,000 tons and 810,000 tons, but there were significant dips, notably 1973–**1975** when exports ran in consecutive years at 132,000 tons, 208,000 tons and 286,000 tons with a further dip in 1978 when exports were 350,000 tons (see Table 4.1 above). Most of Burma's rice exports by 1970 were Government-to-government deals, but small quantities of *Emata* Super 5 per cent brokens and old crop Nos. 2, 3 and 4 mixed brokens were available to the U.K, and Continent (*London Rice Brokers' Association Circular* (*LRBAC*) 27th February 1970 1). Also B1 Extra, B1 and B2 (*LRBAC* 30th May 1970 1). That year there was terrible flooding in East Pakistan (now Bangladesh) (*LRBAC* 30th November 1970 2). The Burma authorities negotiated with the Pakistan authorities a large quantity of broken rice for Dacca (Dhaka) in East Pakistan, and several other cargoes were sold to European Governments for immediate shipment there for relief operations (*LRBAC* 31st December 1970 1). So 1971 saw the best exports from Burma of the decade at 810,000 tons. The exportable surplus for 1972 was estimated at 700,000 tons (*LRBAC* 26th November 1971 1). But there was soon concern about the new crop (*LRBAC* 28th April 1972 1). By September, there were no offers of Burma whole rice for export and brokens from the 1972 crop were unobtainable (*LRBAC* 6th September 1972 1). In December, a reduced export surplus was expected and only limited supplies were being released, and these were for government-to-government contracts only (*LRBAC* 29th December 1972 1).

In January 1973, the *Circular* reported that an extremely serious situation had developed, with the world supply of rice being substantially less than the needs of importing countries. This appears to have been brought on by the "forgotten" *El Nino*/Southern Oscillation (*EN*SO) event of 1972/73 mentioned above. The Philippines required another 200,000 tons of rice and India 300,000 tons. Bangladesh needed enormous unspecified amounts, Indonesia had not covered its needs, nor had a number of other unnamed countries. It was difficult to see where the necessary rice could come from, and many countries would have to do without it. Simultaneously there had been a rise in the price of other food grains (*LRBAC* 31st January 1973 1). Government-to-government negotiations took place between Burma and regular customers, but the amount available for export was down in 1972 (*LRBAC* 31st January 1973 1). Burma exports for 1973 were expected to be far below 1972 (*LRBAC* 28th February 1973 1). They turned out to be 132,000 tons, the lowest for the decade (see Table 4.1 above). This shortfall from Burma was an integral part of the world crisis. In March, the *Circular* reported (in bold) that "Rice prices in the United Kingdom and Continent have now reached their highest level in all time", and further increases were expected before the new crops came on the market (*LRBAC* 30th March 1973 1). No rice was available from Burma (*LRBAC* 30th March 1973 1). The *Circular* then reported (in capitals) that a critical situation had developed in world rice markets. The two major Eastern exporters Burma and Siam had banned further exports and were not even honouring Government-to-government contracts. Demand far exceeded supply. It was not a question of price, stocks were simply not available. Little remained from South America and the U.S. crop was late and would not be available until August/September. Although the current monsoon was normal it would not affect availability until the end of the year (*LRBAC* 30th June 1973 1). All exports from Burma were indeed banned (*LRBAC* 30th June 1973 1). In August, the *Circular* reported (again in capitals) that the world rice market was in a state of acute shortage until the Asian new crop came on the market at the end of the year. World demand for near (i.e. almost immediate) shipment was far greater than could be supplied. But there had been many dubious offers of large quantities from sellers unknown in the rice market and the *Circular* warned Governments not to get involved (*LRBAC* 30th August 1973 1). No rice would be available from Burma until February or March at the earliest (*LRBAC* 30th September 1973 1). However, the new crop was expected to be better than the last one (*LRBAC* 30th October 1973 1). Weather conditions had been reasonably good (*LRBAC* 30th November 1973 1). Then significantly a Government-to-government sale was reported to Indonesia of 100,000 tons *Ngatsein* Small Mills Specials (*LRBAC* 30th December 1973 1).

In 1974 General Ne Win, who had been in power since a military coup in 1962, declared Burma to be a one-party state under the Burma Socialist Programme Party (Andrews 1997 118). However, despite the hopeful crop forecasts, 1974 was another year of low exports. By March the Government was finding it hard to obtain paddy or fulfil Government-to-government contracts (*LRBAC* 29th March 1974 1). The exportable surplus was small, and Government-to-government negotiations were unresolved (*LRBAC* 30th April 1974 1). The *Circular* again warned of fraudulent offers, particularly if the rice contained ash or protein, invariably a warning of potential default (*LRBAC* 30th April 1974 3). Nothing was available from Burma (*LRBAC* 31st May 1974 1). There were more warnings of fraudulent offers (*LRBAC* 31st May 1974 3). In June, the *Circular* reported (again in capitals) that in early 1974 world rice prices had reached the highest levels ever recorded. Since then prices had fallen and would probably fall further when the United States crop came on the market. As only a small proportion of the world crop was actually traded between countries, the supply and demand for rice in the world was very delicately balanced. Population growth was high in the very countries which were the major growers. With the current high price of fertiliser crops were unlikely to keep up with population growth and increasing demand, so rice prices would continue at a high level (*LRBAC* 28th June 1974 3). There were still no offers from Burma (*LRBAC* 27th August 1974 1). More warnings were given about spurious offers of rice (*LRBAC* 27th September 1974 1). The serious situation in Burma was revealed when Burma actually bought rice from Thailand (*LRBAC* 27th September 1974 1). This was a strange event indeed. In October, there were more warnings about offers of non-existent rice (*LRBAC* 29th October 1974 1). Then came news from Burma that at least 970,000 acres of paddy fields had been destroyed by flooding on the Irrawaddy, said to be the worst for 100 years (*LRBAC* 29th October 1974 1). The situation was so bad that it was thought large quantities of rice were being smuggled into Burma from Thailand. However, a tender was held for a limited quantity of Burma brokens, 2, 3 and 4 (*LRBAC* 19th December 1974 1).

1975 was to be another year of low exports. In January, parcels of 10,000 tons Burma old crop brokens B2, B3 and B4 were tendered for sale by the MEIC (Myanmar Export Import Company) but there was no news of a new crop (*LRBAC* 31st January 1975 1). Old crop remained available but not new crop (*LRBAC* 28th February 1975 1). In May, there were reports that severe storms and flooding had damaged rice in storage (*LRBAC* 30th May 1975 1). 100,000 tons were thought to have been destroyed, which would reduce the exportable surplus by that amount (*LRBAC* 27th June 1975 1). In August, 20,000 tons of white rice were sold to a Singapore company for an undisclosed destination (*LRBAC* 26th August 1975 1). In December, the Burmese authorities indicated 10,000 tons of 25 per cent or 35 per cent *Ngatsein* could be shipped promptly, and 30,000 to 40,000 tons in the near future. 7,000 tons of *Zeera* 15 per cent and 7,000 tons of *Ngatsein* full boiled 12 per cent were available, 5,000 tons of B1 and B2 could be shipped in February, and 2, 3 and 4 were available (*LRBAC* 22nd December 1975 1).

But in 1976 the situation improved. Exports for the year were the best for some years at 628,000 tons (see Table 4.1 above). In February, there were substantial Government-to-government sales, and also sales to the private trade, including 105,000 tons of *Ngatsein* Small Mills Specials 25 per cent brokens, sold to a Singapore company for Indonesia (*LRBAC* 26th February 1976 1). At the end of March, the export surplus was understood to be about 450,000 tons. Around 100,000 tons were sold to Ceylon, and there were various Government-to-government sales to Indonesia and the Arab Gulf. Significantly, a delegation even came from Vietnam to negotiate! (*LRBAC* 1st April 1976 1). But loading delays at Rangoon caused problems (*LRBAC* 27th May 1976 1). Because of the declining exports from Burma, the World Bank allocated Burma a substantial sum for further planting and production of rice. Support was to be given to the Government to protect the Delta region from flooding and saltwater intrusion. As background, the *Circular* noted that Burma had exported 1,300,000 tons of rice in 1965, but less than 200,000 tons in 1975 (*LRBAC* 24th 1976 1). But by September Burma was largely withdrawn from the market (*LRBAC* 30th September 1976 1).

1977 turned out to be another good year with 668,000 tons. In January, it was reported that heavy rain in Southern Burma had seriously affected the harvest, but there might be 600,000 tons for export including 100,000 tons of broken rice, although none before March (*LRBAC* 31st January 1977 1). The estimated surplus was updated to 600,000 tons of white and parboiled rice, with 100,000 tons of broken rice ordinary 2, 3 and 4, B1 and B2, etc. The 600,000 tons would also probably include 20,000 tons of raw rice bran and 80,000 tons of extracted rice bran, but mostly it would be *Ngatsein* Small Mills Specials 25 per cent/35 per cent. 100,000 tons of 35 per cent and/or full boiled 12 per cent was being sold to China to supply Sri Lanka under a rubber exchange deal. 54,000 tons of *Milchar* and *Emata* had been sold to Mauritius, covering requirements for that country. Significantly 20,000 tons of *Yawg Yaw* 35 per cent, a low quality, had been sold to Vietnam. Indonesia had bought 30,000 tons of *Emata* 35 per cent and *Zeera* 25 per cent. Other purchasers were Singapore and Yugoslavia, and there was also some *non-faq* or damaged rice which might be difficult to sell (*LRBAC* 28th February 1977 1). Of the 600,000 tons of whole grain rice and 100,000 tons of broken rice, half was sold by March, but it was unlikely much more could be sold until this had been shipped (*LRBAC* 30th March 1977 1). By November all old-crop rice and brokens had been sold. Negotiations were underway with various Governments for new crops, and Indonesia had bought 132,000 tons of *Ngatsein* Small Mills Specials (*LRBAC* 24th November 1977 1). But in December, the market was quiet (*LRBAC* 29th December 1977 1).

No new sales were reported in January 1978 (*LRBAC* 31st January 1978 1). The new crop had again been hit by unfavourable weather, and exports were not expected to exceed 400,000 tons compared with about 630,000 tons in 1977 (*LRBAC* 28th February 1978 1). Official statistics put the 1977/78 crop at just less than 9,500,000 tons, 140,000 tons more than the 1976/77 crop. No whole rice had been available for some time (*LRBAC* 26th April 1978 1). Then the crop estimate was cut to 8,800,000 tons and export availability at 400,000 tons, compared to the 600,000 tons in 1977. The *Circular* commented tellingly that in the 1930s Burma was the world's largest rice exporter, seldom shipping less than 3,000,000 tons (*LRBAC* 31st May 1978 1). But it was reported that the Burmese Government expected rice production in 1978/79 to reach 10,000,000 tons, an increase of about 700,000 tons over the 1977/78 official figures, although bad weather was expected to affect current exports (*LRBAC* 30th October 1978 1).

In February 1979, Indonesia signed an agreement to purchase 50,000 tons of rice from Burma (*LRBAC* February 1979 1). Official forecasts for 1978/79 put production at 10,500,000 tons of paddy compared with 9,500,000 tons the previous year. China had agreed to buy 50,000 tons of rice and Indonesia 50,000 tons at undisclosed prices. Export availability for 1979 was officially forecast at 600,000 to 700,000 tons (*LRBAC* 30th March 1979 1). The quality of the 1978/79 crop was very good, and the export target was 600,000 tons. 300,000 tons had been sold, including 80,000 tons to China for the rubber/rice deal with Sri Lanka, 100,000 tons to Indonesia, 10,000 tons to the Maldives Islands, and 110,000 tons to private merchants, including West Africa and Reunion. No broken rice had been traded, except 15,000 tons to the Gambia (*LRBAC* 30th April 1979 1). The export target for the financial year 1st April 1979 to 31st March 1980 was 600,000 tons. By May Government business and private sales approached 400,000 tons, which included another 80,000 tons to Indonesia, and 100,000 tons *Ngatsein* Small Mills Specials 35 per cent/Long boiled 12 per cent sold Government-to-government to Bangladesh (*LRBAC* 31st May 1979 1). Another 80,000 tons were sold Government-to-government unspecified and to private trade, of which 30,000 tons were *Ngatsein*

Small Mills Specials. By September Burma was effectively sold out until new crops became available in early 1980 (*LRBAC* 28th September 1979 1). In November, it appeared that the new crop would be somewhat below normal. 150,000 tons had been sold to Indonesia of 15 per cent and 25 per cent (*LRBAC* 30th November 1979 1). The 1979 crop was now effectively sold out, although a tender for 15,000 tons of broken rice from 1979 and 1980 crops was to be held in January. Marketing of the new crop would probably start in February 1980 (*LRBAC* 31st December 1979 1).

French Indo-China (Vietnam, Cambodia and Laos) but principally Vietnam and the port of Saigon-Cholon, had been one of the great Asian rice exporters. But these were bleak years of war and disruption, and little export activity is noted. Instead, Vietnam was increasingly an importer. Imports ranged from highs of 1,336,000 tons in 1974 and 1,310,000 tons in 1975 to a low of 35,000 tons in 1978. U.S. Aid in the form of P.L.480 figured significantly in the financing of imports, up to the U.S. withdrawal in 1975. Following Ho Chi Minh's Viet Cong Tet (Spring) offensive of January 1968, the war in Vietnam became increasingly unpopular in the United States, and in 1969 peace talks began in Paris. President Nixon withdrew some of the U.S.'s 500,000 forces and encouraged the Vietnamese themselves to participate more in the South's military struggle. This proved ineffective, as were the peace talks in Paris. Although Ho Chi Minh died in 1969, the United States intensified the war in 1970, attacking Viet Cong bases in Cambodia, and bombing Viet Cong forces in Laos (Andrews 1997 201).

1970 was a year of heavy rice imports of 580,000 tons. The United States, under P.L.480, had agreed to make available 150,000 tons of rice to South Vietnam during late 1969/70 and South Vietnam was given authorisation to purchase another 50,000 tons by the end of January 1970 (*LRBAC* 29th November 1969 3). These allocations were a concern to the authorities in Thailand who had a large crop to sell (*LRBAC* 2nd January 1970 2). Further purchase authorisations under P.L.480 were granted to South Vietnam for 25,000 tons of medium-grain rice and 25,000 tons of long-grain rice for shipment by the end of February. With these authorisations, sales were reported of 25,000 tons to South Vietnam, and there were enquiries for the rest (*LRBAC* 2nd January 1970 3). South Vietnam also bought 10,000 tons from the Thailand government to government (*LRBAC* 30th January 1970 2). This was followed by a U.S. P.L.480 sale of about 73,000 tons long grain rice and 25,000 tons of medium grain rice to South Vietnam, with further authorisation for 10,500 tons for shipment by the end of May (*LRBAC* 30th January 1970 3). In February, South Vietnam bought from the United States about 50,000 tons long grain rice 20 per cent brokens under P.L.480 (*LRBAC* 27th February 1970 3). South Vietnam was again in the market under the P.L.480 "Food for Peace" plan for 50,000 tons of long grain rice from Gulf of Mexico ports (*LRBAC* lst May 1970 3). This sale was finalised in May (*LRBAC* 30th May 1970 3). In June, South Vietnam was given P.L.480 authorisation to buy 50,000 tons for July/August shipment, partly ex-stock pile, at a special discount and partly new crop (*LRBAC* 30th June 1970 3). Agreements were also being negotiated under P.L.480 to supply 150,000 tons to South Vietnam (*LRBAC* 31st July 1970 3). In September, 50,000 tons of rice was reported under P.L.480 to South Vietnam, and further authorisation was granted to purchase

100,000 tons, consisting of 60,000 tons of long grain and 40,000 tons of medium grain for shipment from October 15th to November 10th (*LRBAC* 29th September 1970 3). This purchase took place (*LRBAC* 30th October 1970 3). Authorisation was then awaited for a further 50,000 tons under P.L.480, some of it likely to be long grain (*LRBAC* 30th November 1970 4). In December, South Vietnam did indeed buy 30,000 tons long grain rice, and 19,200 tons of medium grain under P.L.480 (*LRBAC* 31st December 1970 4).

1971 was a quieter year for imports to South Vietnam, with only 137,000 tons being recorded. In June, it was reported from the United States that South Vietnam did not require any more rice currently (*LRBAC* 28th June 1971 3). But in November, purchase authorisation was granted under P.L.480 for 30,000 tons for South Vietnam for November/December shipment, subject to industrial action in the docks in the United States coming to an end (*LRBAC* 26th November 1971 3). This rice was duly purchased, being long grain for shipment in the second half of December (*LRBAC* 29th December 1971 3). 1972 saw overall imports of 272,000 tons and in April 1972, South Vietnam bought 42,000 tons long grain from the United States under P.L.480, shipment first half of May. They were anxious for more, but this would depend on a political decision (*LRBAC* 28th April 1972 4). However, in May, 27,000 tons were indeed bought under P.L.480, being long grain from the Gulf of Mexico (*LRBAC* 31st May 1972 3). Then, in July 1972, the U.S. Secretary of State, Henry Kissinger, began new peace talks in Paris (Andrews 1997 201). By September, South Vietnam had a balance of 85,000 tons outstanding from a previous P.L.480 agreement, which was expected to be shipped in the autumn, some likely to be long grain (*LRBAC* 6th September 1972 2). In September, they bought 50,000 tons under P.L.480, and authorisation was given for a further 30,000 tons to be contracted in the last week of the month for delivery in October/November (*LRBAC* 26th September 1972 3). In October, under P.L.480 South Vietnam bought 47,500 tons of long grain rice, and neighbouring Cambodia bought 30,000 tons of Gulf medium grain (*LRBAC* 30th October 1972 3). In November, South Vietnam bought a further 40,000 tons from the United States for the December shipment, and 30,000 tons for the January 1973 shipment. The usual P.L.480 quality was No.5 long grain 20 per cent brokens (*LRBAC* 30th November 1973 3). In December, a purchase was made under P.L.480 of 40,000 tons to be shipped to Cambodia (*LRBAC* 29th September 1972 4).

In January 1973, an accord was signed under which the United States withdrew from Vietnam, with the 17th parallel dividing the country pending re-unification by "peaceful means" (Andrews 1997 210). This was also the year of the 1972/73 *EN*SO-related world rice crisis. However, imports were relatively modest at 270,000 tons. P.L.480 business during January included 25,000 tons of Gulf medium grain to Cambodia and purchases were pending for South Vietnam (*LRBAC* 31st January 1973 3). In February, 35,000 tons of medium grain were sold under P.L.480 to Vietnam, and 28,000 tons to Cambodia, with Vietnam expected to be in the market for a further 36,200 tons shortly (*LRBAC* 28th February 1973 3). In March, Cambodia bought 5,000 tons of rice from Thailand (*LRBAC* 30th March 1973 2). They also bought 15,000 tons from the United States of P.L.480 quality rice and were negotiating for another 40,000 tons (*LRBAC* 30th March 1973 3). Negotiations between Cambodia and Thailand continued in April (*LRBAC* 30th April 1973 2). South Vietnam then bought 5,000 tons of medium grain and 34,000 tons of long grain under P.L.480. A further 28,000 tons intended for allocation to Cambodia were instead transferred to South Vietnam and a purchase allocation for this amount was expected shortly (*LRBAC* 30th April 1973 2). In July, Cambodia bought 5,000 tons of rice from the Thailand government to government (*LRBAC* 30th July 1973 1). It had been announced in the United States that P.L.480 allocations that season would be restricted to 600,000 tons and the Department of Agriculture did not intend to grant purchase authorisation early in the season. However, they were overruled by the State Department, which insisted allocations be granted to South Vietnam and Cambodia for September and October shipments. It was expected that South Vietnam would be authorised to purchase about 35,000 tons and Cambodia 25,000 tons, although the latter was likely to be cancelled if Cambodia fell into Communist hands (*LRBAC* 30th August 1973 3). There were then floods in Texas and Louisiana, and the purchase authorisation for Vietnam and a re-tender for 10,000 tons for Cambodia were delayed until the flood damage had been assessed (*LRBAC* 30th September 1973 3). In October, Cambodia bought 10,000 tons of unspecified quality, and South Vietnam bought 25,000 tons of medium grain. Under P.L.480 a further purchase allocation of 40,000 tons was made for Vietnam, and another 50,000 tons for later in the year. Also under P.L.480 Cambodia bought 10,000 tons of medium grain from the Gulf of Mexico, and South Vietnam 25,000 tons of medium grain (*LRBAC* 30th October 1973 3). In November, a typhoon caused considerable damage to crops in South Vietnam (*LRBAC* 30th November 1973 2). Again under P.L.480 Cambodia bought another 15,000 tons of Gulf medium grain, and 10,000 tons of Californian medium grain for prompt shipments, and was negotiating for a further 50,000 tons for shipment in December/January. This meant that Cambodia had purchased 60,000 tons under P.L.480 that season and Vietnam 65,000 tons. Under outstanding agreements, Cambodia was to receive a further 75,000 tons and Vietnam 50,000 tons, with more rice likely to be made available for Vietnam (*LRBAC* 30th November 1973 3). In December, sales were made by the United States to both Vietnam and Cambodia (*LRBAC* 30th December 1973 3).

1974 saw the highest imports of the decade at 1,336,000 tons, but details were sparse in the *Circular*. Cambodia bought an undisclosed amount at a high price from the United States under a P.L.480 tender. P.L.480 allocations for 1974 were restricted to 600,000 tons for South Vietnam and Cambodia, with a provisional figure for the following year of 1,000,000 tons (*LRBAC* 28th February 1974 3). In March, at a Vietnam tender, prices were high for a quantity of P.L.480 rice No.5 20 per cent, and about half that quantity was also bought as long grain rice (*LRBAC* 29th March 1974 2). In May, a P.L.480 tender was held for Cambodia, possibly the last of the current crop year (*LRBAC* 31st May 1974 3). By September the P.L.480 programme for 1975 had not even started. The first tender for Cambodia for 30,000 tons did not result in a sale as there was not enough rice available and what there was, was too expensive. P.L.480 purchases expected in the coming months included two lots of 30,000 tons for Cambodia (*LRBAC* 27th September 1974 2).

At the end of 1974 the Communists launched a big offensive in Vietnam, and on April 30th 1975 Saigon surrendered (Andrews 1997 201). That month the Convention of the Rice Millers Association was held in New Orleans. A major issue of concern there was that the U.S. rice industry was facing the loss of their market in Cambodia, and the impending loss of their market in Vietnam. P.L.480 rice afloat to these markets was discharged in Singapore for transshipment and further quantities were likely to be diverted to Bangladesh. It would be hard to replace these markets and could only be done by selling U.S. rice to markets usually supplied by other countries. This would further weaken the world market for lower quality rice (*LRBAC* 28th April 1975 3). Stocks of P.L.480 quality afloat for Vietnam were landed in Singapore and the Philippines and sold off cheaply to merchants (*LRBAC* 27th June 1975 3). In July came rumours that China had purchased 200,000 tons of rice from Thailand for shipment to Vietnam or Cambodia (*LRBAC* 25th July 1975 2). China did indeed buy 200,000 tons from Thailand after prolonged negotiations, in a barter deal for oil spread over twelve months (*LRBAC* 26th August 1975 1).

After this, details in the *Circular* of the rice trade with Vietnam and Cambodia are sparse. In April 1976, a delegation from Vietnam was in Burma to negotiate for rice, but no details emerged of business done (*LRBAC* 1st April 1976 1). On 2nd July 1976 Vietnam was officially re-united as the Socialist Republic of Vietnam (Andrews 1997 201). In February 1977, Vietnam bought 20,000 tons of *Yawg Yaw* 35 per cent, a low quality, from Burma (*LRBAC* 28th February 1977 1). But in November 1977, Thailand closed its borders with Laos and Cambodia, and in consequence had more rice available for export than usual (*LRBAC* 24th November 1977 3). October 1978 saw heavy damage in Vietnam, Cambodia and Laos due to typhoons, continuous heavy rainfall, and flooding. Thailand was unaffected, and broken rice prices there increased due to large Government-to-government sales to Vietnam to alleviate the distress (*LRBAC* 30th October 1978 3). In January 1979, Japan made 90,000 tons originally earmarked for Vietnam available instead as an Aid programme for West Africa. Shipment had not yet been arranged (*LRBAC* 30th January 1979 2). In April, India made a deal with Russia for 200,000 tons of rice 25 per cent brokens. This was within the framework of an exchange for crude oil. Shipments would be 30,000 tons of rice a month, and a large proportion of the rice would be shipped to Vietnam (*LRBAC* 30th April 1979 2).

In Thailand exports during the 1970s ran at between 848,000 and 2,931,000 tons. But as in Burma, there were poor years, in 1973 of 848,000 tons, 1974, 1,046,000 tons, and 1975, 951,000 tons, the years affected by the *EN*SO event. 1978 was also a bad year at 1,606,000 tons as in Burma. But by 1980 exports were running at 2,791,000 tons, more than four times the level of Burma at a mere 653,000 tons. This level was sustained and indeed vastly exceeded in the 1980s.

In January 1970, the *Circular* reported that exports from Thailand in 1969 would probably just exceed 1,000,000 tons due to heavy loadings for Government-to-government contracts late in December. (Ed. It was actually 2,054,000 tons!). But the new crop in 1970 was expected to produce an exportable surplus of 1,250,000 tons, although the crop was late (*LRBAC* 2nd January 1970 2). As a sign of the times, Thailand sold 10,000 tons to South Vietnam, government to government.

Also 30,000 tons of A1 Super to Senegal, government to government (*LRBAC* 30th January 1970 2). This was followed by 40,000 tons to the Indonesian government to government, and similarly 20,000 tons to Mauritius (*LRBAC* 27th February 1970 2). Government-to-government sales continued including 40,000 tons to Indonesia financed by Japan (*LRBAC* 1st May 1970 3). There had been a reduction in the export duty of 25 per cent on parcels of 1,000 tons of parboiled or broken rice, 2,000 tons of white rice and 500 tons of glutinous rice, and this was now applied to any quantities above these amounts (*LRBAC* 30th May 1970 2). Enquiries ceased from South Vietnam and Indonesia and others as they had adequate supplies of American rice supplied under the aid scheme P.L.480 (*LRBAC* 30th June 1970 2). Government-to-government and commercial sales were reported to Hong Kong, the Persian Gulf and the Seychelles (*LRBAC* 1st September 1970 2).

In 1971 the market continued to decline as many of the markets traditionally supplied with Thai rice had received U.S. rice under P.L.480 (*LRBAC* 12th March 1971 3). By May Government-to-government contracts had nearly all been shipped, leaving Thailand with a large surplus. So the Government abolished all export taxes on rice and *Loonzain* containing more than 10 per cent brokens, and also on broken rice. Enquiries flooded in and there was heavy buying of high-quality rice for immediate shipment to Singapore and Hong Kong (*LRBAC* 3rd May 1971 2). The export tax was also cancelled on all types of parboiled rice. 10,000 tons of mostly glutinous rice was sold to Japan, pushing prices up sharply for this quality of rice (*LRBAC* 1st June 1971 2). Now came interest from the Philippines and other Far Eastern countries, and for parboiled rice for quick shipment to India to feed East Pakistan refugees (*LRBAC* 3rd September 1971 2). By the end of September, 1,050,000 tons had been shipped that year and a further 250,000 tons remained to be shipped against contracts already concluded. 1,150,000 tons of all qualities remained to be sold in the current crop year. Container freight was now being introduced by Far East Conference Lines but had not yet been extended to Bangkok (*LRBAC* 4th October 1971 2. See also Meek 2003 142–172). Total exports of rice from 1st January to 14th November 1971 were 1,327,200 tons, an increase of 400,000 tons over the same period in 1970, and total exports for the year were predicted at 1,500,000 tons. The Philippines purchased 43,000 tons of low-grade rice, white rice 15 per cent and A1 brokens for November/December shipment. The British Government financed the Indian Government to purchase about 140,000 tons of Thai rice for East Pakistan refugees (*LRBAC* 26th November 1971 2). The new crop was coming in well, but the Indo-Pakistan war had weakened the market, as contracts for shipment became doubtful. Now peace was being restored Thailand expected substantial demand from that region for low-quality rice through 1972. Heavy demand was also anticipated from the Philippines. 50,000 tons of A1 brokens were sold for spread shipment to Dakar in Senegal (*LRBAC* 29th December 1971 2).

The exportable surplus for 1972 was unofficially forecast at 1,700,000 tons. 300,000 tons had been sold to the Philippines, government to government, being a mixture of white rice 10 per cent and 15 per cent with A1 broken rice (*LRBAC* 28th January 1972 3). 30,000 to 40,000 of A1 brokens was sold to Senegal, and

India was in the market for 140,000 tons government to government, and Sri Lanka for 100,000 tons (*LRBAC* 29th February 1972 3). Around 60,000 tons were sold to India (*LRBAC* 6th April 1972 2). 100,000 tons of white rice special quality 75 per cent brokens was sold to the Philippines for August/December shipment (*LRBAC* 28th July 1972 2). Stocks were running low in Thailand, so the Government decreed permission must be obtained to export any quantity over 1,000 tons. On any export sale, the exporter was required to sell 15 per cent of the quantity to the Government stockpile as 25 per cent broken white rice for local consumption or eventual delivery to Indonesia, a regular customer. The Government would pay well below the current market price (*LRBAC* 6th September 1972 2). Under this scheme, individual exporters were given a monthly quota (*LRBAC* 26th September 1972 3). Unofficial estimates of the exportable surplus for 1973 ranged from 700,000 tons to 1,800,000 tons (*LRBAC* 30th November 1972 2). Government-to-government sales in December included 250,000 tons to Indonesia and elsewhere. Exports for 1972 were expected to reach 2,000,000 tons, which would be an all-time record, but estimates for 1973 were much lower, with one Government estimate as low as 1,000,000 tons (*LRBAC* 29th December 1972 3).

But this was now the period 1973–**19**75 following the *EN*SO event of 1972/73 which devastated Asian rice crops as discussed under Burma above. In the event, 1973 turned out to be the worst year of the 1970s for Thailand's exports, at 848,000 tons. It was a year of crisis in world trade, with the fall in Thailand's exports coinciding with the collapse of exports from Burma. In January 1973, the *Circular* reported a serious shortfall in world rice supplies. Indonesia, the Philippines, India and Bangladesh were all in great need of rice, and it was difficult to see where this rice would come from (*LRBAC* 31st January 1973 1). New crop estimates for Thailand put the crop at 11,600,000 tons compared with 14,200,000 in 1972, with a carryover of only 300,000 tons. Domestic consumption was estimated at 11,750,000 tons annually. The Thai Ministry of Agriculture estimated an exportable surplus of 600,000 tons, but they needed enough for domestic consumption and seed. Yet rice exports were one of Thailand's chief sources of foreign exchange, and forward contracts had already been made by Government and private traders at prices well below current prices. Immediate business was impossible, and price quotations were meaningless. So the authorities decreed that all unshipped contracts would be reviewed by the Thai Ministry of Commerce about a week before shipment, and they might refuse the export licence. A quota of 135,000 tons was set for January/February (*LRBAC* 31st January 1973 2). In February, Thailand sold 20,000 tons to Bangladesh government to government and loading continued on Government-to-government sales to Indonesia and other sales concluded before 15th January. Although Thailand's rice crop was estimated to be 20 per cent below the previous year's crop, export commitments included 250,000 tons to Indonesia, 150,000 tons to West Africa, 120,000 tons to Singapore/Malaysia, Hong Kong and Cambodia, 60,000 tons to the Middle East, Europe, etc., and 20,000 tons to Bangladesh. It was uncertain how much of this rice could be shipped. No offers of Thai rice could now be made (*LRBAC* 28th February 1973 2). Then, as mentioned in Burma above, the *Circular* reported (in bold) that rice prices had reached an all-time high in Europe

(*LRBAC* 30th March 1973 1). The Government hoped that with the second crop, they might achieve exports of 650,000 tons for the year, less than a third of exports in 1972. Government delegations from many countries were turned away empty-handed, and the only sale in March was 5,000 tons to Cambodia at an undisclosed price (*LRBAC* 30th March 1973 2). Limited quantities of low-quality rice and brokens were released by the authorities for export to neighbouring countries, and there were negotiations with Indonesia and Cambodia (*LRBAC* 30th April 1973 2). By May harvest of the second crop had begun, but there was no estimate of the amount. The Government's first concern was to maintain local supplies and keep prices down, but export licences were granted for small quantities to traditional markets (*LRBAC* 31st May 1973 2). The *Circular* now drew attention (in capitals) to the critical situation in world rice markets (*LRBAC* 30th June 1973 1). The summer crop in Thailand was disappointing and trade estimates were only 500,000 tons against hopes of 1,000,000 tons. All exports were banned, except for some quantities outstanding on Government-to-government contracts (*LRBAC* 30th June 1973 2). These they wanted to honour before allowing other sales, but to alleviate shortages they made available Government-to-government 10,000 tons to the Philippines, and 5,000 tons to Cambodia (*LRBAC* 20th July 1973 1). The *Circular* now referred again (in capitals) to the crisis in the world rice market, saying it would continue until Asian new crops came in at the end of the year. Fraudulent offers of rice were circulating (*LRBAC* 30th August 1973 1). Exports of limited quantities of parboiled and broken rice were now permitted from Thailand, but the exporter had to sell to the Government twice the quantity of his exports at a low fixed price. An export tax was imposed. Some limited business was done to Indonesia, the Philippines, Malaysia, Laos, Bangladesh, Mauritius and the Persian Gulf, but prices were far too high for normal commerce. Floods in northern Thailand destroyed a small part of the crop (*LRBAC* 30th August 1973 2). But by October it was expected there would be a good crop of 13,500,000 tons of paddy, giving an exportable surplus of between 1,200,000 tons and 1,500,000 tons of white rice basis. The Ministry of Commerce forecast was 1,500,000 tons (*LRBAC* 30th October 1973 2). This was then cut to 1,200,000 tons, with 400,000–500,000 tons to be licensed for export in the first quarter of 1974 (*LRBAC* 30th November 1973 2). Considerable business was reported to the Persian Gulf, which might not be fulfilled due to lack of freight (*LRBAC* 30th December 1973 3).

1974 was another poor year at 1,046,000 tons. But in a sign that the situation was easing a little, in January 1974, the quantity of rice shippers had to deliver to the Government at a fixed price against exports was reduced from 100 per cent to 50 per cent (*LRBAC* 31st January 1974 2). There was demand from Taiwan (*LRBAC* 28th February 1974 2). The authorities now estimated a crop of 14,000,000 tons of paddy, with an exportable surplus of 1,200,000 tons of milled rice. This did not include a second crop which might produce another 500,000 tons of paddy (*LRBAC* 29th March 1974 2). The May export quota was 40,000 tons, made up of 20,000 tons to the Philippines and 20,000 tons to Taiwan (*LRBAC* 30th April 1974 2). In May, government-to-government sales were 100,000 tons of white rice 25 per cent to Indonesia, 35,000 tons of A1 special to the Philippines, and 12,000 tons of parboiled to Mauritius. The June quota for commercial exports was 51,900 tons but set at unworkable prices (*LRBAC* 31st May 1974 2). The second crop was being harvested in June (*LRBAC* 28th June 1974 2). Substantial business was done to the Middle East and East Africa (*LRBAC* 26th July 1974 2). There were sales to Singapore and Hong Kong of white, parboiled and glutinous rice, and 10,000 tons of white rice 100 per cent were sold to Iraq (*LRBAC* 27th August 1984 2). November saw the export quota system discontinued and a further reduction in the export tax (*LRBAC* 29th November 1974 2). So there was a surge of business with 30,000 tons of 10 per cent white rice sold to Russia, 5,000 tons of A1 brokens to West Africa, 12,000 tons of special mixture to Comoros, 10,000 tons special mixture to Malagasy, and about 20,000 tons of B grade 100 per cent for destinations including Europe, Singapore and Hong Kong. Exports in November were about 35,400 tons taking the total for the first eleven months of the year to about 924,500 tons (*LRBAC* 19th December 1974 3).

But 1975 was the second worst year of the 1970s for Thailand as far as rice exports were concerned, at 951,000 tons. A new minority Government was formed in Thailand which was expected to obtain a vote of confidence on 1st March 1975. 100,000 tons of Thai rice 25 per cent was sold to Indonesia, Peru bought 25,000 tons of Thai rice 25 per cent *faq* (*LRBAC* 28th 1975 2). Around 50,000 tons of A1 broken rice and low-quality whole rice were sold to the Philippines, and the first vessel for Peru was loading. However, the 100,000 tons of Thai white 25 per cent to Indonesia failed to materialise (*LRBAC* 27th March 1975 2). 15,000 tons were being shipped to Singapore, 5,000 tons to Brunei, and as part of Japanese Government Aid, 5,400 tons to the Philippines. 3,500 tons of parboiled had been sold to the United Nations agency for Somalia and Ruanda. Shipments had started to Peru and the Philippines (*LRBAC* 28th April 1975 2). The export levy was reduced by 400 Baht on *Loonzain*, white rice and broken rice, and by 500 Baht on parboiled rice. India bought 100,000 tons of parboiled rice 15 per cent broken (*LRBAC* 27th June 1975 2). The second crop was good and it was rumoured China had bought 200,000 tons for shipment to Vietnam or Cambodia. Government-to-government sales included 100,000 tons of parboiled 15 per cent to India, 2,500 tons white rice A1 super for Okinawa, and 2,000 tons white rice for Singapore (*LRBAC* 25th July 1975 2). India bought 100,000 tons to be shipped by the end of the year, comprising 80,000 tons of parboiled 15 per cent and 20,000 tons of 25 per cent white rice. The sale of 200,000 tons to China was confirmed after prolonged negotiations, thought to be a further agreement against oil spread over 12 months (*LRBAC* 26th August 1975 1). In October, government-to-government sales were 15,000 tons of white rice to Singapore and 4,000 tons of broken rice to Japan (*LRBAC* 24th October 1975 2). To move old crop stocks, the Government cut the amount shippers had to contribute to the stockpile from 100 per cent to 50 per cent of every parcel sold, and reduced export duties (*LRBAC* 25th November 1975 3).

1976 was a much better year with 1,925,000 tons. In January, the Bangkok Authorities cancelled the regulation that exporters must contribute 50 per cent of any quantity exported to the Government stockpile, causing prices to rise and some industrial unrest. They then reduced the export premium and export tax.

These measures made Thai rice more competitive. Government-to-government sales were made to Mauritius of 48,000 tons of 15 per cent parboiled rice, to India of 49,000 tons of 25 per cent and 20,000 tons of 15 per cent, and to the Philippines of 55,000 tons of 55 per cent (*LRBAC* 29th January 1976 3). The official forecast for the export surplus for 1975/76 was 1,500,000 tons of which 600,000 tons would be government-to-government sales including 150,000 tons of old business to China. Recent government-to-government sales included 100,000 tons of white rice to Indonesia, and another 100,000 tons might be required. 40,000 tons of Thai white rice were sold to Malaysia, and 20,000 tons in a private sale to Indonesia (*LRBAC* 26th February 1976 3). Singapore bought another 20,000 tons of white rice 100 per cent B grade for April/June shipment, bringing sales to Singapore for the year to 42,000 tons. A further 100,000 tons were bought for Indonesia, bringing the total to Indonesia to 200,000 tons (*LRBAC* 1st April 1976 3). Singapore took 12,000 tons of Thai rice for May/June shipment and the Malagasy Republic 10,000 tons of 5 per cent white rice (*LRBAC* 27th May 1976 3). Unspecified amounts of broken rice and low-quality rice were sold to Mauritius, Reunion and Seychelles (*LRBAC* 24th June 1976 3). Unspecified amounts of high-grade white rice were also sold to Hong Kong and Singapore. A cargo of broken rice was sold to West Africa, and 70,000 tons to Indonesia, with a prospect of another 100,000 tons government-to-government (*LRBAC* 26th July 1976 2). This was confirmed when 200,000 tons of white rice 25 per cent brokens, double what was expected, were sold government to government to Indonesia for delivery in August/December 1976. Japan purchased about 20,000 tons of parboiled for shipment to Bangladesh under an Aid programme (*LRBAC* 26th August 1976 2). (Ed. Indonesia seemed to be in some difficulty, reflecting the 1976/77 *EN*SO event. Note previous purchases this year of 100,000 tons and 20,000 tons in February, 100,000 tons in April, 70,000 tons in July and now 200,000 tons in August). This was confirmed when an agreement was made to sell 200,000 tons of 25 per cent to Indonesia for delivery in 1977, in addition to the 200,000 tons just purchased. Sri Lanka bought 20,000 to 30,000 tons of A1 super, and the Malagasy Republic bought 20,000 tons of 35 per cent special mixture government to government. 10,000 tons of 10 per cent were sold to Mombasa. Total exports from Thailand from January to August 1976 were 1,147,000 tons compared with 676,700 tons for the same period in 1975 (*LRBAC* 30th September 1976 2). But in October, export duties and quotations for exports were increased and the Ministry of Commerce re-imposed the stockpile system, requiring exporters to deliver to the Government stockpile a given percentage of the amount exported. This was 30 per cent for white rice 100 per cent and 5 per cent, 15 per cent for white rice lower grades, parboiled, *Loonzain* and A1 extra super, and 10 per cent for other broken grades. Exports for the first nine months of 1976 were about 1,388,100 tons of which about half was on government-to-government basis. This compared with total exports of 747,000 tons during the first five months of 1975 (*LRBAC* 28th October 1976 3). The new crop was expected to produce about 13,000,000 – 13,500,000 tons of paddy, which would give an exportable surplus of about 1,250,000 tons (*LRBAC* 25th November 1976 3).

1977 was the best year of the 1970s for exports from Thailand at 2,931,000 tons. By the end of January 1977 government-to-government sales for shipment during the first half of 1977 had already reached 450,000 tons, nearly half the predicted export surplus. Possibly in excess of 60,000 tons of parboiled had been sold to Nigeria (*LRBAC* 31st January 1977 3). Around 60,000 tons of mixed and broken rice was sold to Sri Lanka. In a significant development, rice exports from Thailand were now being handled by a recently formed association of all the merchants concerned (*LRBAC* 28th February 1977 2–3). Total exports for the first three months of 1977 were expected to be 650,000 tons which was 200,000 tons above the export target. So the target for the year was increased from 1,100,000 to 1,300,000 tons. A substantial sale of parboiled rice 5 per cent was made for shipment to Nigeria, and 50,000 tons were sold to Senegal, with another 50,000 tons under negotiation (*LRBAC* 30th March 1977 3). 20,000 tons of white rice 100 per cent was sold to Iraq, and Bangladesh agreed to buy 60,000 tons of parboiled rice. There were unconfirmed reports that Ghana had bought 25,000 tons of medium grain (*LRBAC* 26th April 1977 3). By May export commitments for the year totalled 1,500,000 tons, well above the revised export target of 1,300,000 tons. The authorities were now prepared to allow total exports of up to 1,800,000 tons for the year. But any commercial sale over 200 tons had to be reported to the authorities for their approval, and no sales were permitted beyond June shipment. Letters of credit had to be received within ten days of approval and registration of such sales (*LRBAC* 26th May 1977 3). Shipments for the first half of the year were now expected to be just under 1,500,000 tons and the latest estimate for the year was 2,200,000 tons, almost double previous estimates. Commercial sales were now permitted for shipment up to the end of September, but any business over 200 tons had still to be approved. Recent business included 10,000 tons of white rice to Iraq and a government-to-government sale to Singapore of 10,000 tons of lower quality rice (*LRBAC* 29th June 1977 2–3). Exports for the first half of 1977 totalled 1,520,000 tons and commitments for the rest of the year were already over 700,000 tons. A limit of 10,000 tons had been imposed on commercial sales for export. Sales during July included 50,000 tons to Bangladesh, 5000 tons of glutinous rice to Indonesia, and 6000 tons of *Loonzain* to Reunion. Malaysia bought 125,000 tons government to government for spread shipments from July to December, and 24,000 tons of 100 per cent white rice was sold to Iran for July/August shipment (*LRBAC* 28th July 1977 2). The Nigerian market was a good customer for Thai parboiled rice, and it was estimated that 235,000 tons had been exported to Nigeria up to lst September, with another 50,000 tons to be shipped that month. But the Thai authorities were increasingly worried about the large quantities of rice exports being made, and reduced the maximum size of individual commercial sales from 10,000 tons to 2,500 tons, and it was becoming difficult to get a licence for export (*LRBAC* 31st August 1977 3). No export licences were granted in October, and sales only made "subject to export licence". 2,250,000 tons had already been exported in 1977, and there was a danger the home market would be left short. One report said only 100,000 tons more would be authorised for export, including 70,000 tons on a government-to-government basis. There had been good rains, but they were late and it seemed the new crop would be delayed by a month (*LRBAC* 28th September 1977 2). Commercial quotations were strictly subject to export licences, which would be considered for November shipment to regular customers. A Government-to-government agreement had been made with Indonesia for 220,000 tons 20 per cent brokens for new crops to be shipped between January and April 1978 (*LRBAC* 27th October 1977 2). In November, new export regulations were announced with a quota for private trade of only 50,000 tons for December and 75,000 tons for January. Traders had to sell 1 ton of white rice 25 per cent super to the Government at a substantial loss to obtain 1 ton of the quota. The stockpile ratios were increased for all qualities of rice, causing prices to rise considerably. There had been insufficient rain in many of the rice-growing provinces, and the harvest was in any case late. But as regards the export surplus for 1978, the closure of the borders of Laos and Cambodia meant there was actually more rice available for overseas export than previously. These closures and the outstanding crop of 1976/77 had produced exports which would exceed 2,500,000 tons by the end of 1977. But it was thought that exports during the first half of 1978 might be down to around 1,000,000 tons, this being when the greater part of the rice surplus was expected (*LRBAC* 24th November 1977 3).

Exports for 1978 turned out to be well down in 1977 at 1,606,000 tons. The export quota for January 1978 was 75,000 tons. Then the authorities announced increases in the rice export premium (Ed. Export levy) on white rice, cargo rice, boiled rice, glutinous rice and broken rice. The authorities expected the 1978 main crop to be about 12,700,000 tons, with about 800,000 tons from the second crop. The export target was 1,200,000 tons (*LRBAC* 29th December 1977 3). Prices rose when the increase in the rice export premium was announced and rose again when the amount of rice to be put in the Government stockpile was announced. Nigeria remained a huge market for parboiled rice, and total sales to Nigeria in 1977 had been 360,000 tons (*LRBAC* 31st January 1978 3). In February, the Bangkok authorities increased the amount of rice private exporters had to contribute to the Government's stockpile at a fixed low price. On all whole rice, a quantity (100 per cent) equal to the quantity of the sale had to be contributed. The latest official forecast was for 1,000,000 tons but private sources suggested 1,500,000 to 2,000,000 tons. 40,000 tons of Thai white rice 5 per cent was sold by one exporter for Iraq (*LRBAC* 28th February 1978 3). In April, it was announced there would be no quota for whole grain on commercial terms, but there would be a quota of 40,000 tons for brokens. Around 20,000 tons were sold to Iraq, and the rest of the March quota was mainly parboiled rice for Nigeria. 30,000 tons were sold to Singapore for April/July, in addition to 35,000 tons already shipped (*LRBAC* 30th March 1978 3). Export quotas to the end of May were 30,000 tons of broken rice and 30,000 tons of other grades. The estimate for the summer crop was around 1,000,000 tons of paddy (*LRBAC* 26th April 1978 3). An additional 50,000 tons for export was granted of which at least half was to be low-grade rice. Severe difficulties were being experienced in the important Nigerian market, and one vessel loaded for Nigeria was under arrest in Singapore (*LRBAC* 31st May 1978 3). In June, the Bangkok authorities announced a special export quota in addition to those already granted, of 50,000 tons of low-grade white rice, parboiled rice, and A-grade broken rice. The second crop was expected to yield 1,500,000 tons of paddy, 50 per cent more than the original forecast. There was continued demand for parboiled from Nigeria (*LRBAC* 30th June 1978 3). Then the authorities announced a further export quota of 40,000 tons for August shipment, which could include any grade of rice. Most types of broken rice were free from quota if shipped before 31st October. Demand for parboiled continued from West Africa, but many vessels carrying rice to Nigeria were getting into trouble for non-payment of debts at ports of call. 17 vessels were under arrest in Singapore (*LRBAC* 26th July 1978 3). The percentage of rice which exporters had to sell to the Government was cut from 100 per cent to 50 per cent to increase the export of low-grade rice and was confined to 25 per cent, 35 per cent and 45 per cent white rice, 15 per cent, 25 per cent and 35 per cent parboiled rice, and all grades of *Loonzain*. The second crop was expected to be 1,800,000 tons, giving a total rice production over the 1977–78 season of 14,500,000 tons compared with just over 15,000,000 tons in 1976–77. Exports were now expected to reach 1,600,000 tons. Problems continued with shipments to Nigeria (*LRBAC* 31st August 1978 3). Exports over the first 8 months of 1978 were 1,000,000 tons, about half the figure for the same period in 1977 (*LRBAC* 28th September 1978 3). One of the main qualities now being offered was 5 per cent parboiled long grain packed in double 50 kilo sacks for shipment to Lagos, Nigeria. Broken rice prices had advanced due to large Government-to-government sales to Vietnam where foodstuffs were urgently needed to alleviate the distress caused by recent heavy flooding (*LRBAC* 30th October 1978 3). Exports from Thailand over the first ten months of the year totalled 1,230,000 tons and the Government's export target for the year was 1,400,000 tons. The Nigerian market had 120,000 tons of parboiled rice under contract, but the Nigerian Central Bank was checking the price of every contract, and it was becoming difficult to get prices approved. The Nigerian Government was worried over the very large quantities of rice being imported into the country (*LRBAC* 30th November 1978 3). By December, it was expected that exports for 1978 would be slightly under 1,500,000 tons compared with 2,800,000 tons in 1977 (*LRBAC* 30th December 1978 3).

1979 was a very good year with exports at 2,796,000 tons, second only to 1977, the best year of the decade. In January, the government took control of all exports. A syndicate of exporters was formed and all sales were pooled between exporters, regardless of who did the business. Small sales, however, were not distributed this way. Prices were now worked out between the government and exporters, and a weekly list was published. These prices were the minimum levels at which exporters could sell. This way the authorities were able to stop the downward slide of prices of the previous three months. A considerable amount of government to government and private business was concluded. Gambia bought 24,000 tons of A1 super broken rice for shipment in four lots of 6,000 tons each over the following twelve months. Business in Nigeria was disrupted by new rules introduced by the Nigerian authorities. Thai paddy production for the current season was expected to be 16,000,000 tons, assuming about 2,000,000 tons would come from the second crop. This compared with 14,500,000 tons in the previous season (*LRBAC* 30th

January 1979 1). Indonesia bought 300,000 tons of Thai white rice, with shipments from March at 40,000 to 50,000 tons per month. Other Government-to-government sales included 24,000 tons to Mauritius, and Malaysia with 140,000 tons of white rice, broken rice and white glutinous rice for spread shipment to the end of the year (*LRBAC* 28th February 1979 3). Export controls were eased, and approval was no longer required for quantities under 1,000 tons for delivery within a month. But official sanctions were still required for sales of over 1000 tons (*LRBAC* 30th March 1979 3). By June the authorities had limited further exports, as 2,300,000 tons had been sold government to government and commercially against an export target of 1,800,000 tons. Government-to-government sales from the current crop would only take place in special cases, and commercial sales over 1,000 tons would require Government approval (*LRBAC* 29th June 1979 3). 209,000 tons were sold to Brazil (*LRBAC* 31st July 1979 3). In October, the authorities eased export controls until March 1980 to encourage exports from the new crop, and private exporters were free to export as much as they liked without prior approval. 18,000 tons of high grade white rice were sold to Singapore. Exports for the current year were expected to reach 2,800,000 tons against a previous target of 2,600,000 tons (*LRBAC* 31st October 1979 3). The 1979–1980 crop was officially estimated at just under 18,000,000 tons, with 16,900,000 tons from the new crop to be harvested, and 1,000,000 from the second crop in mid-1980. Around 615,000 tons of the new crop had already been sold to Indonesia, made up of 400,000 tons of 25 per cent super, 200,000 tons of white rice 10 per cent and 15,000 tons of glutinous rice 10 per cent. Around 100,000 tons of high-quality white rice was sold to the Middle East, including Iran, Iraq and Syria for December/January/February shipment. Export controls were relaxed so private exporters no longer had to obtain Government approval before concluding business (*LRBAC* 30th November 1979 3). But in December, the official estimate of the 1979–80 crop was reduced from 18,000,000 tons to 14,000,000 tons of paddy, with the second crop 1,000,000 tons. The export target for 1980 was set at 1,500,000 tons, but other sources suggested exports might reach 2,200,000 tons (*LRBAC* 31st December 1979 3). They actually turned out to be 2,791,000 metric tons, another excellent year.

Of the rice-importing countries, Indonesia was the most important, with imports rising from 956,000 tons to 2,011,000 tons in 1980. But *EN*SO events are marked by low rainfall and drought in Indonesia (and heavy rain in South America), so sudden increases in rice imports to Indonesia are key markers of these events (Latham 2009). The high imports of 1,657,000 tons in 1973, and 1,132,000 tons in 1974 were clear responses to the *EN*SO event of 1972/73 as were the highs of 1,301,000 tons in 1976 and 1,973,000 tons in 1977 in response to the 1976/77 event. But imports continued at a high level until the end of the decade.

1970 was a year of some difficulty in Indonesia, with rice imports of 956,000 tons. These came from many sources, some of them quite surprising. The United States was a leading supplier, and P.L.480 purchase authorisation was granted for 75,000 tons for Indonesia by the end of February (*LRBAC* 2nd January 1970 3). Also, Japan negotiated with Thailand for rice to be shipped to Indonesia under an Aid programme (*LRBAC* 30th January 1970 2). Indonesia also bought from the

United States. Around 36,000 tons of long grain rice and 36,000 tons of medium grain (*LRBAC* 30th January 1970 3). This was followed by a small unspecified amount from Japan (*LRBAC* 27th February 1970 1). Indonesia bought another 40,000 tons from Thailand, government to government (*LRBAC* 27th February 1970 2). In May, Thailand also shipped 40,000 tons to Indonesia on Government-to-government terms but financed by Japan (*LRBAC* lst May 1970 3). Indonesia also bought 24,500 tons of Gulf (of Mexico) medium grain rice from the United States (*LRBAC* 30th May 1970 3). This seems to have eased the situation, and as Indonesia now appeared to have sufficient supplies of American rice under P.L.480, it no longer needed rice from Thailand (*LRBAC* 30th June 1970 2). But then Indonesia proceeded to buy from the United States a further 22,500 tons of medium grain, and 27,000 tons of long grain Gulf ports (*LRBAC* 30th June 1970 3). Japan also sold Indonesia 35,714 tons of rice, with shipment from Japanese ports in August/September with deferred payment over 30 years. By another U.S. P.L. 480 agreement Indonesia was to be supplied with 175,000 tons from the new crop, with Indonesia anxious to obtain some of this for August shipment (*LRBAC* 31st July 1970 3). Another P.L.480 authorisation followed for Indonesia to purchase about 30,000 tons for shipment September/October/November, probably of medium grain (*LRBAC* 1st September 1970 3). Buying rice wherever it could, Indonesia had also imported 1,397,131 quintals (139,713.1 metric tons) from Italy, between 1st September 1969 and 31st August 1970 (*LRBAC* 29th September 1970 2). There was a further P.L.480 purchase of 30,000 tons (*LRBAC* 29th September 2). Yet another 25,000 tons were then bought under P.L.480 and Indonesia was granted an additional allocation by which 80,000 tons of medium grain and 30,000 tons of long grain were purchased, and further purchases rumoured (*LRBAC* 30th October 1970 3). This turned out to be true, and Indonesia was waiting for a further P.L.480 allocation of 100,000 tons (*LRBAC* 30th November 1970 4). So in January 1971, Indonesia purchased about 106,730 tons of Gulf medium grain rice (*LRBAC* 29th January 1971 4).

Such were the purchases by Indonesia and other countries under P.L.480 that many markets traditionally supplied by Thailand had received U.S. rice instead (*LRBAC* 12th March 1971 3). But Indonesia's import needs were at last relieved as 1970 domestic rice production turned out at 11,767,000 tons, some 8.9 per cent up on 1969. The Government calculated that the country would achieve self-sufficiency by the end of 1973. But the *Circular* commented that similar predictions in the past had not been fulfilled, possibly because of population growth and/or higher *per capita* consumption (*LRBAC* 1st June 1971 1). (See also Latham 1994 and 2011. Also Latham 1999). Nevertheless, a large unspecified quantity of rice was made available to Indonesia under P.L.480 for shipment from the Gulf of Mexico to beat an anticipated U.S. dock strike in September 1971 (*LRBAC* 30th July 1971 3). This turned out to be a massive 350,000 tons, of which 100,000 tons were to be shipped by the middle of September (*LRBAC* 3rd September 1971 3). The 100,000 tons were duly shipped, and it was expected that Indonesia would be in the market for the October shipment of some of the remaining 250,000 tons (*LRBAC* 4th October 1971 4). A further P.L.480 authority was due to be given for another

250,000 tons (*LRBAC* 29th October 1971 3–4). P.L.480 authorisation was given to Indonesia for 50,000 tons for November/December shipment, subject to normality returning to the docks (*LRBAC* 26th November 1971 3). Indonesia bought another 50,000 tons under P.L.480 for very early delivery and was interested in another 50,000 tons before the strike deadline (*LRBAC* 29th December 1971 3).

In January 1972, again under P.L.480, Indonesia bid for 50,000 tons of long grain rice prior to the dock strike (which had been postponed) (*LRBAC* 28th January 1972 4). It did indeed buy 50,000 tons from the Gulf of Mexico for early shipment (*LRBAC* 29th February 1972 3). This was followed by another 50,000 tons of Gulf long grain under P.L.480 (*LRBAC* 6th April 1972 3). A further 33,000 tons were authorised under P.L.480 for shipment June/15th July (*LRBAC* 31st May 1972 3). Then there was a quiet period. But in September, after a typhoon disaster in the Philippines which required relief supplies, there was again P.L.480 authorisation for Indonesia to purchase 26,000 tons (Ed. 25,000 tons? See December below). This replaced rice for Indonesia which had been diverted to South Vietnam to replace rice sent from there to relieve the emergency in the Philippines. A further P.L.480 agreement was expected for 100,000 tons to Indonesia, probably long grain (*LRBAC* 6th September 1972 2). But remarkably China stepped in and made a large sale to Indonesia, believed to be 100,000 tons (*LRBAC* 26th September 1972 1). Clearly, Indonesia was having to widen its base of suppliers. But in December, in a return to something like normality, Indonesia bought 250,000 tons from Thailand government to government, with a further 100,000 tons "being worked" (*LRBAC* 29th December 1972 3). However, supplies from the United States were still needed and Indonesia purchased 25,000 tons of medium grain under P.L.480 (*LRBAC* 29th December 1972 4).

But by January 1973, as has been noted, an extremely serious situation had developed in the world with the supply of rice substantially less than the essential requirements of the importing countries. This was the time of the "forgotten" *El Nino*/Southern Oscillation (*EN*SO) event referred to at the start of this chapter. Indeed, Indonesia is a country particularly affected by such events (See Latham 2009). The Philippines (which had imported heavily in 1971 and had made substantial imports in 1972 as a consequence of a typhoon disaster) still required 200,000 tons of rice. India needed 300,000 tons and Bangladesh had enormous unspecified requirements. But Indonesia had also not covered its needs, nor had several other countries. It was difficult to see how this rice could be obtained and many countries would have to go without. Unfortunately, there was also a simultaneous increase in the price of wheat and other alternative food grains (*LRBAC* 31st January 1973 1). Fortunately, in the United States, P.L.480 business was pending for Indonesia (*LRBAC* 31st January 1973 3). In Thailand, loading continued for the government-to-government sales to Indonesia, some 250,000 tons (*LRBAC* 28th February 1973 2). To help relieve the situation the Thai authorities released limited quantities of low-quality rice and broken rice to neighbouring countries, and there were negotiations with Indonesia (*LRBAC* 30th April 1973 2). In July, Indonesia bought 150,000 tons from China, said to be the first business between the countries since diplomatic relations were restored some year ago (*LRBAC* 30th July 1973 1). (Ed. China had actually sold 100,000 tons to Indonesia in September 1972. See above *LRBAC* 26th September 1972 1). In August, Indonesia bought an undisclosed quantity of *Joshi*/parboiled IRRI-8 from Pakistan (*LRBAC* 30th August 1973 1). Also, in August, Thailand sold a limited but unspecified amount to Indonesia (*LRBAC* 30th August 1973 1). This was followed in December by a purchase of 100,000 tons *Ngatsein* Small Mills Specials from Burma, government to government, and government-to-government negotiations with Burma were continuing (*LRBAC* 30th December 1973 1).

But although the disastrous year of 1973 was over, in which Indonesia had imported 1,657,000 metric tons, much of it not specified, Indonesia still needed substantial amounts of rice. It bought from Pakistan 120,000 tons of white rice 55 per cent brokens or similar (Ed. A very low quality) government to government (*LRBAC* 31st February 1974 2). In May, 100,000 tons of white rice, 25 per cent brokens was purchased from Thailand government to government (*LRBAC* 31st May 1974 2). Then came the strange news that Indonesia had bought 200,000 tons from North Korea, shipment to start in October, but the bulk in the first half of 1975 (*LRBAC* 27th August 1974 1). With this the crisis seemed to have been over and details in the *Circular* for Indonesia are few. Yet 1974 was in fact a year of high imports of 1,132,000 tons. It was not until 1975 that imports fell to more normal levels of 692,000 tons, and the crisis appeared to be over. Again details in the *Circular* are sparse, but in February, Indonesia bought 100,000 tons of white rice 25 per cent from Thailand, and it was thought another 100,000 tons would be required. But according to reports from Indonesia and elsewhere, there were doubts this business would go through (*LRBAC* 28th February 1975 2). It did not, for reasons not disclosed (*LRBAC* 27th March 1975 2). Otherwise little was reported.

But in 1976 imports were again higher at 1,301,000 tons, coinciding with the lesser *EN*SO event of 1976/77 mentioned at the start of the chapter. In February, Indonesia bought 105,000 tons of *Ngatsein* Small Mills Specials 25 per cent brokens from Burma through a Singapore company (*LRBAC* 26th February 1976 1). It also bought a substantial but unspecified amount via the same Singapore company from China, this being long-shaped white rice 25 per cent (*LRBAC* 26th February 1976 1). Indonesia then bought 100,000 tons of white rice from Thailand government to government, and it was thought that another 100,000 tons would be required (*LRBAC* 26th February 1976 3). Indonesia also bought an unknown amount of rice from Burma, which had more rice to export than it had had for some time (*LRBAC* 1st April 1976 1). Another 100,000 tons was indeed purchased from Thailand, bringing the total for the year so far from Thailand to 200,000 tons (*LRBAC* 1st April 1976 3). In May, there were rumours of another Government-to-government purchase of 100,000 tons from Thailand (*LRBAC* 27th May 1976 3). But Indonesia also bought an unquantified amount of long-grain rice from the United States under a P.L.480 tender and intended to buy more (*LRBAC* 27th May 1976 3). In July, another 70,000 tons were bought and shipped from Thailand, and there was a prospect of another 100,000 tons of white rice 25 per cent brokens, government to government (*LRBAC* 26th July 1976 2). This turned out to be 200,000 tons of white rice 25 per cent brokens, government to government, shipment August/December

1976 (*LRBAC* 26th August 1976 2). Clearly, Thailand was a preferred choice of origin, as Indonesia then signed an agreement with Thailand to buy 200,000 tons of 25 per cent white rice for delivery in 1977, in addition to the 200,000 tons for August/December delivery 1976 just mentioned (*LRBAC* 30th September 1976 2). But the United States remained important, and under P.L.480 200,000 tons were to be shipped to Indonesia in October/December 1976 (*LRBAC* 30th September 1976 3). Also, under P.L.480, Indonesia purchased at the end of October about 47,000 tons No. 5 medium grain 20 per cent brokens and over 50,000 tons in mid-November (*LRBAC* 25th November 1976 3).

If 1976 had been a year of high imports to Indonesia, 1977 at 1,973,000 tons, 1978 at 1,841,000 tons and 1979 at 1,922,000 tons were even heavier years, continuing into 1980 at 2,011,000 tons. Indonesia was soon buying rice wherever it could, including some very unlikely places such as Taiwan, North Korea, South Korea and Japan. The strange thing, and indicating how desperately they needed supplies, is that rice from these countries was usually round grain, not the medium and long grain which Indonesia normally consumed. However, some, particularly from Japan, might have been old emergency stocks of long grain which had previously been imported and were now being sold off.

So 1977 turned out to be a year of exceptionally high imports, continuing the effects of the minor *EN*SO event of 1976/77. The United States continued to be an important supplier. In February, Indonesia purchased from Burma 30,000 tons of *Emata* 35 per cent and *Zeera* 25 per cent (*LRBAC* 28th February 1977 1). But in April, Indonesia obtained a P.L.480 agreement with the United States for 150,000 tons, with tenders for the grain to take place in the next fortnight. In return for this agreement, Indonesia also undertook to buy from the United States. Around 30,000 tons of rice on commercial terms (*LRBAC* 26th April 1977 3). Then in June came the unusual news that Taiwan had up to 200,000 tons of round grain rice for export. (Ed. Presumably, Taiwan had round grain as it had previously been the Japanese colony of Formosa, and Japan preferred round grain!). It was mainly old crop but would be available freshly milled as it was still paddy. Both 15 per cent and 25 per cent milled rice were available, and Indonesia was conducting negotiations (*LRBAC* 29th June 1977 2). These resulted in Indonesia buying a substantial but unspecified amount (*LRBAC* 28th July 1977 2). Indonesia also bought 5,000 tons of glutinous rice from Thailand (*LRBAC* 28th July 1977 2). A considerable surplus remained in Taiwan, and Indonesia was conducting further negotiations (*LRBAC* 31st August 1977 3). Taiwan continued as an exporter, and it was forecast that 200,000 tons would be exported by the end of January 1978, some of which had been sold already, but sales to Indonesia were not specified (*LRBAC* 28th September 1977 2). Ultimately Indonesia bought 200,000 tons from Taiwan during 1977 (See below *LRBAC* 31st May 1978 3). In October, Indonesia bought from Pakistan government-to-government 100,000 tons of long grain 20 per cent brokens, shipment January/April 1978 (*LRBAC* 27th October 1977 2). Then came a government-to-government agreement with Thailand for 220,000 tons of new crop 20 per cent brokens for shipment January/April (*LRBAC* 27th October 1977 2). There was also a government-to-government purchase from Burma of 132,000 tons of new crop *Ngatsein* Small Mills Specials (*LRBAC* 24th November 1977 1). Even more remarkably, Indonesia bought a substantial but unspecified quantity of white rice from North Korea (*LRBAC* 24th November 1977 2). But the United States remained important and U.S.D.A. (United States Department of Agriculture) announced an initial P.L.480 allocation for Indonesia of 300,000 tons (*LRBAC* 24th November 1977 2). In December, Japan agreed to sell 100,000 tons of rice to Indonesia at a subsidised price, partly for cash, but mainly against a loan (*LRBAC* 29th December 1977 2. See also *LRBAC* 30th June 1978 2). South Korea also was now able to export rice for the first time and signed an agreement with Indonesia for 70,000 tons on a loan basis for prompt shipment (*LRBAC* 29th December 1977 2).

1978 was again a year of high imports, even though the effects of the minor *EN*SO 1976/77 had theoretically diminished. But problems clearly remained, and Indonesia's search for sources of rice continued. In January, 100,000 tons were bought from Pakistan (*LRBAC* 31st January 1978 2). In the United States, the main export activity of the month was 60,000 tons of medium grain purchased by Indonesia under P.L.480. A further tender for 100,000 tons for Indonesia was held later, but details were not specified (*LRBAC* 31st January 1978 4). Then, surprisingly, Indonesia bought 10,000 tons from the neighbouring Philippines, approved by the Manila Government, despite their own recent problems (*LRBAC* 28th February 1978 3). The Indonesian authorities were also in government-to-government negotiations with Thailand for a large quantity of rice undetailed (*LRBAC* 28th February 1978 3). In 1977 Indonesia had purchased 200,000 tons from Taiwan and was likely to draw more of its supplies from Taiwan (*LRBAC* 31st May 1978 3). Taiwan had a surplus possibly as large as 1,000,000 tons and was considering exporting another 100,000 tons, but Indonesia was not mentioned (*LRBAC* 30th June 1978 2). However, demand from Indonesia appeared to be declining, and in China, prices were dropping, partly because shipments to Indonesia of rice purchased previously had been postponed (*LRBAC* 26th July 1978 1). From Japan, there were reports that Indonesia had asked Japan to supply rice on a long-term loan basis, but quantity and delivery dates were not known (*LRBAC* 26th July 1978 2). The Philippines had a 1978 surplus of 138,000 tons for export, in addition to 80,000 tons earmarked for Indonesia and Malaysia (*LRBAC* 31st August 1978 3). That Indonesia's needs were becoming less was indicated when in Taiwan, 200,000 tons of *Bonlai* rice from the 1976/77 crop, and 40,000 tons of off-standard rice were put up for tender for export. But there was only one bid, and the tender was cancelled and the rice was put up for private negotiation. Again, Indonesia was not mentioned (*LRBAC* 31st August 1978 3). In the Philippines there was rice for sale, but no reports of business. Some growing areas in the Philippines had reported damage by locusts to the growing crop, but the level of damage had yet to be assessed (*LRBAC* 29th September 1978 2). A large quantity of Chinese rice coming onto the market had been diverted from sales previously made to Indonesia for shipment this year, and more might come from this source (*LRBAC* 30th October 1978 1). But then the situation changed again, and in October 1978, it was reported from Sri Lanka that the Trade Ministry in Colombo was to supply 8,700 tons of rice to Indonesia during

November. This was Sri Lanka's first export of home-grown rice for 32 years (*LRBAC* 30th October 1978 3). Meanwhile, in Taiwan, the decline in demand from Indonesia seemed to have had an effect, as the Government wanted to reduce output in 1979 by 150,000 tons because of overproduction. This would give a 1979 production target of 2,350,000 tons (*LRBAC* 30th November 1978 3).

If demand from Indonesia had slackened towards the end of 1978, 1979 again saw heavy imports at 1,922,000 tons. In February, Indonesia signed an agreement to buy 50,000 tons from Burma, full details not known (*LRBAC* 28th February 1979 1). Indonesia also agreed to buy 300,000 tons of white rice from Thailand, shipments expected to commence in March at 40,000 – 50,000 tons per month (*LRBAC* 28th February 1979 3). In a P.L.480 tender, Indonesia also bought from the United States 143,000 tons, 80,000 tons of which from California (Ed. Presumably round grain) and the rest from the Gulf of Mexico (Ed. Presumably medium or long grain)(*LRBAC* 28th February 1979 3). Indonesia then agreed to take 50,000 tons from Burma, presumably in addition to the 50,000 tons mentioned above (*LRBAC* 30th March 1979 1). Then it was reported that the 300,000 tons bought from Taiwan last year, and later cancelled, had now been re-instated. Taiwan then withdrew from the market (*LRBAC* 30th March 1979 2). Indonesia then bought 100,000 tons from Burma (*LRBAC* 30th April 1979 1). Quantities (not specified) of rice that had been earmarked in Pakistan for government-to-government sale to Indonesia were yet to be traded (*LRBAC* 30th April 1979 3). It was reported from Rangoon that Indonesia had bought 80,000 tons of Burmese rice, in addition to the 50,000 tons bought earlier in the year (*LRBAC* 31st May 1979 1). (Ed. The earlier figures appear to be 50,000 tons, 50,000 tons and 100,000 tons, see above *LRBAC* 28th February 1979 1, *LRBAC* 30th March 1979 1 and *LRBAC* 30th April 1979 1). In June, it was reported that Japan was to export 200,000 tons of rice to Indonesia on deferred payment terms. These government-assisted sales had been made to reduce Japan's current rice surplus, said to be in the region of 5,000,000 tons (*LRBAC* 29th June 1979 2). Then the Philippines sold 50,000 tons of rice to Indonesia, from an export availability up to August of approximately 500,000 tons (*LRBAC* 29th June 29th 3). But it was reported from Pakistan that Indonesia's requirements remained unsatisfied (*LRBAC* 31st July 1979 3). In August, Indonesia arranged to take the first shipments that month of the 100,000 tons they had agreed to buy from the Philippines, the quality being 30 per cent brokens (*LRBAC* 31st August 1979 2). This was followed by a purchase by Indonesia from Pakistan of 100,000 tons of 15 per cent brokens (*LRBAC* 31st October 1979 2). Further government-to-government negotiations were to take place between Indonesia and the Philippines (*LRBAC* 31st October 1979 3). In the United States, a P.L.480 authorisation was issued for 120,000 tons medium grain No. 5 20 per cent for Indonesia (*LRBAC* 31st October 1979 3). Indonesia also bought from Burma 150,000 tons of new crop, made up of 15 per cent and 25 per cent (*LRBAC* 30th November 1979 1). In Japan government-to-government sales for 1980 included 63,000 tons to Indonesia, but there still remained a surplus (*LRBAC* 30th November 1979 2). Then Indonesia bought 100,000 tons of North Korean rice for shipment during 1980 (*LRBAC* 30th November 1979 2). This was followed by a government-to-government purchase of 100,000 tons of 15 per cent brokens from Pakistan (*LRBAC* 30th November 1979 3). Next came a huge purchase from Thailand of 615,000 tons of new crop, comprising 400,000 tons of 25 per cent Super, 200,000 tons of white rice 10 per cent and 15,000 tons glutinous, shipment from January 1980 at 50,000–60,000 tons per month (*LRBAC* 30th November 1979 3). Yet again Indonesia bought from the United States under P.L.480, being 94,000 tons out of a total authorisation of 120,000 tons (*LRBAC* 30th November 1979 3). In Pakistan, a sale originally reported as 100,000 tons of Punjab rice 15 per cent for Indonesia was not finally confirmed, as Indonesia wanted to reduce the price but the Pakistan authorities refused (*LRBAC* 31st December 1979 2). Indonesia's purchase of 615,000 tons from Thailand's new crop was confirmed (*LRBAC* 31st December 1979 3). Indonesia also purchased 200,000 tons from Taiwan, leaving remaining stocks in Taiwan for export limited (*LRBAC* 31st December 1979 3).

Although the Philippines were a relatively minor importer, they are of interest because of their proximity to Indonesia and also influenced by *EN*SO climatic events. Imports fluctuated considerably, creating some instability in world markets. 1970 saw few imports but 1971 did see imports of 370,000 tons, and they were in the market for an unspecified amount of Thai rice in September (*LRBAC* 3rd September 1971 2). The United States also made an unspecified P.L.480 allocation for the Philippines, 25,000 tons of which were for prompt shipment. But no sellers of rice could be found as the mills were fully engaged in meeting commitments before the threatened dock strike (*LRBAC* 3rd September 1971 3). The Philippines were then back in the market for October shipment if the dock strike was delayed (*LRBAC* 4th October 1971 4). Clearly, they were in difficulty because in October, they bought some long grain from Italy (*LRBAC* 29th October 1971 2). However, P.L.480 authority was due for another 42,000 tons for the Philippines (*LRBAC* 29th October 1971 3–4). This was followed by unconfirmed reports of 50,000 tons purchased from China (*LRBAC* 26th November 1971 1). They also bought about 43,000 tons of low-grade rice from Thailand, a mixture of white rice 15 per cent and A.1. brokens for November/December shipment (*LRBAC* 26th November 1971 2). Thailand was expecting heavy buying from the Philippines in 1972 (*LRBAC* 29th December 1971 2). This was confirmed in January when the Philippines bought 300,000 tons from Thailand on government-to-government terms, understood to be white rice 10 per cent/15 per cent brokens with A.1. white broken rice (*LRBAC* 28th January 1972 3). In June, negotiations took place with Thailand for a further 200,000 tons, but very long-term credit would be required to bring this business about (*LRBAC* 30th June 1972 3). However, in July, the Philippines did buy from Thailand 100,000 tons of white rice special quality 75 per cent brokens (Ed. A very low milling quality) for August/December shipment, with an enquiry for a further 100,000 tons (*LRBAC* 28th July 1972 2). But then a major typhoon hit the Philippines, with disastrous consequences, and by September 500,000 tons of rice was needed for relief. 100,000 tons was bought from Japan on a 25-year credit basis, and 100,000 tons from China. 100,000 tons from the United States destined for South Korea were diverted to the Philippines, and a further 100,000 tons were to be bought from Thailand (*LRBAC* 6th September 1972 1).

In the United States under P.L.480, it was intended to divert 100,000 tons bought by South Korea to the Philippines to meet the emergency, but this was only partly possible. So either the Philippines or South Korea were expected to be in the U.S. market for 50,000–75,000 tons of rice, the Philippines probably for medium grain (*LRBAC* 6th September 1972 2). Further substantial purchases were still required, but the imposition of martial law in the Philippines made negotiations very difficult (*LRBAC* 26th September 1972 2). The background to this was that Ferdinand Marcos had been re-elected in 1969, but there had been demonstrations and strikes. An insurrection began. Marcos declared martial law, and a programme of land redistribution to give rice and corn land smallholdings to landless peasants (Andrews 1997 180). In September, the Philippines were given P.L.480 authorisation by the United States for 30,000 tons for delivery in October/November (*LRBAC* 26th September 1972 3). P.L.480 activity continued and the Philippines were in the market for 20,500 tons for shipments to South Korea in repayment of a loan (See above *LRBAC* 6th September 1972 1, *LRBAC* 6th September 1972 2). This would probably come from California (Ed. As round grain rice) (*LRBAC* 30th October 1972 3). It was reported from Pakistan that exports of coarse rice were being restricted to the Philippines, Indonesia and Nepal (*LRBAC* 30th November 1972 2).

So 1971 and 1972 were years of heavy imports to the Philippines, at 370,000 tons and 455,000 tons respectively. Then came the news in January 1973 of the serious situation in world rice markets (Ed. Linked to the 1972/73 *EN*SO event) and that the Philippines required another 200,000 tons of rice (*LRBAC* 31st January 1973 1). To alleviate shortages, the Thai authorities made 10,000 tons available to the Philippines (*LRBAC* 30th July 1973 1). The Philippines then bought a limited but unspecified amount of rice from Thailand in August (*LRBAC* 30th August 1973 1). Although the Philippines did import 336,000 tons of rice this year, other details are not clear. After the crisis year of 1973 imports to the Philippines began to decline, with only 166,000 tons in 1974. In April 1974, the Philippines bought 20,000 tons from Thailand (*LRBAC* 30th April 1974 2). In May, they purchased 35,000 tons of A.1. Special from Thailand, government to government (*LRBAC* 31st May 1974 2). But in August, it was reported that there had been severe flooding in some of the main rice-growing areas of the Philippines. It was not clear how much damage had occurred, and how this would affect import requirements for the following year (*LRBAC* 27th August 1974 1).

Fortunately the situation was not too serious, and 1975 was not a year of exceptionally heavy imports at 134,000 tons. In March, the Philippines bought from Thailand 50,000 tons of A.1 Broken rice and low-quality whole rice (*LRBAC* 27th March 1975 2). In April, 5,400 tons of rice were being shipped to the Philippines from Thailand as part of Japanese Government Aid, and shipments were taking place from Thailand against earlier sales (*LRBAC* 28th April 1975 2). Then P.L.480 quality rice from the United States, which had been afloat for Vietnam was landed in the Philippines and Singapore, and re-sold to merchants at cheaper prices (*LRBAC* 27th June 1975 3). In 1976, it was reported that the Philippines was heading towards self-sufficiency and even an export surplus. The *Circular* commented that it was not always easy to distinguish the factual situation from reports which may have been intended primarily for internal information, but self-sufficiency did appear to have been achieved (*LRBAC* 27th May 1976 3). Nonetheless, 55,000 tons were imported that year. (Ed. From Thailand. See *LRBAC* 29th January 1976 3). 1977 was a year of imports of 30,000 tons, with no details in the *Circular*. But in 1978, confirming that the Philippines might even have an export surplus, 10,000 tons of Philippines rice was sold to Indonesia, and 10,000 tons to Malaysia, approved by the Manila Government (*LRBAC* 28th February 1978 3). Later it was reported that the Philippines would have a surplus of 138,000 tons for export that year, in addition to 80,000 tons already earmarked for Indonesia and Malaysia (*LRBAC* 31st August 1978 3). In September, the Philippines had rice to sell, but this would depend on Indonesian requirements during the coming months. Some growing areas had reported locust damage to the growing crop, but the extent had yet to be assessed (*LRBAC* 29th September 1978 2). In May 1979, the rice production estimate for the Philippines from the 1978/79 crop was 4,450,000 tons of milled rice. This would give an export surplus of about 500,000 tons, almost double earlier expectations (*LRBAC* 31st May 1979 3). The Philippines then sold 50,000 tons of rice to Indonesia and 25,000 tons to Malaysia, with expected export availability up to August 1979 confirmed at about 500,000 tons (*LRBAC* 29th June 1979 3). In August, Indonesia arranged to take the first shipment from the total of 100,000 tons they had now agreed to buy from the Philippines, the quality being 30 per cent brokens (*LRBAC* 31st August 1979 2). Further government-to-government negotiations were to take place with Indonesia (*LRBAC* 31st October 1979 3).

References

Andrews, John (1997) *Pocket Asia*, London: The Economist-Profile Books Ltd.

Cushing D.H. (1982) *Climate and Fisheries*, London: Academic Press.

Flynn, D.O., Frost, L. and Latham, A.J.H. (Eds) (1999) *Pacific Centuries: Pacific and Pacific Rim History since the 16th Century*, London and New York: Routledge. Paperback 2014.

Glanz, Michael H. (1996) *Currents of Change. El Ninos Impact on Climate and Society*, Cambridge; Cambridge University Press.

Latham, A.J.H. (1994) (2011) "Rice Moves to Areas where Incomes are Rising", a reinterpretation of Asian Economic Development since 1800, in Latham and Kawakatsu (1994) 17–26, and Latham and Kawakatsu (2011) 72–79.

Latham, A.J.H. (1999) "Rice is a Luxury, Not a Necessity", The Sources of Asian Growth, in Flynn, Frost and Latham, 110–24.

Latham, A.J.H. (2009) Climatic Fluctuations and the International Rice Trade: A Preliminary Investigation, in Latham and Kawakatsu (2009) 221–233.

Latham, A.J.H. and Kawakatsu, Heita (Eds) (1994) *The Evolving Structure of the East Asian Economic System since 1700: A Comparative Analysis*, Milan: Universita Bocconi. (Proceedings of the Eleventh International Economic History Congress, B6). See Latham and Kawakatsu (2011).

Latham, A.J.H. and Kawakatsu, Heita (Eds) (2009) *Intra-Asian Trade and Industrialisation. Essays in Memory of Yasukichi Yasuba*, Abingdon and New York: Routledge. Paperback 2014.

Latham, A.J.H. and Kawakatsu, Heita (Eds) (2011) *The Evolving Structure of the East Asian Economic System since 1700: A Comparative Analysis*, Abingdon and New York: Routledge. Paperback 2016.

Meek, Marshall (2003) *There Go The Ships*, Spennymoor: The Memoir Club.

5 The Asian rice trade 1980–1989

In the 1980s, Burma continued to export modest amounts of rice with exports running at between 452,000 and 858,000 metric tons from 1980 to 1987. They then fell away significantly, associated with domestic political difficulties. Meanwhile, Vietnam contributed little in the aftermath of the Vietnam War. But in 1989 it suddenly returned to the world market with exports of 1,420,000 metric tons. The gap in the Asian market left by the shortfalls from Burma and Vietnam was filled by Thailand with huge increases in exports from 2,791,000 metric tons in 1980 to 6,311,000 metric tons in 1989. But in the midst of these great changes, the intra-Asian rice trade was again disrupted by significant *El Nino*/Southern Oscillation (*EN*SO) events in 1982/83 and 1986/87 (Glantz 1996 66–68).

Table 5.1 Rice exports (selected countries) 1980–1990 (metric tons 000)

	1980	*1981*	*1982*	*1983*	*1984*	*1985*	*1986*	*1987*	*1988*	*1989*	*1990*
Myanmar	653	673	701	858	720	452	635	485	63	168	213
Vietnam	33	–	8	46	16	–	3	153	97	1420	1624
Thailand	2791	3027	3782	3476	4615	4061	4523	4443	5267	6311	4017
China	1376	684	775	1112	1369	1045	1122	1261	802	383	405
India	472	940	633	200	200	250	200	350	350	421	505
Pakistan	1086	1243	951	904	1265	718	1316	1270	1210	854	743
U.S.A.	3054	3132	2540	2384	2141	1939	2392	2471	2259	3061	2473

Source: FAO *Trade Yearbooks*.

Table 5.2 Rice imports (selected countries) 1980–1990 (metric tons 000)

	1980	*1981*	*1982*	*1983*	*1984*	*1985*	*1986*	*1987*	*1988*	*1989*	*1990*
India	19	82	43	315	550	67	35	16	684	544	660
Bangladesh	584	78	263	316	166	689	53	259	673	62	380
Sri Lanka	168	154	111	176	20	40	210	79	194	313	131
Malaysia	167	316	403	358	436	428	191	196	283	367	330
Singapore	188	183	192	197	210	185	240	214	212	210	220
Indonesia	2011	538	309	1168	414	33	27	54	32	268	49

(*Continued*)

DOI: 10.4324/9781003492917-6

Table 5.2 (Continued)

	1980	*1981*	*1982*	*1983*	*1984*	*1985*	*1986*	*1987*	*1988*	*1989*	*1990*
Philippines	–	–	–	–	–	–	–	–	119	195	592
Vietnam	134	30	184	11	284	422	500	344	175	55	1
China	130	273	223	77	102	213	326	544	314	1206	62
Hong Kong	359	360	365	370	365	378	367	372	363	406	374
Japan	13	75	65	13	165	19	20	17	16	15	18

Source: FAO *Trade Yearbooks*.

In Burma, government-to-government sales began in January 1980, but rice was not available to the commercial market until March, suggesting rice was in short supply. Two cargoes earmarked for Government deals were sold to Angola (*London Rice Brokers' Association Circular* (*LRBAC*) 31st January 1980 1). Government-to-government negotiations continued, but no rice was released for private sale (*LRBAC* 29th February 1980 1). An official forecast for 1979/80 put production at 10,500,000 tons, some 500,000 tons above earlier estimates, and about the same as 1978/79. It was hoped exports would reach 630,000 tons against an earlier target of 600,000 tons, but no rice had been made available from the 1979/80 crop for private sale. Severe drought in the interior made it impossible to forecast how much would be allocated for the local market. So far 400,000 tons had been traded government to government to Indonesia, Bangladesh, Sri Lanka and (surprisingly), the People's Republic of China (*LRBAC* 31st March 1980 1). In July, there was a private sale of some *Emata* and *Ngatsein*. Some stocks of *Ngatsein* Small Mills Specials 35 per cent were made available and a tender was held for 30,000 tons but prices were too high (*LRBAC* 31st July 1980 1). Around 10,000 tons of broken rice were sold for export, and some whole rice (*LRBAC* 30th August 1980 1). In September, 50,000 tons were sold to the Malagasy Republic but stocks were now sold out until the new crop (*LRBAC* 30th September 1980 1). Then it was reported from Indonesia that due to a record harvest and lack of storage space, imports scheduled for later in the year had been put back. Burma agreed to postpone outstanding shipments, as did Japan, whilst Thailand deferred shipments of about 150,000 tons until April 1981 (*LRBAC* 30th September 1980 1). Indeed Burma agreed to waive contacts of approximately 68,000 tons to Indonesia for shipment that year, provided Indonesia bought 100,000 tons of Burma rice in 1981 (*LRBAC* 31st October 1980 1).

Forecasts for the Burma 1980/81 crop were good (*LRBAC* 28th November 1980 1). Over and above government-to-government deals, total sales of new crops were expected to be more than 200,000 tons, and some rice was sold to the private trade (*LRBAC* 31st December 1980 1). Reports of good crops continued in January and sales were made for shipment in April (*LRBAC* 31st January 1981 1). The total tonnage to be exported from Burma was now expected to be 800,000 tons, half of which would be Government business. 400,000 tons had already been committed, and most of it exported. The business in April was expected in 15 per cent to 35 per cent brokens of *Emata*, *Zeera* and *Ngatsein*. No broken rice from the new crop had been tendered as it was all being consumed domestically. The *Circular* noted that when shipping from Rangoon there was a problem with the depth of the river as there were two sand bars. So a fully loaded vessel had only a few days each month when it could sail (*LRBAC* 31st March 1981 1). In April, the Government sold 100,000 tons of *Emata* 10 per cent and *Emata* 25 per cent to Indonesia bringing the total for the season exported or committed for export to 550,000 tons (*LRBAC* 30th April 1981 1). 60,000 tons of rice 35 per cent brokens was sold in June for spread shipments to October, and 40,000 tons more might be available. This would take exports for the season to 800,000 tons, half government to government and half private trade (*LRBAC* 30th June 1981 2). In July, bids were invited for 50,000 tons of white rice 35 per cent brokens (*LRBAC* 30th July 1981 2). These were bought by an international merchant (*LRBAC* 31st August 1981 1). A further 30,000 tons remained from the 1980/81 crop, being 10,000 tons of *Emata* 15 per cent for October shipment, and 20,000 tons of *Emata* 25 per cent divided into 10,000 tons for October and 10,000 tons for November. A tender of 10,000 tons of good quality broken rice, comprising 3000 tons of A1 and A2, and 7000 tons of B1 and 2 was to be held in October, shipment November (*LRBAC* 30th September 1981 1). Not much interest was shown, and some medium grain *Emata* 15 per cent and 25 per cent was available for export (*LRBAC* 31st October 1981 1). There were several sales of *Emata* 15 per cent and *Ngatsein* 35 per cent, and a little 35 per cent *Emata* remained for sale and one cargo of 15 per cent. The new crop was likely to start selling in December, but the authorities were worried about heavy rain, flooding and typhoons which had also affected Bangladesh and other neighbouring countries (*LRBAC* 30th November 1981 1). In December, sales of *Emata* 35 per cent and *Ngatsein* 35 per cent increased but prices fell. Reports of damage to the new crop had been exaggerated, prospects looked good and the new crop would be traded on a government basis in the next month or so (*LRBAC* 31st December 1981 1).

In January 1982, Burma was still keen to sell *Emata* 25 per cent and 35 per cent. Negotiations were held for 30,000 tons of 25 per cent and 20,000 tons of 35 per cent. Prices were for loading at Rangoon, and one other port unspecified (*LRBAC* 29th January 1982 1). 35 per cent *Emata* could be purchased easily, stowed Rangoon. Superior quality *Emata* 15 per cent or 10 per cent was also available, but little demand. There had been recent sales of small broken rice, 20,000 tons of A2, 3 and 4, and B2, 3 and 4, which was likely to go to Northern Europe. There had also been a tender for 10,000 tons of bigger mixed brokens (*LRBAC* 27th February 1982 1). Burma exports for 1982 were officially forecast at 700,000 tons, and about half had already been sold. But the exportable surplus might be even greater. *Emata* 35 per cent was available from Rangoon. A Burma trade mission was trying to sell rice in West Africa and elsewhere (*LRBAC* 31st March 1982 1). The exportable surplus was then raised by 300,000 tons to 1,000,000 tons. *Emata* 35 per cent was quoted from Rangoon, and other qualities were available at prices competitive with Thailand (*LRBAC* 30th April 1982 1). In June, efforts were still being made to make sales from the 1981/82 crop surplus, but Thailand was offering cheaper prices. Buyers of 35 per cent brokens were covering their needs at the last minute. *Emata* Super 5 per cent and 10 per cent, as well as Small Mills Specials 35 per cent were available. A small amount of 35 per cent was traded stowed Rangoon (*LRBAC* 30th June 1982 1). Although the Burma Government had set an export target of 1,000,000 tons, by July sales were well down on 1980/81, and seemed unlikely to exceed last year's official figures of 700,000 tons. 20,000 tons of good quality broken rice was sold stowed Rangoon (*LRBAC* 30th July 1982 1). The monsoons were good, and the crop was likely to be comparable with the previous year (*LRBAC* 31st August 1982 1). But in October, there were still stocks of the old crop for export, and with the new crop coming in soon, Burma was keen to sell. Some *Emata* 35 per cent was sold at prices below Thailand, and rice with more than 35 per cent brokens was available, as also some better quality *Emata* (*LRBAC* 29th October 1982 1). Burma's rice production for 1982/83 was officially estimated at around 14,400,000 tons of paddy. The 1982/83 new crop was also expected to be good, so the authorities were keen to make sales to avoid storage problems. There was a considerable carryover from 1981/82, particularly 35 per cent, 45 per cent and 55 per cent brokens. 10,000 tons of Burma brokens was tendered in late November, and results awaited (*LRBAC* 30th November 1982 1). In a tender in December, 10,000 tons of A1 and A2 mixed, 1982 crop, was purchased for shipment second half of December, and another tender was held at the end of the month for 10,000 tons A Extra and/or A1 Extra/Mixed, and A1 and/or Al and A2 mixed (*LRBAC* 31st December 1982 1).

In January 1983, large stocks of lower qualities of rice, mainly *Emata* 35 per cent were available. The sale of 50,000 tons *Emata* 5 per cent to Iran stowed Rangoon took all available top quality rice until May. There was a tender for large broken rice, A1 and 2, B1 and B2, in bags. Another tender was to be held in February for small broken rice, 2s, 3s and 4s (*LRBAC* 31st January 1983 1). It was sold and shipped to Europe as cattle feed (*LRBAC* 28th February 1983 1). All the carryover from 1981/82 had now been sold, and it seemed exports from the 1982/83 crop would be about the same as 1981/82, some 800,000–900,000 tons. Half of this would be sold government to government and was already being negotiated with traditional buyers. For the moment Burma was only a seller of *Emata* 25 per cent and 35 per cent (*LRBAC* 31st March 1983 1). In April, qualities traded included *Emata* 15 per cent, 25 per cent and 35 per cent, also *Ngatsein* 15 per cent. As much as 200,000 tons might have been sold, significantly reducing the stocks remaining for sale in 1983. So the Burmese authorities increased their prices (*LRBAC* 29th April 1983 1). In June, a government-to-government sale of 100,000 tons of 25 per cent brokens was reported to India. Otherwise, the Myanmar Export Import Company (M.E.I.C.) was largely withdrawn from the market (*LRBAC* 31st June 1983 1). About 810,000 tons of rice had been committed from the current crop, and it seemed unlikely much more would be sold. The sale to India of 100,000 tons was confirmed (*LRBAC* 29th July 1983 1). Burma remained inactive as far as whole grain was concerned, but there was a tender in September for broken rice A1 and A2 mixed (*LRBAC* 30th September 1983 1). Deliveries from existing contracts of white rice 10 per cent to 35 per cent brokens continued (*LRBAC* 31st October 1983 1). In November, nothing was for sale because a large number of shipments were being moved out of Rangoon and other ports, and there was considerable congestion and delays (*LRBAC* 30th November 1983 1). Despite the congestion, exports of the 1982/83 crop continued at a rapid rate. When the last of these ships had sailed, nothing would be left from the old crop. The new crop would not be marketed until the middle of February. The harvest appeared normal, although a little late rain had delayed it slightly. Exports were likely to be about the same as 1982/83, some 800,000 tons (*LRBAC* 30th December 1983 1).

Moving to 1984 there was to be a tender in early February for 10,000 tons broken rice A1 and Extra and 10,000 tons of B2, 3 and 4, from the 1983 and 1984 crops, March shipment. *Emata* rice 35 per cent, 25 per cent and 15 per cent was available for export and shipment from mid-February onwards. Congestion in the ports had been reduced and vessels could expect to berth straightaway (*LRBAC* 31st January 1984 1). In the early February tender, 10,000 tons of A1 and Extra were sold and some B2, 3 and 4 mixed, and at a subsequent tender 10,000 tons of and B2 brokens were sold (*LRBAC* 29th February 1984 1). Some 25 per cent and 35 per cent were sold to West Africa, but nothing was available for the next two or three months. Despite some adverse weather, Burma production for 1983/84 was officially estimated at 14,800,000 tons compared with 14,500,000 tons for 1982/83. Exports for 1982/83 were 726,000 tons (*LRBAC* 30th March 1984 1). Government estimates for exports for 1983/84 were 800,000 tons compared to the 726,000 tons of 1982/83 (*LRBAC* 30th April 1984 1). (Ed. These figures suggest that Burma was not adversely affected by the 1982/83 *EN*SO event!). Current monsoon conditions were hampering the loading of vessels in port, and congestion was building up again. Some merchants were told to delay the arrival of their vessels by up to a month because previous vessels had not been completed (*LRBAC* 31st May 1984 1). The Myanmar Export Import Corporation (M.E.I.C.) was still having problems with congestion and was not anxious to make sales until the situation improved (*LRBAC* 29th June 1984 1). But shipments were going ahead on contracts concluded earlier in the year, some having been delayed by the port congestion (*LRBAC* 31st July 1984 1). There was to be a tender in September for 10,000 tons of white broken rice, A1 and A1 Extra (*LRBAC* 31st August 1984 1). At this, the 10,000 tons were sold stowed Burma ports. But the M.E.I.C. was still not keen to sell at this time (*LRBAC* 28th September 1984 1). In October, the market was quiet, although some cargoes of previous sales had still to be lifted. Congestion at Rangoon had eased (*LRBAC* 31st October 1984 1). A cargo of broken rice was put up for sale for shipment in December/January (*LRBAC* 30th November 1984 1). The authorities expected to export 1,000,000 tons from the 1984/85 crop, of which half would be 35 per cent broken quality, mostly *Emata*, and the rest 25 per cent brokens with a limited amount of higher grade qualities and parboiled. 120,000 tons of 35 per cent brokens was available in the first quarter of 1985. At a tender for broken rice, A1 and Extra were sold (*LRBAC* 31st December 1984 1).

In 1985 there was to be a tender in March for 10,000 tons of B1 and B2 brokens, and 5000 tons of B2, 3 and 4 (*LRBAC* 28th February 1985 1). The B2, 3 and 4 sold at this tender, but not the B1 and B2. Burma prices looked high compared to other Far Eastern origins, including rice re-sold by Indonesia. There were no other sales other than Government to Government business (*LRBAC* 29th March 1985

1). There was a tender for broken rice in May (*LRBAC* 31st May 1985 1). 162,018 tons were exported in January/June 1985 compared with 427,713 tons in the same period in 1984. One reason for this was that nothing was shipped to India in this period compared with 139,028 tons in 1984. At the end of July, the authorities held a tender for one cargo of 25 per cent and one cargo of 35 per cent (*LRBAC* 31st July 1985 1). Between January and July Burma exported 214,000 tons compared with 484,314 tons in 1984. This was due to a reduction in shipments to Asia from 339,939 tons to 100,907 tons. Shipments to Africa fell slightly from 128,081 tons to 101,794 tons. Shipments to Africa in 1985 included 20,576 tons to Mauritius, and 26,392 tons to Reunion, neither of which figured in the same period of 1984. Burma had been reluctant to compete with Pakistan for medium and lower quality rice (*LRBAC* 30th August 1985 1). Large amounts of rice were still available for export in the current crop year which ended in December. About 100,000 tons of *Emata*, *Zeera* and *Ngatsein* 35 per cent were available at prices more in line with Pakistan. The authorities wanted to sell this and some long boiled (sic) rice (Ed. full boiled? See *LRBAC* 30th June 1987 below) and 5 per cent rice before the new crop became available in January (*LRBAC* 30th September 1985 1). In October, heavy shipments were being made from Burma to Vietnam, purchased by Russia, and there were shipments to other buyers. There was likely to be congestion until mid-December (*LRBAC* 31st October 1985 1). When the congestion at Rangoon eased, both *Emata* and *Ngatsein* would be available for shipment. A small amount of broken rice was available, but it was under negotiation for barter trade (*LRBAC* 30th November 1985 1). As the season came to a close it was clear that exports in 1985 had been disappointingly low, and there were still stocks of the old crop left for sale (*LRBAC* 31st December 1985 1).

In January 1986, prices were high compared with Pakistan (*LRBAC* 31st January 1986 1). Some rice was exported in January, and there were export sales of 35 per cent *Emata*. A tender was held for 10,000 tons of broken rice (*LRBAC* 28th February 1986 1). Some business was done with 25 per cent and 30 per cent brokens, with the authorities keen to make sales before the end of March, as this was the end of the financial year (*LRBAC* 17th March 1986 1). By the end of April, the authorities had managed to sell a good percentage of the 1985/86 crop. Interestingly sales included 180,000 tons to Russia for delivery to Vietnam, and 135,000 tons to the People's Republic of China, of which perhaps 40,000–50,000 tons would be delivered to Sri Lanka under Tripartite Compensation arrangements. Senegal had purchased 40,000 tons of broken rice, nearly all the brokens available. *Ngatsein* and *Emata* 35 per cent were available in small quantities for shipment from June onwards (*LRBAC* 30th April 1986 1). So far exports had gone well in 1986 but logistical problems were appearing again at the docks. A cargo of *Emata* 25 per cent was available for June shipment, and some *Zeera* and *Ngatsein* 35 per cent. *Emata* 35 per cent was now sold out until August shipment (*LRBAC* 31st May 1986 1). Exports for the four-month periods January/April 1986 were 316,262 tons, comprising Africa 121,509 tons, Asia 164,011 tons, Europe 9,880 tons and Brazil 20,862 tons. This compared favourably with the same period in 1985 when only 102,794 tons were exported, comprising Africa 62,794 tons, Asia 40,000 tons,

Europe nil and Brazil nil (*LRBAC* 30th June 1986 1). There was a tender for 30,000 tons of B2, 3 and 4 mixed, shipment in August/September Rangoon, but no outcome. 10,000 tons *Emata* 25 per cent were for sale for August shipment (*LRBAC* 31st July 1986 1). The export figure of 400,000 tons to the end of June was a considerable improvement on the 162,000 tons exported over the same period in 1985. *Emata* 25 per cent long grain rice remained available for export (*LRBAC* 30th August 1986 1). Some sales of broken rice were made at reasonable prices, including A1 and Extra, B1 and B2, and B2, 3 and 4. There were sales to Iran of high-quality rice, both for the end of 1986 and from the new crop in 1987 (*LRBAC* 31st October 1986 1). Burma's exports to the end of 1986 were 542,000 tons compared with 333,400 tons over the same period in 1985. Most shipments were to Third World countries in Africa and Asia, and a high percentage were government to government (*LRBAC* 31st December 1986 1).

In January 1987, a number of contracts previously concluded were being shipped. 35 per cent 25 per cent and 5 per cent brokens were available at prices comparable with Thailand (*LRBAC* 30th January 1987 1). Then came news that Burma had suddenly sold out for the next two or three months (*LRBAC* 31st March 1987 1). Around 150,000 tons of 35 per cent had been sold to China for consumption in Southern China, and 50,000 tons had been sold to Russia, probably destined for another country unspecified. Whole grain and broken rice were sold out (*LRBAC* 31st March 1987 1). There was a tender in May for 10,000 tons of broken rice B2, 3 and 4, shipment end of June, and 10,000 tons of broken rice B1 and B2, shipment end of July, at high prices (*LRBAC* 29th May 1987 1). In June, there was a tender for B2, 3 and 4 brokens packed in 50-kilo bags, and they were also selling a limited quantity of full boiled (sic) *Ngatsein* (*LRBAC* 30th June 1987 1). (See *LRBAC* 30th September 1985 1 above). In September, it was reported that Burma had not been affected by the poor monsoon which other parts of Asia including Thailand had experienced (*LRBAC* 30th September 1987 1). (Ed. The poor monsoon seems to have been associated with the *EN*SO event of 1986/87. As in 1982/83, Burma seems to have been largely unaffected by this event). But in December, it was reported that nothing had been offered for shipment to commercial markets from the new crop. Shipment from the previous business was taking place, and the Indian government was seeking a large parcel of rice, thought to be 100,000 tons (*LRBAC* 31st December 1987 1).

In January 1988, it was rumoured that 200,000 tons had been sold to India. A tender was held for 7500 tons of Burma broken rice 1987 crop, Al and A2 mixed, and B2, 3 and 4 mixed (*LRBAC* 29th January 1988 1). Another tender was held in February for 7000 tons of Burma full boiled rice old crop for the second half of March shipment (*LRBAC* 29th February 1988 1). However there had not been any sales from the 1987/88 crop, other than the sale of some small broken rice B2, 3 and 4, and the intention to deliver 100,000 tons of rice to India. The *Circular* commented cryptically "It will be interesting to see if, when and how Burmese rice will be exported in 1988." (*LRBAC* 31st March 1988 1). Clearly, they were aware of developing problems. At the beginning of June, a tender was held for 10,000 tons of mixed quality broken rice, and a further tender was to take place in July for

15,000 tons, but nothing else was available (*LRBAC* 30th June 1988 1). The tender for 10,000 tons of small broken rice B2, 3 and 4 was awarded at the beginning of the month (*LRBAC* 29th July 1988 1). Then came a political crisis. In July 1988, Ne Win resigned as chairman of the Burma Socialist Programme Party (BSPP). Demonstrations were suppressed by the army, which established in September the State Law and Order Restoration Council under General Saw Maung, with Ne Win behind the scenes (Andrews 1997 118). Against this background, exports from Burma in 1988 had been minimal. There was widely reported civil unrest and the struggle to find a new leader made it difficult to know what was possible, and many thought there would be no further sales from the current crop (*LRBAC* 31st August 1988 1). The disturbed political situation continued and it was difficult to see how exports could take place (*LRBAC* 30th September 1988 1). In October, the civil strikes and unrest lessened. Shipments of outstanding contracts were to continue from mid-November (*LRBAC* 31st October 1988 1). In November, the new crop was about to be harvested but the authorities were not ready for export business (*LRBAC* 30th November 1988 1). In December, 10,000 tons of B1 and B2 were sold, but there was no indication when or how much whole grain would be sold from the new crop (*LRBAC* 30th December 1988 1).

In February 1989, a sale of rice was reported of 30,000 tons, 25 per cent brokens, in a "compensation" or barter business (*LRBAC* 28th February 1989 1). After several months without news, the *Circular* reported in June that little or nothing further was expected that year (*LRBAC* 30th June 1989 1). Then in August, it was reported that rice exports for the year had actually amounted to nearly 100,000 tons, mostly Government to Government, with a little private trade, especially for broken rice. Conditions for the new crop were said to be normal (*LRBAC* 31st August 1989 1). Rice exports for 1989/90 were expected to be 200,000 tons, a considerable improvement on 1988/89 but not comparable with the early 1980s when Burma was exporting 600,000 –700,000 tons a year (*LRBAC* 29th September 1989 1). (Ed. Or the pre-war days when Burma exports were over 3,250,000 tons annually, see *LRBAC* 22nd April 1952 1). In the future, rice would be available from private exporters, whilst the government would also continue to be exporters although they had none at that moment (*LRBAC* 31st October 1989 2). As export policy had now been relaxed, offers were expected from many places although no prices had been suggested (*LRBAC* 30th November 1989 1). Whilst there was a greatly increased crop, as noted, Burma was unlikely to increase exports in 1989/90 to above 200,000 tons (*LRBAC* 29th December 1989 1).

Although Vietnam had been one of the great Asian rice exporters before the Second World War, exports in these years were negligible and Vietnam largely figured as an importer. But in 1989 Vietnam suddenly re-entered Asian markets in a big way with exports of 1,420,000 tons. The *Circular* carries nothing on Vietnam exports for most of these years, although there are occasional references to imports. Then in May 1989, it was reported that exports of rice from Vietnam had increased considerably that year, and Vietnam was becoming an important supplier of 35 per cent broken rice, a low quality. It might export as much as 600,000 tons that year (*LRBAC* 31st May 1898 3). Vietnam was now in competition with

Thailand for low-quality white rice (*LRBAC* 30th June 1989 1). By June, 400,000 tons had been exported, and exports for the whole year might reach 700,000 tons, almost all white rice 35 per cent, and mostly shipped to African countries (*LRBAC* 30th June 1989 3). Indeed the market in West Africa was depressed because of the large number of vessels loaded with Vietnamese 35 per cent white rice which were on their way there. The other major market for Vietnam was India, which was said to have purchased 275,000 tons. The big question was whether there was enough rice in Vietnam to cover the order, and could the port facilities at Ho Chi Minh City (Saigon-Cholon) take all the vessels needed to ship the rice to India by mid-September (*LRBAC* 31st July 1989 1). India had indeed bought 270,000 tons of Vietnam rice 35 per cent brokens to arrive before the end of September (*LRBAC* 31st July 1989 2). It was confirmed that 270,000 tons had been sold to India, some for guaranteed shipment by the 15th September and some for guaranteed arrival by the 30th September, all with a 10 per cent performance bond. The business had been done by various traders, and it was of interest to see if it could all be shipped in time. Altogether over 700,000 tons of Vietnamese rice had been shipped out, or earmarked for vessels chartering to load in 1989 (*LRBAC* 31st July 1989 3). By the end of August, exports totalled 860,000 tons including vessels in port and vessels about to load. Total exports for the year would be well over 1,000,000 tons, which was in sharp contrast with 100,000 tons the previous year. Conditions for the crop were good, but Vietnam was very much at the mercy of typhoons, and the situation could change quickly (*LRBAC* 31st August 1989 3). There would have been a serious shortage of low-quality rice in world markets in 1989 had it not been for the re-entry of Vietnam into export markets in a big way. Shipments from Vietnam had gone on and on and showed no sign of diminishing (*LRBAC* 29th September 1989 1). Vietnam continued to be a seller of 25 per cent and 35 per cent rice with export volumes remaining high. There were typhoons in September, but it was too early to assess any damage (*LRBAC* 29th September 1989 3). Rice continued to be available both by direct purchase from Vietnam and through barter agreements. The outlook for the new crop was good, and Vietnam was expected to be a big exporter in 1990 (*LRBAC* 31st October 1989 3). In November, the *Circular* commented "The emergence of Vietnam as a substantial exporter is of major importance. If they succeed in exporting two million tons next year (as forecasted by certain sources), the Thais will have a hard time keeping their paddy prices high." (*LRBAC* 30th November 1989 1). In December, it added "The incidence of Vietnam as a major exporter over the last year has been one of the most significant changes in the rice market for many years. We have seen an exported tonnage which was negligible in 1987 rise to one hundred thousand tons in 19888 and a staggering 1.5 million tons in 1989 with a target of two million tons in 1999." (*LRBAC* 29th December 1989 2). (Ed. How this was all achieved is not explained!).

The main story of the 1980s is the huge expansion of rice exports from Thailand, which made up for the shortfalls from Burma and Vietnam. In December 1979, the main crop was expected to produce 14,000,000 tons of paddy, and the minor second crop was about 1,000,000 tons. This was considerably less than an earlier forecast for the year of 18,000,000 tons. The official export target for 1980 was 1,500,000 tons, but some suggested that exports might reach 2,200,000 tons. This would still be 300,000 tons down from the 2,500,000 tons in 1979. Export sales so far from the new crop were 1,000,000 tons, which included a large government-to-government sale of 615,000 tons to Indonesia. Iran was looking to Thailand for rice they used to get from the United States (*LRBAC* 31st December 1979 3). Dry weather affected the second crop, so the export estimates for 1980 were reduced from 2,200,000 tons to 1,800,000 tons (*LRBAC* 31st March 1980 3). Then came rain in the growing areas and the 2,200,000 target was restored (*LRBAC* 30th April 1980 3). During the first four months of the year, Thailand exported 1,400,000 tons and demand continued despite higher prices. To prevent the export target of 2,200,000 tons from being exceeded, the authorities imposed restrictions. Exporters had to obtain approval for sales over 500 tons up to the end of August. Quantities for export in this period were to be no more than 300,000 tons of any quality of white rice, and for parboiled rice, the limit was 100,000 tons to any market providing the business was done through the Rice Exporters' Association (*LRBAC* 30th May 1980 2). Rice exports for the first five months of the year were 1,600,000 tons, only 600,000 tons short of the year's target of 2,200,000 tons. But exports were now expected to exceed 2,400,000 tons and good rainfall in June meant that the second crop might reach 1,000,000 tons. Iran bought 40,000–50,000 tons of white rice 5 per cent for July shipment and Nigeria was interested in parboiled rice (*LRBAC* 30th June 1980 2–3). Exports during the first half of the year were over 1,800,000 tons compared with 1,200,000 tons in the same period in 1979 and were still expected to be around 2,400,000 tons. In July, the second crop was being harvested. There was demand from Nigeria for parboiled rice, but rumours they had bought 70,000 tons were exaggerated. Shipments of brokens to Vietnam were cancelled for political reasons (*LRBAC* 31st July 1980 3). There were large sales of broken rice to West Africa (*LRBAC* 30th August 1980 2). In September, the Bangkok authorities fixed an export quota for September/October shipment of only 10,000 tons to Hong Kong, and 40,000 tons to other markets. This was because 140,000 tons had yet to be delivered from previous allocations. Some parboiled rice was sold to Nigeria (*LRBAC* 30th September 1980 2). In October, the Thai Government increased the quantity which traders had to sell to the Government stockpile for home consumption. It was raised from 50 per cent to 60 per cent of the amount they were allowed to export. But the export premium (tax surcharge) on rice was reduced. Demand from the Middle East for high grade rice continued (*LRBAC* 31st October 1980 3). From lst January to 31st October rice exports were 2,329,000 tons compared with 2,339,000 tons in the same period of 1979. Shipments during 1980 were now expected to reach 2,500,000 tons compared with the earlier target of 2,200,000 tons, and the Government had already set a target of 2,800,000 tons for 1981. Existing commitments included 150,000 tons of white rice to Iran and 100,000 tons to Brazil. South Korea was negotiating for a further 100,000 tons and Singapore had agreed to buy 30,000 tons for delivery in the first half of 1981 (*LRBAC* 28th November 1980 3). Exports during November were 138,000 tons bringing total exports for the period lst January to 30th November to 2,470,000 tons and total exports for the year were now expected to be just over 2,500,000 tons. The quota system was dropped for shipments to March, and only high qualities of rice had been in demand for export. However, Senegal bought 200,000 tons of broken rice government to government (*LRBAC* 31st December 1980 3).

Total exports from Thailand during 1980 were just over 2,500,000 tons as expected. For 1981 the combined first and second crop was expected to be 18,000,000 tons compared with 15,700,000 tons in 1980, and the export target for 1981 was 2,800,000 tons, although local merchants estimated 3,200,000 tons (*LRBAC* 31st January 1981 3). The authorities imposed new export restrictions. Ministry of Commerce approval had to be obtained before any exporter could offer 100 per cent white rice, whole rice up to 15 per cent brokens, or lower grades and broken rice over 500 tons. Around 60,000–70,000 tons of 5 per cent non-smell parboiled rice was sold to Nigeria (*LRBAC* 31st March 1981 3). Rice exports for the first quarter of the year were 855,000 tons. There had been more business to Nigeria in parboiled rice, and 82,000 tons of 100 per cent Grade B had been sold to Iran (*LRBAC* 30th April 1981 2–3). The Government stated export authority for top-quality white rice would not be given for the time being. Bangladesh purchased 50,000 tons of parboiled rice for delivery to India, and more business was done with Nigeria (*LRBAC* 29th May 1981 3). The *Circular* now quoted a bulletin of the United States Department of Agriculture (U.S.D.A.). This said that the Thai share of the world rice export market had recovered from the 12–15 per cent share of the late 1960s and early 1970s and was now 20 per cent and more of the market. Thailand had recently focussed on providing enough rice at low prices for the home population. Cheap rice shops had been set up where people could buy a week's supply of rice below retail prices. An export tax imposed in 1954 to generate revenue was removed in 1971 when the world rice market slackened. It was re-established in 1973 when rice prices soared, and the Government later adjusted it in line with world market conditions. The export tax and trade restrictions in years when supplies were short had discouraged production for export and held back Thailand from increasing its share in world markets. But the measures had ensured adequate domestic supplies. A change in policy allowing producers to get higher prices might have a huge influence on rice output. Farmers would have a bigger incentive to use fertilisers, improve storage facilities (loss to rats was a big problem), and use irrigation to increase double cropping (*LRBAC* 30th June 1981 3). On 17th July 1981, the Thai currency was devalued against the US$Dollar by approximately 9 per cent, resulting in substantial external price reductions, particularly for lower grades. But prices for lower grades were still above the world level, and there was no increase in demand except for a few cargoes of 100 per cent for Iraq (*LRBAC* 31st July 1981 3). Sales from the current crop were already over 3,000,000 tons, but stocks were still good and with the devaluation, prices were easier. Thai whole rice however was still above long grain prices from other international exporters. Exporting merchants in Thailand were divided into two main groups, but any business had to be referred to the Export Board to check the price before a contract could be made. There was much activity in broken rice and low quality rice such as Special Mixture 45 per cent, mainly to Africa (*LRBAC* 31st August 1981 3–4). There was more trade in low-grade and broken rice to West Africa (*LRBAC* 30th

September 1981 2–3). More sales of brokens to West Africa followed. On 28th October the Government reduced the export premium and stockpile level on all grades, and prices fell substantially (*LRBAC* 31st October 1981 2). Demand for brokens continued (*LRBAC* 30th November 1981 2). Despite the reduction in the export quota restrictions there was little increase in demand, so with a large new crop about to come in, the Ministry of Commerce reduced further the minimum price Bangkok (*LRBAC* 31st December 1981 2–3).

The new crop was expected to produce 16,500,000 tons in 1982, with a further 2,500,000 tons from second crop, making a total of 19,000,000 tons. Exports were expected to be over 3,000,000 tons, and some forecast 3,300,000 tons (*LRBAC* 29th January 1982 2–3). There were more cuts in export taxes, and export prices drifted down. There was strong demand for good quality rice from traditional markets, and also Tehran. 50,000 tons of Thai white rice 100 per cent Grade B was sold to Indonesia, and there were large shipments to Malaysia (*LRBAC* 27th February 1982 2). Then demand slowed. Estimates for the first crop, just harvested, were for 15,700,000 tons, and the Government hoped there would be 2,000,000 tons from the second crop, giving a total of just less than 18,000,000 tons. Earlier estimates had been for 19,000,000 tons (*LRBAC* 30th April 1982 2). There was interest in high-grade rice from the Middle East and 250,000 tons of broken rice was sold to China and the Malagasy Republic, although how much to each was not given (*LRBAC* 31st May 1982 2). Prospects for the second crop were good, and sales of brokens steady (*LRBAC* 30th June 1982 2–3). The export target for the year was then increased to 4,000,000 tons although the actual exportable surplus was thought to be 4,500,000 tons. Exports during the first six months of the year were 1,800,000 tons, 3 per cent above the same period in 1981. The business was done with Nigeria, probably for 50,000 tons of parboiled 5 per cent, and there were sales to Iran of 100 per cent Grade B. Some areas planted for the new main crop due in December were affected by drought, and forecasts for the summer crop were somewhat lower (*LRBAC* 30th July 1982 2). (Ed. This seems to have been related to the 1982/83 *EN*SO event). The export target for the year remained 4,000,000 tons (*LRBAC* 31st August 1982 2). But assessments of the 1982/83 crop harvested at the end of the year were less than 1981/82 due to the unfavourable growing conditions (*LRBAC* 30th September 1982 2). By October 3,000,000 tons had been exported, and the carry-forward was approximately 1,500,000 tons (*LRBAC* 29th October 1982 2). The new crop harvested was expected to yield 15,000,000 tons of paddy. If the second cop was 2,200,000 tons there would be a combined 1982/83 production of about 17,200,000 tons, down by 1,500,000 tons on the 18,700,000 tons of the 1981/82 season. Exports for 1982 were now revised down to 3,600,000 tons and an export target for 1983 of 3,000,000 tons was announced (*LRBAC* 30th November 1982 3). (Ed. Clearly, a reduced crop was anticipated because of the *EN*SO-related drought conditions). In December, there were shipments of parboiled to Nigeria, and the government announced a scheme to boost paddy prices to help farmers. The total parboiled sold was 100,000 tons, and there was government-to-government business of 150,000 tons of white rice in Indonesia. A further 150,000 tons were under review for Indonesia and Malaysia (*LRBAC* 31st December 1982 3).

During the period lst January to 1st May 1983, exports were 1,257,365 tons, slightly up on the 1,151,700 of the first four months of 1982. This was made up of 434,785 tons on government-to-government basis, and private sales of 822,580 tons. (Ed. 34.5 per cent to 65.4 per cent or roughly one-third to two-thirds). In May, business was done in high-grade white rice to the Middle East, and about 20,000 tons of broken rice A1 Super was sold to Madagascar. There was heavy demand for high-quality rice from Iran and Iraq (*LRBAC* 31st May 1983 2–3). Business was done in high-grade milled rice to the Middle East and there were sales of broken rice to West Africa, including 20,000 tons to Senegal (*LRBAC* 31st June 1983 2). Exports during the first six months of 1983 were 1,660,000 tons of which government-to-government sales were 575,634 tons and private trade 1,084,366 tons (Ed. 34.6 per cent to 65.3 per cent, or approximately one-third to two-thirds again). Crucially, shipments were about 15 per cent down on the same period in 1982. In July, the export market was active to West Africa, Iran and Iraq (*LRBAC* 29th July 1983 3). Recent sales included 60,000 tons of white rice 100 per cent grade B to Iran and 30,000 tons of white rice 15 per cent to Peru. There was also parboiled business to Nigeria, and India had bought a further 100,000 tons of 25 per cent brokens. 3,200,000 tons had been sold for shipment by the end of December, which was close to the target of 3,400,000 tons (*LRBAC* 31st August 1983 2). With the year's export target of 3,400,000 tons almost achieved, prices were expected to remain firm for the rest of the year (*LRBAC* 30th September 1983 2). Then the Thai government unexpectedly reduced the export premium and the export tax by 50 per cent. The government explained that they did not wish to penalise rice farmers by taxing them on exports when tapioca and corn farmers were not taxed. Prices dropped drastically but lower grades were not so badly affected. The Ministry of Commerce's plan for stabilising paddy prices in the coming season included an increase in the contribution to the Government stockpile, which stood at 500 tons per exporter (*LRBAC* 31st October 1983 2). Iraq bought about 130,000 tons of high-grade rice, and some parboiled rice was sold to Nigeria. But new crop forecasts were good, and many Bangkok merchants were nervous with prices weaker for forward sales (*LRBAC* 30th November 1983 3). Exports from the 1982/83 crop were now expected to be above target and reach 3,800,000 tons. The 1983/84 first main harvest crop was expected to be 16,000,000 tons of paddy. The Government announced that contrary to previous practice they would allow some exports of paddy from the 1983/84 crop to European markets subject to guarantees they would not be diverted or re-exported to other markets. At current prices, Thai rice was very competitive against U.S. rice and substantial amounts of new crop rice had already been sold for shipment in 1984 (*LRBAC* 30th December 1983 2–3).

In January, there was renewed interest from Middle East Markets. Nigeria could not buy any more parboiled for the time being as all outstanding export licences had expired on 31st December. Total exports for 1983 were 3,700,000 tons, about 12 per cent above target (*LRBAC* 31st January 1984 2–3). (Ed. Clearly, the 1982/83 *EN*SO event did not have too much impact on Thailand!). Demand for the new crop was good, and there was some government-to-government business including 200,000 tons of white rice and 25 per cent brokens to India. Bangladesh was interested in 100,000 tons of parboiled rice, and Nigeria in 250,000 tons of parboiled and white rice. Mexico bought 20,000 tons of 25 per cent Super for quick shipment, having already bought 20,000 tons earlier in the month (*LRBAC* 29th February 1984 2). 40,000 tons of white rice 100 per cent Grade B were sold to Iran, 13,000 tons of broken rice to the Malagasy Republic, and about 20,000 tons of broken rice to West Africa. About 3500 tons of *Loonzain* (cargo rice) suitable for milling 100 per cent Grade B was sold to destinations in the European Economic Community (E.E.C.) (*LRBAC* 30th March 1984 3). If the second crop in June was as good as anticipated, total production for the year might be 18,000,000 tons, with an export target of 3,900,000–4,000,000 tons. Around 510,000 tons were exported from Bangkok during March. There were two government-to-government sales of 12,000 tons each of Thai broken rice A1 Special, destination not given. 100,000 tons which had been sold to Bangladesh were cancelled. 420,000 tons of rice to Nigeria was finalised. Vessels were being fixed for 20,000 tons of parboiled rice 5 per cent in April, and 40,000 tons in May. Of this tonnage, 20,000 tons was broken rice A1 Special and the Government was in the market for a vessel during April (*LRBAC* 30th April 1984 3). Prospects for the second crop appeared very good. Exports from January to mid-May totalled 1,600,000 tons compared with 1,340,000 tons in the same period in 1983. Zanzibar had purchased 50,000 tons of Thai white rice 10 per cent brokens government to government for shipment spread over one year. But there were big uncertainties over 400,000 tons were reportedly sold to Nigeria. There was a problem over credit, and the first vessel which put in for 20,000 tons parboiled sailed away (Ed. Presumably unloaded?) having waited eighteen days. The fate of this contract would significantly affect the Thai parboiled market (*LRBAC* 31st May 1984 3). The Nigerian letter of credit proved useable, so the 400,000 tons were to be shipped as planned. Bangladesh completed a purchase of 375,000 tons, and Japan was expected to buy 100,000 tons of 25 per cent Super to implement aid programmes (*LRBAC* 29th June 1984 3). Bangladesh's purchase of 375,000 tons was later confirmed as 425,000 tons, but Bangladesh still needed more rice, and a delegation was expected in Bangkok seeking more. Overall Thailand had sold 4,300,000 tons, of which 2,600,000 tons had already been shipped. India, Japan, Senegal and others were in the market, and exports could reach 5,000,000 tons (*LRBAC* 31st July 1984 2–3). Total exports of rice to 31st August were just over 3,000,000 tons, and it was expected that exports would exceed 4,000,000 tons by the end of the year (*LRBAC* 28th September 1984 2). Estimated production from the current crop was reduced from 18,500,000 tons to 17,500,000 tons, but stocks were plentiful, and apparently, the carryover from the 1983/84 record crop of 19,000,000 tons was greater than estimated. Rice exports for 1984/85 were likely to exceed 4,500,000 tons, and by mid-October, 3,750,000 tons had already been shipped (*LRBAC* 31st October 1984 3). On 2nd November the Thai Government announced a devaluation of the Baht by 17.39 per cent against the US$Dollar, to improve the country's trade and balance of payments, and there was to be a flexible exchange rate based on a "basket" of currencies. Local rice prices advanced sharply for a few days, but the improvement was short-lived, as world buyers naturally expected a reduction in

Thai export prices because of the devaluation. There was no Government business but there were several transactions in the private sector. These included 165,000 tons of white broken rice A1 Special to Senegal, 24,000 tons of white rice 100 per cent white Grade C to Syria by tender, 15,000 tons of white broken rice A1 Super to Malagasy, 14,000 tons parboiled rice 5 per cent brokens to undisclosed destinations, 12,500 tons parboiled rice 5 per cent brokens to the Cameroons and 21,000 tons white rice 20 per cent brokens to Mexico. Rice exports since the beginning of the year were estimated at over 4,000,000 tons compared with 3,330,000 tons for the same period the previous year, and total exports that year of 3,700,000 tons. Total exports for 1984 could exceed 4,500,000 tons (*LRBAC* 30th November 1984 2–3). The devaluation of the Baht against the US$Dollar in November meant a fall in the price of all grades of rice for foreign buyers. Then the Government announced a new policy. From 1st January the stocks of all exporters were to be checked every month. The authorities would then decide what percentage of the crop could be exported in the coming months, and each exporter told what percentage of his stocks he would be allowed to export. This had the desired effect and merchants were collecting stock and prices had risen (*LRBAC* 31st December 1984 2–3).

Demand for export was slow in January, and with new crops starting to come on the market, prices eased (*LRBAC* 31st January 1983 2–3). In February, export activity was mainly shipments of rice sold the previous year for forward delivery (*LRBAC* 28th February 1985 1). Exports in the first quarter were expected to be over 2,000,000 tons. The export quota for March was 70 per cent of merchant stocks, but it was not certain enough would be sold abroad to fill the quota. Total exports for 1985 were expected to be 4,000,000–4,500,000 tons, but this would depend on the second crop which might be reduced due to shortage of fertiliser (*LRBAC* 29th March 1985 3). Congestion had built up at the ports as ships awaited cargoes, but this had now eased and a good supply of rice was now flowing from up-country growing areas down to Bangkok (*LRBAC* 30th April 1985 3). There was considerable interest from Iran and Senegal in May, but nothing sold. More rice was moving from Bangkok to Europe (*LRBAC* 31st May 1985 2–3). In June, the *Circular* reported that according to the FAO, the international rice market in 1985 was likely to see large supplies for export, but weak import demand. This would result in lower prices and the large end-of-season stocks. India and Indonesia might import less, and Indonesia was already selling off surplus stocks and was expected to be largely self-sufficient. Interestingly Bangladesh would import less rice as it was making large imports of wheat instead, but Kampuchea (Cambodia) and the Philippines were expected to import more, as their 1984 crops had been hit by floods. Meanwhile, imports to Sri Lanka had increased sharply, and in the first quarter were 150,000 tons, six times as much as in 1984. Purchases by Iran, Iraq and Saudi Arabia, which were about 1,700,000 tons in 1984, were expected to increase more slowly. Africa was difficult to judge, due to shortages of foreign exchange, and the Ivory Coast, a major buyer, might have had a larger than usual crop in 1984. World rice stocks at the end of 1985 were forecast to rise by nearly 7,000,000 tons to a record level of 51,000,000 tons. China and the United States would account for most of the increased stocks in exporting countries, and stockpiles of imported rice were already large in India and Indonesia (*LRBAC* 28th June 1985 1). Exports from Thailand during the first five months of 1985 were over 2,000,000 tons, but fell in June, and might only have been 200,000 tons. Bangkok needed to watch the situation in Indonesia, Pakistan and China, but Europe took more rice from Thailand than from the United States, and two shiploads had sailed in June. This was in addition to normal liner trade which continued all the time (*LRBAC* 28th June 1985 3). In July, the *Circular* reported that there was a heavy surplus of rice and a shortage of buyers who could afford to pay for it. Indonesia was trying to sell large amounts of old-stock rice, and buyers were encouraged to bid below the indicated level to shift the rice in order to make room for the new crop. Taiwan and Burma were keen to export, but Pakistan had chosen to reject unacceptably low bids for its exports. Prices in Thailand were falling and had reached a ten-year low. The outlook remained weak (*LRBAC* 31st July 1985 1). Prices did indeed hit a ten-year low at the end of July. Then a dispute between a major Thai exporter and Iran was settled. The exporter should have shipped rice from the December 1984 harvest, but stocks were not available, and the deal was now reached for shipment from the summer 1985 crop, meaning 52,000 tons would be exported. There was further business with Iran by other exporters for 150,000 tons. In the middle of the month, cargoes loaded at Bangkok included one cargo to Iraq of Thai fragrant 25 per cent. (Ed. This is very significant as it is the first reference to Thai fragrant rice, a quality which was to become a premier grade and a direct competitor for the highest grade of *Basmati* from India and Pakistan. See Miyata 2007, cited in Kano 2007). Other shipments included one cargo to Syria of white rice 100 per cent C, four cargoes to Iran of white rice 100 per cent B, two cargoes to the Philippines of white rice 55 per cent, one cargo to Yugoslavia of white rice 5 per cent, one cargo to China of white rice 25 per cent, and one cargo to Malaysia of white rice 100 per cent. government-to-government talks were taking place with Nigeria for 100,000 tons of parboiled (*LRBAC* 31st July 1985 3). In August, there were sales of 100,000 tons of broken rice to Senegal, 150,000 tons to Brazil, and negotiations were re-opened with Nigeria. The sale to Brazil fell through, and the negotiations with Nigeria were stopped by an attempted "coup" in Bangkok. The Thai Government cancelled substantial purchases by exporters from local suppliers (Ed. presumably to preserve domestic supplies in a time of disturbance). There was a tender for Reunion in September by which Thailand hoped to sell *Loonzain* 5 per cent in two lots of 6000 tons (*LRBAC* 30th August 1985 2–3). There was uncertainty about whether the deal with Brazil for 150,000 tons had been finalised (*LRBAC* 30th September 1985 1). But it had, and shipment began. There were enquiries from Nigeria, but nothing materialised. To obtain more competitive prices internationally, the Government removed the 2.5 per cent export tax. The recent abortive coup in Thailand did not affect rice trading, but there was a temporary shortage of stocks at the port in Bangkok which delayed some shipments (*LRBAC* 30th September 1985 2–3). Having removed the 2.5 per cent export tax, the Government now fixed a minimum price for paddy below which the mills were forbidden to buy. The Government also tried to get the traders to work together to eliminate excessive competition between them. Vessels were loading for Iran, Brazil and Vietnam, and more were expected in November for Iran, Brazil and elsewhere. Up to 26th October, 230,000 tons had been exported that month, and there would probably be another 60,000 – 80,000 tons by the end of the month (*LRBAC* 31st October 1985 2–3). The Government continued to try to force up prices by fixing a minimum price at which the mills must buy paddy from the farmers (*LRBAC* 30th November 1985 1). During the first ten months of the year, the major buyers included Malaysia 325,000 tons, Nigeria 290,000 tons and Iran 260,000 tons. Sales to Iran and Iraq in the future were to be Government to Government, but within the rice export trader's system (*LRBAC* 30th November 1985 3). In December, the *Circular* commented that the feature of the month had been the uncertainty over the US Farm Bill, which had now been finally passed and signed by President Reagan. The effect of this bill would be to reduce the price of U.S. rice on the U.S. domestic market, and exporters from other countries feared they would now get less for their own rice. Thailand had been trying to force up export prices with a scheme for minimum prices on the home market, but the market looked weak with the expected drop in U.S. prices. It was difficult to see where prices would settle (*LRBAC* 31st December 1985 1). Merchants in Thailand were increasingly concerned about the U.S. Farm Bill. With a considerable carryover from 1985, and the new crop coming in, the market looked weak. Exports during December had been unusually low with less than 200,000 tons (*LRBAC* 31st December 1985 3).

In January, the *Circular* commented that it was still uncertain at what level the United States would market rice abroad under the Farm Bill. The idea was that rice should be sold at "world market prices", but it was not clear how these would be calculated (*LRBAC* 31st January 1986 1). In Thailand, there were many Government resignations, and a new Minister of Commerce was appointed. To improve rice exports he abolished most of the previous Government's control regulations. The support scheme was dropped, and so was the system by which the Commerce Minister allocated export quotas. Stock-holding requirements by exporters were also dropped, except for the compulsory 2000 tons per exporter. Premiums on low-quality rice were dropped but still remained on high-quality rice, parboiled rice and cargo rice. So free trade had returned with prices fluctuating according to supply and demand (*LRBAC* 31st January 1986 1). There followed a drop in the official Board of Trade prices. Substantial sales were made affecting the market and causing logistical problems in the port. The main sales were 100,000 tons of white rice 10 per cent to Brazil, shipment 15th February/15th March, 200,000 tons of white rice 25 per cent to China, by shipment of 50,000 tons a month from February (with 110,000 tons of maize to be shipped in the same way), and 100,000 tons broken rice sold to Russia for delivery to Vietnam. Normal sales included 50,000 tons of broken rice to West Africa (*LRBAC* 31st January 1986 3). Thailand had a near record 800,000 tons of rice to export in February/March (*LRBAC* 28th February 1986 1). But trade was slow (*LRBAC* 28th February 1986 3). Anxiety continued over the U.S. Farm Bill (*LRBAC* 27th March 1986 2). In April, the *Circular* commented that in Thailand the price of broken rice A1 Special had fallen so much that the local market was using it as animal feed, which pushed down the price of yellow maize (*LRBAC* 30th April 1986 1). Broken rice now reached a level below which it would be difficult to fall further (*LRBAC* 30th April 1986 2). The U.S. Rice Millers' Association held their annual conference in Florida in May. Discussion turned to the Farm Bill, and it was clear that the rice industry in the United States was determined to force prices down, to be competitive with Thailand and others. European millers were now starting to think of U.S. rice rather than Thai rice (*LRBAC* 31st May 1986 1). The *Circular* then noted that the published "world market price" in the United States and the lowering of prices had taken effect. Northern European markets were now thinking of U.S. rice before others, and sales from the United States had increased. Thailand was finding it difficult to compete (*LRBAC* 30th June 1986 1). Purchases from Brazil were less than anticipated. Thai quotes for the higher grades of white rice eased slightly where exporters were concerned with the sharp fall in U.S. prices (*LRBAC* 30th June 1986 3). The *Circular* commented that in world terms the main interest of the private trade was in shipments to Africa from the Far East, but exporters were using Brazilian buying as an excuse to force up the market (*LRBAC* 31st July 1986 1). There was a sharp increase in prices, particularly for parboiled, because paddy was in short supply due to a small second crop. It was also difficult to produce parboiled in the rainy season. Despite the loss of some markets to the U.S. total exports to June were good at 2,592,000 tons. Some demand was expected from Peru and North Korea and Vietnam had recently bought large quantities of broken rice for prompt shipment (*LRBAC* 31st July 1986 3). But in September, the *Circular* commented that prices had fallen in Thailand, and this had lowered the "world market price" in the United States and with it U.S. export prices (*LRBAC* 30th September 1986 1). Export figures to the end of August were 3,297,310 tons compared with 2,964,380 tons at the same time in 1985 (Ed. An increase of 332,930 tons or 11.2 per cent). This was a record quantity. But the value was much less than in 1985 because prices were so low. China had been the largest buyer with 232,000 tons, followed by Brazil with 218,000 tons, and other leading purchasers were the U.S.S.R., Singapore, Saudi Arabia, Madagascar, Malaysia and the Netherlands. Forecasts for the new crop varied, with some reports of drought. The latest Government figures were for 19,000,000 tons of paddy including the main and second crop, compared with 18,000,000 tons last year (*LRBAC* 30th September 1986 2). World prices continued to fluctuate, as there was too much rice available, and not enough money. As usual in Bangkok prices went up when vessels came in for loading, and merchants were covering their requirements. In October, prices edged up as contracts to Iran were about to be loaded (*LRBAC* 31st October 1986 1). The export figures to the end of September were 3,601,844 tons, an 8.35 per cent (sic) increase over the same period in 1985. In October, between 280,000 and 300,000 tons of rice would be exported. Prices firmed because of a possible large government-to-government sale to Senegal. 60,000 tons of 100 per cent Grade B had also been sold to Iran by two local merchants and was being collected for loading (*LRBAC* 31st October 1986 3). The *Circular* commented that when Christmas approached it was normal to hear that problems in the Far East would produce smaller crops and higher prices. This was usual just before the new crop in Thailand, in the hope that prices would be pushed up. But this year

Bangkok merchants were quoting discounts for forward shipment, so a weaker market was expected (*LRBAC* 29th November 1986 1). Then the authorities reported that in 1986/87 the main crop would be down by 10–15 per cent. Based on the 1985/86 main crop of 17,700,000 tons this indicated a crop of 15,000,000 to 16,000,000 tons (*LRBAC* 29th November 1986 3). The *Circular* commented that although forecasts at this time of the year were usually widely inaccurate, they thought the world quantity for export in 1987 might be slightly down in 1986. But demand from importers would also be less, with no heavy demand from any Asian countries. There would also be less demand from West Africa due to better crops and a shortage of money, and they expected a sharp reduction in demand from Brazil. They thought the world rice market would continue for another year at price and quantity levels distressing to producers (*LRBAC* 31st December 1986 1). Although in recent years price falls were normal at the end of the year, this year prices were unchanged. This was due to the decrease in the main crop of 10–15 per cent, and the government's intention to buy 200,000 tons of white rice in the local market in January. Despite the decrease in the crop, price increases were not expected until the second half of the year because of the financial position of the exporters, and the need to sell (*LRBAC* 31st December 1986 3).

The Government purchases in January turned out to be greater than expected, at 337,500 tons. The aim was to increase the total to 700,000 tons, and then negotiate large-scale government contracts around the world (*LRBAC* 30th January 1987 1). Prices were forced up by the Government purchase of 337,500 tons, made up of Thai white rice 100 per cent, 10 per cent and 25 per cent and brokens A1 Special. When the total had reached 700,000 tons the intention was to sell 150,000 tons of white rice 100 per cent to Iran and Iraq, 60,000 tons A1 Special to Senegal, and 200,000 tons of white rice 100 per cent to Malaysia. The private sector was asking for offers for 85,000 tons of A1 Special for shipment to Senegal. At this point, the *Circular* discontinued the Thailand Board of Trade price lists as they no longer bore much relation to prices at which it was possible to buy (*LRBAC* 30th January 1987 3). The Government purchases increased prices, and the private sector purchases pushed them even higher (*LRBAC* 28th February 1987 1). In the end, the Government bought 750,000 tons of rice of which 250,000 tons were sold to Iran, 150,000 tons to West Africa and South America combined, 200,000 tons to China, 60,000 tons to Senegal, 50,000 tons to Malaysia and 30,000 tons to Comoros Islands, mostly for February/March shipment. So the local market was very active as exporters bought to sell to the Government, and as always in Bangkok, the market was strengthened by the number of vessels in port to collect cargoes from previous trades. Five vessels had been tendered to pick up cargoes for China in February/early March (*LRBAC* 28th February 1987 3). Then the Government bought another 120,000 tons of 100 per cent grade B, 10 per cent, 15 per cent and broken rice A1 Special, bringing Government purchasing to well over 1,000,000 tons and ensuring prices remained high (*LRBAC* 31st March 1987 3). Prices for white rice were unchanged despite a fall in activity, and prices for broken rice were firm due to sales to the U.S.S.R. and North Korea. Prices for parboiled increased as traders anticipated a tender for 50,000 tons for Bangladesh in May (*LRBAC* 30th April 1987 3). Bangladesh actually purchased 150,000 tons of parboiled for shipment May/June/July and might need more. Iran made regular purchases. A delegation from Malaya asked for offers of 100 per cent B white rice from the Government and exporters and was thought to have bought 60,000 tons 10 per cent white rice and would need more. The Thai Government bought 66,000 tons, being 50,000 tons 100 per cent B, 10,000 tons 10 per cent, and 6000 tons A1 Special broken rice. The second crop was estimated at 2,000,000 tons paddy, down by 500,000 tons from the previous year and just coming on the market (*LRBAC* 29th May 1987 2). Prices fell with the second crop. Because of its high moisture content, it was not possible to store it for long. It needed to be sold quickly and mixed with old crops before export (See also *LRBAC* 31st May 1988 3). This is why prices normally fell at this time of year. Exports from January to May were extremely good with 1,970,000 tons shipped. Major shipments in June were for Iran, China, Bangladesh, Benin and Cameroons, and shipments expected in July were for Iran, the U.S.S.R. and North Korea (*LRBAC* 30th June 1987 3). The *Circular* commented that Bangladesh had entered the market, but as always with that country the details were shrouded in mystery. Authorisation had been given for quantities of rice imports, both government to government and by the private sector. How much was not known because payment from the private sector was a problem. This had a dramatic effect on the market in Bangkok, where merchants were already worried about the severe drought affecting the main growing areas. Drought was a traditional rumour at this time of year, so the *Circular* had it checked independently, and found the reports correct. The maize crop was already damaged. Rice needs more water than maize, so the rice crop would certainly be delayed a few weeks. Supplies would be limited until then, and the situation could become even more serious if rain did not come (*LRBAC* 31st July 1987 1). Even if the rains came soon the main crop due in November/December would be late, and of reduced quantity. There were rumours of purchasing by Bangladesh, and Iran bought 45,000 tons of 100 per cent B and Malaysia 100,000 tons of white rice 10 per cent. Parboiled stocks were low because of the 170,000 tons exported to Bangladesh in June (Ed. *LRBAC* 29th May 1987 2 gives a figure of 150,000 tons). Broken rice was hard to find. Up to July 14th Thailand had exported 2,539,000 tons of rice of all kinds (*LRBAC* 31st July 1987 3). The *Circular* commented "The monsoon!!! Historically if the rice bowl does not get enough water in the early and middle stages of the growing season, then a shortage of rice can be expected." There had been some dramatic price increases, particularly from Thailand. The monsoon was late, which would mean the crop there would be smaller and late. But Burma, India and Pakistan had also been affected. The Pakistan crop might be down 30 per cent, and India might need to import 600,000 tons. Burma could not even say what their position was. Prices had rushed up all over the world, including the United States, where the "world market price" had moved up strongly (*LRBAC* 31st August 1987 1). (Ed. This presumably was the consequence of the 1987/86 *EN*SO! See Glantz 1996 66–68). The drought in Thailand ended in the middle of August, but the new crop would be delayed and smaller. Thailand would not have more than 3,000,000 tons of milled rice to export in 1988. This, and the reduced crop of the previous year, plus very good sales, resulted in the most bullish market for many years. Prices rose sharply for white rice and parboiled. The increase for parboiled was particularly spectacular because of a tender for 100,000 tons held by Bangladesh on 31st August, at which 92,000 tons of Thai parboiled were bought. Iran continued to purchase, and Tanzania bought 20,000 tons of 15 per cent white rice. Vessels had been loading for Malaysia, Cuba, Russia, Benin, the Cameroons, Laos, Indonesia and the Ivory Coast (*LRBAC* 31st August 1987 3). The *Circular* then commented that Thailand had almost run out of rice, although the Government still held stocks, and prices were likely to continue rising until the new crop became available. There were reports of a serious drought in Kampuchea (Cambodia) which had affected their rice crop and could result in famine. Other countries affected by the poor monsoon were Vietnam, Laos, the Philippines, Sri Lanka, Thailand, India and Pakistan. By contrast flooding in Bangladesh was causing grave concern (*LRBAC* 30th September 1987 1). Milled white rice prices and parboiled prices continued to rise. Bangladesh bought 100,000 tons of white rice 20 per cent at especially low "friendship" prices from the Thai Government, and they were likely to buy more. Other enquiries came from Malaysia and the Comoros Islands. Vessels had loaded for Iran, France, Mozambique, Reunion, Italy and Indonesia. Up to the end of August exports were 3,027,000 tons compared with 3,297,000 tons in 1986 (*LRBAC* 30th September 1987 2). The *Circular* commented that the year had seen a steady rise in prices throughout the world, and many qualities particularly from Thailand had doubled in price. But there had not been a single default from an exporter in Thailand covering a trade concluded on a London Rice Brokers' Association contract (Ed. This comment turned out to be premature, see *LRBAC* 29th January 1988 1). But now prices in Thailand had dropped sharply. Business cancelled with Bangladesh had also had an effect. Prices were now only half what they were in 1974, and if the Editor of the *Circular* was speculator he would prefer to buy than sell! (*LRBAC* 30th October 1987 1). Prices had fallen considerably due to limited business, and traders who held stocks of rice were cashing their profits. Up to the end of October exports for the year were between 3,500,000 and 3,600,000 tons and shipments were made to Dubai, Mozambique, Madagascar, Benin and the Cameroons. The new crop was still expected to be considerably reduced with estimates at 3,500,000 tons for export (*LRBAC* 30th October 1987 3). The *Circular* commented that demand for rice on world markets in 1988 would be higher than in 1987 because of larger imports by various Asian countries. But supplies for exports would be less, particularly from Thailand. The final amount to be exported from Thailand in 1987 was larger than seemed possible, and stocks carried forward would be low. There was also great nervousness about the Thai new crop. Some compared the present situation with 1973 (Ed. Also an *EN*SO year!). But the situation was different in one important respect. In 1973, the reduction in paddy crops in the world by about 5 per cent resulted in an increase in the prices of white rice of about 300 per cent. At that time, wheat was also in short supply, whereas in late 1987, wheat was plentiful, prices were extremely low and wheat would be substituted for rice wherever possible (*LRBAC* 30th November 1987 1). The Thai government estimated exports for 1988 at 2,600,000 tons against 1987 exports of 4,000,000 tons. Exporters, however, expected a surplus of 3,000,000 to 3,500,000 tons, but some private estimates were as low as 1,500,000 tons. Conditions varied so much in the different rice-growing regions that assessment was difficult. The second crop would be reduced due to lack of water in the irrigation dams, but this would be offset by some new areas coming into cultivation. There were sales of 60,000 tons of 100 per cent B to Iran and 40,000 tons of 100 per cent B to Malaysia. Rice would be loaded during November/December to Benin, Iran, the U.S.S.R., Angola, the Cameroons, Sierra Leone, Italy, Senegal and Indonesia (*LRBAC* 30th November 1987 3). In December, there were rumours in world terms of forthcoming imports to Indonesia, the Philippines, Vietnam and other countries in the Far East. Iran had made substantial purchases in Thailand, and Malaysia was negotiating for a substantial quantity. Prices were beginning to rise in Bangkok (*LRBAC* 31st December 1987 1). Exports from Thailand from January to November 1987 were over 4,000,000 tons and were expected to be about 4,350,000 tons when the December figures were added. Iran was the largest importer, with purchases so far in 1987 of over 500,000 tons, and it was expected this would be 560,000 tons by the end of December (*LRBAC* 31st December 1987 3).

In January 1988, the Circular commented:-

"DISASTER!!"

"What a shameful performance we have seen on the part of a good number of Bangkok exporters in the last month. There has been a shower of defaults on contracts made which in some cases have been re-negotiated with enormous losses chalked up by the unfortunate international traders concerned. Indeed it would seem that there are very few of the well-known international operators who have been unaffected. Whatever the reasons behind this behaviour we totally deplore what has happened.

We have also noticed that there has been very little comment from the authorities but one thing is certain and that is that the Bangkok market will not be the same again for a very long time. In one case a contract had been re-negotiated at considerable loss to the overseas buyer and when the vessel was presented shortly afterwards the contract was defaulted a second time and the vessel did not load. There are many examples we can quote and the result is that the whole trade has lost confidence in the Bangkok market. Happily there are some well-known names that are exceptions and which shine like a light on a dark night.

How premature we were in our October 1987 issue when there had been some defaults in Bangkok and we pointed out that the L.R.B.A. contracts had been honoured. Even the added strength of protection from the London contract has not been of much help this time – so far.

If exporters expect to default when the market goes up, then how can they expect their buyers not to default if the market goes down? We have already seen one example of this and the Thai exporters (with or without official pressure) simply must put their house in order if total chaos is to be avoided.

The sanctity of the contract must be preserved at all costs."

(*LRBAC* 29th January 1988 1).

The background to all this was that prices had suddenly advanced in Thailand at the end of December when the new crop was harvested, and farmers and merchants alike realised how small it was (Ed. The *EN*SO effect!). Local merchants tried to buy all the paddy available and would not release much to the mills. So Thai exporters who had been expecting prices to fall at harvest as usual, had to pay very high prices or be unable to cover sales they had already made. Defaults resulted. Subsequently, prices stabilised, as less rice was shipped due to defaults and some improvement in the availability of rice. Estimates of the export surplus varied but it would be greatly reduced from the 4,360,000 tons of 1987 (*LRBAC* 29th January 1988 3). In January 1988, only 230,000 tons of rice were exported, and February would be about the same. This was about two-thirds of what was exported in January/February 1987. Current estimates of exports in 1988 were as low as 2,000,000–2,500,000 tons. A larger area of the second crop had been planted, but irrigation reservoirs were at low levels, and not enough water would be available for all the rice planted. As could be seen from the export figures, the market had been very quiet. A delegation from India was in Bangkok discussing the purchase of 100,000 tons of rice. An Iraqi delegation had visited but were looking for three years credit, which they were unlikely to obtain (*LRBAC* 29th February 1988 2–3). The *Circular* commented that the world rice crop was down about 5 per cent in total, which should have reduced supply and increased demand. Supply had indeed fallen, but so had demand. Countries in Asia had reduced their stockpiles, and Iran and the Ivory Coast had built up stocks fearing a strong market, and so had not recently been buyers. Also cheaper grains (Ed. like wheat) had been substituted for rice because of the unusually large differential (Ed. in price). During March prices fell in Thailand but sales did not pick up. Then prices bounced back (*LRBAC* 31st March 1988 1). Prospects for the second crop looked good as the rains had kept going. Then China purchased 200,000 tons of white rice 25 per cent on a government-to-government basis for April/June shipment. There was a delegation from Bangladesh in Bangkok, and the Indian negotiators were again trying to purchase rice. There were sales of broken rice, including 10,000 tons for Gambia, 20,000 tons for Vietnam, and 16,000 tons for Mauritania. Syria bought 12,000 tons of white rice 100 per cent Grade B and Somalia 10,000 tons of parboiled 10 per cent brokens (*LRBAC* 31st March 1988 3). The April edition of the *Circular* began:-

"If a man has not eaten breakfast today, it is unlikely that he will eat two breakfasts tomorrow. The month has seen a remarkable lack of demand and lack of enquiry which must mean that the stock situation for international trade is a little easier. This fact, coupled with the gradual improvement in prospects for the second crop in Thailand has depressed the market in that country. The US market has tumbled down in the last few days and export prices from other areas are stagnant." (*LRBAC* 29th April 1988 1).

The second crop in Thailand looked promising, with possibly 2,500,000 tons of milled rice for export and prices had declined. Fragrant rice and *Loonzain* were not affected, as the second crop was not suited for high quality. Broken rice was firm as some had been sold for shipment to Vietnam, and a further sale of 30,000 tons was announced for Vietnam (*LRBAC* 29th April 1988 3). There was a rapid drop in prices as the summer crop arrived on the market in larger quantities than expected, but demand remained small. It was therefore difficult to mix new crop with old crop to dry the second crop. The second crop has to be sold quickly because it is harvested early (Ed. in the ripening process) and if millers do not have mechanical dryers they cannot dry it properly (See also *LRBAC* 30th June 1987 3 above). The Government purchased 166,000 tons from a large number of exporters to prop up the market, made up of 40,000 tons of white rice 15 per cent, 74,000 tons white rice 25 per cent, 7000 tons white broken rice A1 Super, and 45,000 tons parboiled 10 per cent. Merchants sold 30,000 tons of white rice 10 per cent to Zimbabwe and another 20,000 tons of broken rice to Vietnam. Iran was negotiating to ship 60,000 tons of white rice 100 per cent Grade B which they contracted in 1987 (*LRBAC* 31st May 1988 3). At the beginning of June came the biggest single sale ever made from Thailand, when India purchased from the Thai Government 500,000 tons of rice with 15 per cent and 25 per cent brokens for shipments from June to October 1988. (Ed. India had been devastated by *EN*SO). When the first Indian vessel arrived for its rice, prices moved up in Thailand by 17 per cent for whole grain and brokens, and 10 per cent for parboiled (*LRBAC* 30th June 1988 1). Then the Thai government sold Malaysia 84,000 tons of 100 per cent Grade B and 17,000 tons of white rice 10 per cent, shipment from July to December. Government rice exports for the second half of the year now reached 700,000 tons, including 500,000 tons for India, 80,000 tons of 25 per cent for China, 30,000 tons A1 brokens for Mauritania and 84,000 tons for Malaysia. Interestingly rice was now usually sold in 50 kilo new single polypropylene bags (*LRBAC* 30th June 1988 3). In July, India wanted to buy another 200,000 tons of white rice 25 per cent brokens, but prices were rising as an Iranian delegation also wanted 200,000 tons of high-quality rice (*LRBAC* 29th July 1988 3). In August, Iran purchased 165,000 tons of 100 per cent Grade B for quick shipment, and there were purchases of 60,000 tons by Malaysia and 90,000 tons of 100 per cent Grade B by Iraq (*LRBAC* 31st August 1988 2). In September, under the heading "A BOTTOMLESS PIT?" the *Circular* commented that at the beginning of 1988 forecasts for exports from Thailand had been very low, between 1,700,000 and zero. But as the year progressed more and more business had been done, and it was now thought that exports for 1988 would be 4,000,000 to 4,200,000 tons. Exports from 1st January to 31st September had already reached 3,020,000 tons (*LRBAC* 30th September 1988 1). Parboiled rice was in short supply and prices had risen, and there was some high moisture rice with a moisture level of 15/17 per cent which was trading at a discount. The Government of Bangladesh was negotiating for 100,000 tons of parboiled rice 10 per cent (*LRBAC* 30th September 1988 2). In October, the *Circular* commented that "Bangkok still makes the market". There had been good reports from Thailand about the new crop, until it became apparent that heavy rains were continuing with damage to standing crops (*LRBAC* 31st October 1988 1). The heavy rains and cyclones meant the harvest was delayed during October, with rice fields submerged in some areas and the crops damaged. But a large crop was expected with harvesting to commence at the end of November, which was still early. The market had been squeezed for shipment in October, because merchants were covering their sales to India and stocks were low prior to the new harvest (*LRBAC* 31st October 1988 2). In November, the estimate for Thailand's exports in 1988 was raised to 4,300,000 tons. With increased demand, a good second crop, and an earlier than expected harvest of the main crop, Thailand shipped over 1,000,000 tons during August and September, and this seemed likely to continue (*LRBAC* 30th November 1988 1). The new crop began to arrive at the end of November, with excellent quality and high milling yields. There were commitments for 500,000 – 600,000 tons to be shipped during December. Delegations from Iran and Senegal had been in Bangkok, an Indian delegation was expected, and Malaysia was about to purchase 100,000 tons. In North Yemen, tender 10,000 tons of parboiled 100 per cent sortexed rice was sold. In a recent Iraq tender three cargoes of Thai, 100 per cent Grade B was sold, and the result of a Syrian tender for 6000–12,000 tons of 5 per cent rice was awaited. Recent reports of floods in Bangladesh meant more purchasing was expected from there, but floods in the south of Thailand would have little effect as only 5 per cent of the crop was grown in that region (*LRBAC* 30th November 1988 3). The market in Bangkok fell very little in December despite the arrival of the new crop, due to heavy commitments for December and January, and continuing new demand from China. A surprise was the small difference in price between high-quality whole rice and low-quality broken rice. This was due to the good quality of the rice, and heavy demand for 25 per cent and lower quality rice for China. Parboiled prices were also high because of a shortage of paddy with low milling yield. 91,000 tons 100 per cent Grade B was sold to Malaysia, stowed in Bangkok for January to May shipment. The price was a special case and below cost. Other sales included 200,000–400,000 tons of rice with 25 per cent brokens to China, 45,000 tons 100 per cent Grade B to Iraq and around 30,000 tons 100 per cent Grade B to Iran. Senegal and India were expected to purchase soon. Demand was good, and exports in 1988 were expected to be between 4,500,000 tons and 4,700,000 tons. The forecast for 1989 was at least 4,700,000 tons. Quotations were for rice in 50-kilo new polypropylene bags (*LRBAC* 30th December 1988 3).

In January 1989, demand for rice in Asia kept coming, and it was difficult for Thai exporters to buy sufficient rice for their needs. Total exports from Thailand during 1988 had reached an astonishing 4,783,000 tons (Ed. Actually 5,267,005 tons see Table 5.1 above). End-of-year stocks were minimal and a substantial tonnage included in the Thai government statistics for 1989 was actually exported at the end of 1988. The main paddy crop was estimated at 17,000,000 tons of good quality and high milling yield. Much demand had been for low-quality rice, and a shortage of brokens had developed, so there was only a small difference in price between the high and the low qualities. A big second crop was needed and prospects were good with high prices, and reservoirs at a satisfactory level. But early rains were required and farmers were trying to produce a big second crop. Supplies in the world were at a critical level, and the world needed good crops in 1990 (sic) (*LRBAC* 31st January 1989 1). Prices rose in January 1989 despite the arrival of the new crop. The farmers and the rice millers "squeezed" the exporters by holding back their stock, knowing exporters had many vessels to load. Exports in January were 500,000 tons, of which 400,000 tons might have been purchased by

Indonesia. China had also been buying, but how much was not clear. India might purchase soon to replenish their stockpile (*LRBAC* 31st January 1989 3). The farmers continued to hold back rice from the market, so exporters were still short of rice and had to purchase supplies for loading when vessels arrived. Exports were made to Malaysia, Iraq, Peru, Sudan, Cuba, Dakar, Angola, China, Indonesia and Vietnam. In a Syrian tender, 12,000 tons of 100 per cent Grade B was sold in March/April shipment to Latakia (Al Ladhiqiyah). 30,000 tons A1 Special broken rice was sold to Mauritania, government to government (*LRBAC* 28th February 1989 2). China needed another 250,000 – 300,000 tons of rice. Although they had purchased 500,000 tons from Thailand, they were experiencing delays in shipments (*LRBAC* 31st March 1989 1). The farmers continued to hold back rice, leaving exporters to purchase supplies when vessels arrived. Exports in March were 600,000 tons, with forward commitments for April and May of 900,000 tons. New (second) crop rice would arrive on the market in May, but it seemed there would not be much decrease in prices. Because of very hot weather, it was thought some second crop would be damaged. 40,000 tons of broken rice A1 Special was sold to Senegal, Government to Government, 20,000 tons in June and 20,000 tons in July, at a special "political" price. China purchased 12,500 tons of 100 per cent Grade B, and 12,500 tons of 5 per cent, and needed another 250,000 tons, but their purchases would depend on the progress of existing commitments (*LRBAC* 31st March 1989 3). The *Circular* reported in April that in the previous three months, Thai exporters had been striving to keep prices stable whilst they covered their "shorts". (Ed. For immediate loading). But market levels began to rise sharply with news of high prices at a tender in Pakistan for Pakistan rice. This news was published in Thailand and had a dramatic effect on both the Thai and U.S. markets. A heavy shipping programme was continuing from Thailand (*LRBAC* 28th April 1989 1). Prices rose as a response to the high prices paid in Pakistan, and Russia bought a very large quantity of rice with 10 per cent brokens for May/June shipment, which added to the excitement. Many vessels had been arriving in port, and exporters were forced to pay higher and higher prices to cover their needs. The second crop estimates were about 3,500,000 tons of paddy. But there was still no rain! (*LRBAC* 28th April 1989 3). The unspecified business was done with Russia and Iran, and a large trade in parboiled was reported to Bangladesh but not confirmed. Heavy forward sales ensured that prices did not fall. Exports in May were expected to be 600,000 tons, bringing the total to 2,800,000 tons for the year so far (*LRBAC* 31st May 1989 2). Thailand was showing signs of stress as a result of the huge exports they had achieved already in 1989, and exports showed no signs of slackening despite continuing competition from Vietnam for low-quality white rice (*LRBAC* 30th June 1989 1). The market was extremely excited, with increased demand for the high grades from Iran, Syria and Malaysia, and for parboiled from Sri Lanka and Bangladesh. The Philippines and India were also making enquiries. Iran purchased at least seven cargoes of 100 per cent B and Bangladesh bought 200,000 tons parboiled 15 per cent. Exports for the first five months of 1989 were 2,880,000 tons against 1,390,000 tons for the same period in 1988, an increase of 107.5 per cent. In May, 620,000 tons were shipped and the quantity in June would be about 500,000 tons. China was the largest buyer with 742,000 tons shipped in the first five months, and about 200,000 tons yet to be shipped (*LRBAC* 30th June 1989 3). Prices rose in July in anticipation of purchasing by India and Sri Lanka. But significantly India bought 270,000 tons from Vietnam and only 100,000 tons of Thai 25 per cent, and Sri Lanka bought 70,000 tons from Vietnam and none from Thailand. The market fell dramatically with the arrival of the second crop, which has a high moisture content and needs to be sold quickly. To meet the Thai export standard it had to be mixed with rice of lower moisture content from the main crop or which had been dried mechanically. Exports up to the end of June were 3,500,000 tons (*LRBAC* 31st July 1989 3). In Thailand, prices can drop quickly when there are few vessels in port and little demand, as happened in August. The second crop arrived in quantity and was a record 4,000,000 tons. In the first week of August, there were seven ships in port for India, but since then not much has been shipped. Interestingly the bulk of demand from Africa for low-quality rice was now being met by Vietnam, and China and India had covered their needs. Rumours of Bangladesh needing 100,000 tons did not result in business. Export figures to the end of July were 4,100,000 tons, with 580,000 tons shipped in July, but the figure for August was likely to be 400,000 tons. Exports for 1989 would probably reach a record 6,000,000 tons (Ed. Actually 6,311,000 tons see *Table 5.1* above). In a tender, Malaysia purchased 47,000 tons 100 per cent Grade B for September shipment (*LRBAC* 31st August 1989 3). Negotiations continued with India, whilst Iran bought eight cargoes of 100 per cent Grade B, for October/December shipment. Iraq and Syria also made purchases and Malaysia bought 55,000 tons of 100 per cent Grade B (*LRBAC* 29th September 1989 2). A delegation from Thailand visited China proposing to sell 1,500,000 tons but the Chinese gave no indication of how much they wanted (*LRBAC* 31st October 1989 2). Prices fell in October with large quantities of the wet second crop on the market. This was no surprise as the new (main) crop was only a month away and there was an excellent forecast. Iraq held a tender for two cargoes of 100 per cent B for November/December shipment basis one-year payment but could find no sellers who would accept their payment terms. Syria bought another cargo. The export figure for September was low at 371,120 tons taking the total up to the end of September to 4,997,581 tons (*LRBAC* 31st October 1989 3). The Thai new crop was estimated at 21,500,000 tons of paddy (*LRBAC* 31st November 1989 1). In November, many buyers stayed out of the market expecting lower prices. But prices did not fall much because the Government promised to make purchases to support the market. In the last week of November, they bought 100,000 tons of rice, 25 per cent brokens, paying well over the market rate. Also, a substantial sum had been set aside for loans to farmers, which would cover about 1,600,000 tons of rice. Iran bought six cargoes, each of 15,000 tons of 100 per cent B white rice, in November/December shipment, including one year's credit. Malaysia tendered 100,000 tons 100 per cent B for various shipment positions, but eventually only bought 25,000 tons for the December shipment. Syria bought 12,000 tons of 100 per cent B for December/January shipment. So far exports in 1989 totalled 5,314,835 tons (*LRBAC* 30th November 1989 3). The *Circular* commented that as they moved into 1990, the Thai Government was expected to purchase up to

1,500,000 tons of rice to stabilise the market but there was pressure from Vietnam for low quality rice (*LRBAC* 29th December 1989 1). In Thailand Government buying calmed the market and a repeat operation for 100,000 tons of 25 per cent Super for January delivery to the warehouses helped. The market currently wanted 100 per cent grade B, not 5 per cent brokens or other qualities. Malaysia bought another 193.000 tons of 100 per cent grade B, half for shipment in January/April, the remainder in May/August. A tender was to be held in Sri Lanka for 100,000 tons in January, split between white and parboiled rice 25 per cent brokens, for shipment in March/August 1990. The tender was for trade offers, with possibly an additional 100,000 tons of parboiled to be negotiated from government to government. Burkina Faso bought 65,000 tons 35 per cent brokens (with an option for delivery from Pakistan for arrival February/August shipment divided between the ports of Abidjan (Cote D'Ivoire) and Lome (Togo). Peru bought 15,000/25,000 tons spread between 10 per cent standard and 15 per cent maximum for December/ January shipment (*LRBAC* 29th December 1989 3).

Of the importing countries, Indonesia figured heavily but erratically, being subject as it is to the vicissitudes of the *El Nino*/Southern Oscillation (*EN*SO). 1982/83 and 1986/87 were *EN*SO years, as was 1992/92 (Glantz 1996, 34, 59–69). For Indonesia, the story of these years is that from being a major Asian rice importer, it moved to rice self-sufficiency, and then became a rice exporter. This had important consequences for the Asian rice trade. 1980 was a year of heavy imports, some 2,011,000 tons and so was the *EN*SO year of 1983, a year when 1,168,000 tons were imported. The *EN*SO year of 1986/87 did not seem to cause such serious problems.

In 1979 the Philippines had exported about 100,000 tons of rice to Indonesia, and intended to raise this to 150,000 tons in 1980. In February 1980, 33,000 tons of rice were shipped from the Philippines to Indonesia in exchange for crude oil (*LRBAC* 29th February 1980 2). Pakistan had hoped to sell 100,000 tons of rice to Indonesia, but the deal fell through (*LRBAC* 29th February 1980 2). In March, Burma sold 400,000 tons government to government to Indonesia, Bangladesh, Sri Lanka and the People's Republic of China, although how much of this went to Indonesia is not clear (*LRBAC* 31st March 1980 1). The Philippine Government agreed to sell a further 100,000 tons to Indonesia, for shipment in May 1980. This was in addition to the 33,000 tons reported in February (*LRBAC* 31st March 1980 3). Meanwhile, in the United States, the P.L.480 market was subdued by the news that the current agreement with Indonesia was for 93,000 tons, not the 117,000 tons expected. Shipment was to be during the calendar year 1980, not the rice marketing year, and it was noted that Indonesia's current requirements might be satisfied by the recent purchases from Thailand and the Philippines (*LRBAC* 31st March 1980 3–4). In the United States, the P.L.480 market continued depressed, as the main interest had been on the April tender for up to 150,000 tons for Indonesia. But Indonesia only bought 50,000 tons, comprising 45,000 tons long grain No.5 20 per cent, and 5000 tons medium grain (*LRBAC* 30th April 1980 3–4). In the United States, it was expected that Indonesia would tender in July for 60,000 tons under P.L.480 for shipments July/September (*LRBAC* 30th June 1980 3). But Indonesia itself was expected to produce a record 20,000,000 tons of rice in 1980, about 2,000,000 tons more than in 1979. Rice stocks were 2,500,000 tons, and it was expected that imports scheduled for later in the year might be delayed due to lack of storage space (*LRBAC* 30th August 1980 1). So Thailand agreed to defer shipments to Indonesia of about 150,000 tons contracted for 1980/81 shipment, with deliveries not expected before April 1981. Burma and Japan also postponed outstanding shipments. The import target for the fiscal year ending April 1981 had been 2,500,000 tons but it was now hoped to reduce this to 1,000,000 tons (*LRBAC* 30th September 1980 1). Indonesia then asked the Rice Export Corporation of Pakistan to reserve 50,000 – 100,000 tons of 20 per cent/25 per cent rice for shipment during 1981 (*LRBAC* 30th September 1980 2). Burma agreed to waive contracts for 68,000 tons sold to Indonesia for shipment in 1980, provided Indonesia bought 100,000 tons of Burma rice in 1981 (*LRBAC* 31st October 1980 1, *LRBAC* 31st October 1980 2). Reports were coming in of good crops in Indonesia, so imports during 1981 were likely to be less than in 1980 (*LRBAC* 28th November 1980 2).

An Indonesian delegation was expected in Karachi in March/April 1981 to negotiate for Sind 15 per cent/20 per cent (*LRBAC* 28th February 1981 2). In March, Indonesia bought 51,000 tons of long grain No.5 20 per cent from the United States under P.L. 480 and was negotiating for another 20,000 tons (*LRBAC* 31st March 1981 4). This was followed by 100,000 tons from Burma of *Emata* 10 per cent and *Emata* 25 per cent bought government to government (*LRBAC* 30th April 1981 1). In May, Indonesia purchased a further 22,000 tons of U.S. No. 5 20 per cent long grain shipped Gulf ports (*LRBAC* 29th May 1981 3). This seems to have been a relatively quiet year for Indonesia, for there appears to have been no more recorded activity for Indonesia in 1981.

But in February 1982, it was reported from Thailand that there had been a recent sale to Indonesia of 50,000 tons of Thai white rice 100 per cent Grade B (*LRBAC* 27th February 1982 2). (Ed. This was a high grade!). But clearly, difficulties were emerging in what turned out to be an *EN*SO year, for it was reported from Thailand in December that there had been a Government sale of white rice to Indonesia of 150,000 tons of white rice, with another 150,000 tons under review for Indonesia and Malaysia (*LRBAC* 31st December 1982 3).

Then in February 1983, it was reported that Indonesia's rice crop had been affected by drought (Ed. A typical *EN*SO consequence, although *EN*SO is not mentioned). The crop was now expected to be around 20,300,000 tons against 22,300,000 tons in 1982 and there would have to be substantial imports to make up the shortfall. In November 1982, import requirements had been forecast as low as 300,000 tons, but now it seemed as much as 1,000,000–2,000,000 tons might be required (*LRBAC* 28th February 1983 1). Estimates of import requirements continued to rise, and it was now clear that 2,000,000 tons would be required and many thought 2,500,000 tons would be needed (*LRBAC* 31st March 1983 1). In April, the 1982/83 crop estimate was revised to 24,100,000 tons (Ed. Given as 34,100,000 tons but obviously in error, see *LRBAC* 31st October 1984 2 below). This was an increase on earlier reports, but import requirements still looked like being between 2,000,000 and 2,500,000 tons (*LRBAC* 29th April 1983 1). Reports changed again, and it was suggested that imports in 1983 would be unlikely to be more than

2,000,000 tons, and the eventual total might be much less (*LRBAC* 31st May 1983 2). But Pakistan reported that Indonesia had bought substantial quantities of 15 per cent/20 per cent government to government (*LRBAC* 31st June 1983 2). Nothing more was reported from Indonesia for the rest of the year. However actual imports for 1983 are listed as 1,168,000 tons, a substantial amount! (see *Table 5.1* above).

In March 1984, it was reported from Taiwan that Indonesia had been allocated 200,000 tons from the Taiwan 1984 crop (*LRBAC* 30th March 1984 2). The Indonesian crop for 1984/85 was then forecast as 25,050,000 tons compared with the 1983/84 crop of 24,000,000 tons (*LRBAC* 31st October 1984 2). Then in November, it was reported that there was an excellent current crop, resulting in a lack of storage space. So some rice purchased from abroad during the year, and not yet delivered, might be resold (*LRBAC* 30th November 1984 1). In December, it was reported that Indonesia could now be considered a net exporter in the short term. Local crops had improved over the last two years, and rice already purchased to import had been offered for resale. So far 130,000 tons of this had been sold to the Philippines on three year's credit. Other quantities were available for export, including some home-grown rice. The *Circular* commented "This turn-around must be one of the major factors in the weakness of world rice markets today when it is considered that Indonesia was an importer of up to two million tons of rice per year which must be about 15 per cent of the world export" (*LRBAC* 31st December 1984 2).

Indonesia continued to make strenuous efforts to sell quantities of Taiwan rice it had purchased, and also Burmese and Chinese rice. But they were not very successful, despite asking competitive prices (*LRBAC* 31st January 1985 1). In March, it was reported that Indonesia was now an exporter of rice, although it had previously been the world's largest importer, with imports of 2,000,000 tons a year or more. The first quantities Indonesia had on offer were re-sales of previous imports, and one of the leading international companies had purchased 126,000 tons in stock in Indonesia. The price was not clear as financing arrangements had not been disclosed. However, it seemed that 32,000 tons of Burma *Emata* 10 per cent 1983/84 crop, 34,000 tons of Pakistan 15 per cent/20 per cent 1982/83 crop, and 60,000 tons of 25 per cent 1984/85 new crop Java rice had been sold. There remained for sale 74,000 tons of Chinese 25 per cent 1983/84 crop, 30,000 tons of North Korean 10 per cent 1983/84 crop and 30,000 tons of Taiwan *Bon Lei* 15 per cent 1982/83 crop. There was also a further 300,000 tons of Java 25 per cent new crop in 1984/85. As the *Circular* commented, "This obviously alters the balance of trade in the Far East and will probably go a long way to helping the deficiency in the Philippines which was originally reported as 300,000 tons although later comment puts it at a level considerably above this." (*LRBAC* 29th March 1985 2). By April the export of non-Indonesian rice had started, and two or three vessels were now loading Taiwan and Pakistan rice for African destinations. But there were still substantial quantities of previously imported rice for export (*LRBAC* 30th April 1985 2). These exports continued, and it was probable that some home-grown Indonesian rice would also be exported as soon as the remaining stocks of imported rice had been marketed. Prices seemed favourable when compared with similar quantities (Ed. qualities?) available from the Far East (*LRBAC* 31st May 1985 1). In June, the *Circular* commented that according to the FAO, the international market was likely to see large export supplies, weak import demand, low prices and larger end-of-season stocks. Indonesia and India were amongst the principal countries which might import much smaller quantities in 1985, and indeed Indonesia had already been selling off stocks surplus to requirements and was likely to remain self-sufficient. Imported stockpiles were high in Indonesia, as they were in India (*LRBAC* 28th June 1985 1). Indonesian home-grown rice was now available for export, in addition to the previously imported stocks that were being moved out. It was expected Indonesia would have sufficient rice to export later in the year (*LRBAC* 28th June 1985 2). Substantial quantities of old stock rice were now being offered by Indonesia, and buyers were urged to bid below the indicated level to move stocks out to make way for the new crop (*LRBAC* 31st July 1985 1). Indonesia then put 250,000 tons of previously imported rice on the market, together with 70,000 tons of the home crop in 1983/84. Prices were open to negotiation. One international rice merchant had exported 120,000 tons over the preceding three months, and also the 100,000 tons previously purchased by the Philippine Government. Storage space was needed badly for new crop paddy, and it was important to move out these old stocks as soon as possible. One unconfirmed report said there were 2,700,000 tons of Indonesian new crop paddy stored in the open, but as the *Circular* commented, it was always difficult to see how see how such a statistic had been worked out (*LRBAC* 31st July 1985 2). There were substantial sales of this previously imported rice, and also some of the Indonesian home-grown rice. Very good domestic crops were reported, and Indonesia was no longer a major importer, but an exporter. This was the fundamental reason for the weakness in the world rice market (*LRBAC* 30th August 1985 2). In September, uncertainty was now the main factor in the world rice market, one element being the unknown quantity of the remaining stocks in Indonesia (*LRBAC* 30th August 1985 2). Indonesia still had for sale possibly as much as 350,000 tons of previously imported rice (*LRBAC* 30th September 1985 2). Annual consumption of rice in Indonesia was about 20,000,000 tons, and it was Government policy to maintain a stockpile sufficient to cover three months' requirements, about 5,000,000 tons. But present stocks were about 3,000,000 tons. Meanwhile, considerable pressure had been put on the Indonesian government by fellow members of the ASEAN pact not to export rice, as it would damage the trade of other members who had previously relied on sales to Indonesia. Domestic crop prospects were good, and unless there was a drought or other disaster, it seemed Indonesia was at least self-sufficient in rice (*LRBAC* 31st October 1985 2). In November, Indonesian traders who had purchased a considerable tonnage of stocks were busily exporting this and the only rice now still available for sale were some parcels of previously imported rice which was old and slightly damaged. Domestic crop prospects still looked good (*LRBAC* 30th November 1985 2). Some 1985 crops were available, and prices were likely to be competitive with Thailand, although the market had not been tested recently. Prices were slightly higher than possible prices out of Pakistan (*LRBAC* 31st December 1985 2).

There were no further reports of the trade from Indonesia in January 1986, although it should have been possible to purchase some old crop stocks (*LRBAC*

31st January 1986 2). Old crop stocks continued to be available, but there were no reports of business (*LRBAC* 28th February 1986 2). There was little news during the rest of 1986. It was not until November 1987 that there was any news, and that was of Thailand loading rice destined for Indonesia (*LRBAC* 30th November 1987 3). (Ed. That Indonesia was importing again suggests that it was indeed affected by the 1987/87 *EN*SO). In December, the *Circular* noted, "We are already beginning to see speculation on the possibility of imports by Indonesia, the Philippines, Vietnam and other countries of the Far East" (*LRBAC* 31st December 1987 1). This was presumably on the basis of reports of the incoming harvest. Nonetheless, imports for 1987 are only given as 54,000 tons and 32,000 tons in 1988 (see *Table 5.1* above). But little information was available in 1988. However, at the end of the year, it was noted that in the United States a P.L.480 allocation for Indonesia was expected to be announced in December (*LRBAC* 39th December 1988 3). In February 1989, it was reported from Thailand that rice exports of an unspecified amount had been made to Indonesia (*LRBAC* 28th February 1989 2). The next news came in July 1989 when Indonesia asked Washington for permission to export 300,000 tons of rice, which they needed because they had in place a P.L.480 agreement to import rice from the United States under this aid programme (*LRBAC* 31st July 1989 1). There was no further news of Indonesia this year.

In the Philippines, historically another important regular Asian rice importer, rice production for the crop year 1979/80 was estimated at 4,650,000 tons compared to just under 4,400,000 tons in 1978/79. The surplus for export was expected to be between 150,000 and 200,000 tons (*LRBAC* 31st January 1980 3). In February 1980, it was reported that about 33,000 tons of rice were shipped from the Philippines to neighbouring Indonesia in February in exchange for crude oil. In 1979 the Philippines had exported about 100,000 tons of rice to Indonesia and it was said that it was intended to increase this by 50 per cent to 150,000 tons in 1980 (*LRBAC* 29th February 1980 2). In March, it was reported that the Philippine Government had agreed to sell a further 100,000 tons of rice to Indonesia for shipment in May 1980. This was in addition to the 33,000 tons reported in February (*LRBAC* 31st March 1980 3). Nothing more was heard from the Philippines until October 1982 when it was reported that there was a possibility of the Philippines exporting rice, but prices were not competitive with comparable quantities from other origins. But it was interesting to find the Philippines back in the market again despite price levels being at least 10 per cent higher than Thailand (*LRBAC* 29th October 1982 2). There was no further news until December 1984 when it was reported that 130,000 tons of rice Indonesia had previously imported, had been sold to the Philippines on a three-year credit scheme (*LRBAC* 31st December 1984 2) (Ed. This presumably reflects problems in the Philippines resulting from the 1982/83 *EN*SO!). In March 1985, it was reported that although Indonesia had been the world's largest importer of rice, it had now become an exporter. They had quantities of previously imported rice for sale, and also considerable quantities of homegrown Java 25 per cent crop. This would go a long way in helping the deficiency in the Philippines, which was originally reported as 300,000 tons but was later thought to be considerably more (*LRBAC* 29th March 1985 2). In June, it was reported that the import requirements of the Philippines were expected to increase as their 1984 crops had been badly damaged by floods (*LRBAC* 28th June 1985 1). In July, it was reported that an international merchant had exported from Indonesia the 100,000 tons previously purchased by the Philippine Government (*LRBAC* 31st July 1985 2). Yet the Philippines were still in need of rice as that month it was reported from the United States that the Philippines were negotiating for about 130,000 tons of medium grain rice on P.L.480 terms, expected to be sold from California (*LRBAC* 31st July 1985 3–4). Little more was heard from the Philippines until September 1987 when the *Circular* included the Philippines in a list of countries hit by the poor monsoon, the other countries being Vietnam, Laos, Sri Lanka, Thailand, India and Pakistan (*LRBAC* 30th September 1987 1) (Ed. The 1987/87 ENSO!). By December the *Circular* was noting that there was already speculation on the possibility of imports by the Philippines, Indonesia, Vietnam and other countries of the Far East (*LRBAC* 31st December 1987 1). Nothing more was heard of the Philippines until June 1989 when it was reported from Thailand that the Philippines had been making enquiries for rice (*LRBAC* 30th June 1989 3).

References

Andrews, John (1997) *Pocket Asia*, London: The Economist-Profile Books Ltd.

Glantz, Michael H. (1996) *Currents of Change. El Nino's Impact on Climate and Society*, Cambridge: Cambridge University Press.

Kano, Hiroyoshi (Ed) (2007) *Proceedings of the IOC UT Symposium, Sugar, Coffee, Tea and Rice in Economic History of Modern Asia,* Tokyo: Institute of Oriental Culture, University of Tokyo, March 7–8.

Miyata, Toshiyuki (2007) 'Jasmine' Rice and the Thai Rice Export Economy in the 20th Century (Economic History of Jasmine Rice in the World Rice Market: *Khao Dok Mali 105* and *Pathumthani 1*) in Kano (2007) 65–77.

6 The Asian rice trade 1990–1999

The 1990s saw the continued weakness of Burma (Myanmar in 1989) as an exporter, with figures as low as 28,000 tons in 1997 and 54,000 tons in 1999. By comparison, Vietnam had come back into the market and was now a major exporter rising from 1,033,000 tons in 1991 to 4,508,000 tons in 1999. But Thailand remained the anchor of the Asian rice market, with 4,017,000 tons in 1990 increasing to 6,838,000 tons in 1999. These years also saw the devastating effect of the *EN*SO phenomenon in 1997/98 with Indonesia and the Philippines badly affected and importing huge quantities.

Table 6.1 Rice exports (selected countries) 1990–2000 (metric tons 000)

	1990	*1991*	*1992*	*1993*	*1994*	*1995*	*1996*	*1997*	*1998*	*1999*	*2000*
Myanmar	213	173	204	209	933	353	92	28	120	54	251
Vietnam	1624	1033	1945	1764	1983	1988	3003	3574	3730	4508	3477
Thailand	4017	4333	5151	4989	4266	5533	4737	4713	5740	6838	6141
China	405	817	1034	1506	969	234	251	943	3681	2819	3070
India	505	678	580	767	890	4893	2505	2328	4888	1895	1532
Pakistan	743	1204	1511	1032	984	1852	1600	1767	1971	1791	2016
U.S.A	2473	2242	2164	2679	1996	2267	1786	1467	1446	2668	2736

Source: FAO *Trade Yearbooks*.

Table 6.2 Rice imports (selected countries) 1990–2000 (metric tons 000)

	1990	*1991*	*1992*	*1993*	*1994*	*1995*	*1996*	*1997*	*1998*	*1999*	*2000*
India	66	12	102	75	6	–	–	–	–	34	13
Bangladesh	380	15	17	20	66	500	586	1456	966	2215	260
Sri Lanka	131	132	237	181	32	–	206	290	155	206	14
Malaysia	330	399	444	389	340	427	568	630	657	612	595
Singapore	220	211	234	242	232	238	262	243	230	404	355
Indonesia	49	170	609	24	271	1309	2040	–	2793	4748	1355
Philippines	592	–	–	201	1	263	866	722	2414	834	642
Vietnam	1	6	1	–	–	–	–	–	–	5	–
China	62	145	106	99	495	1613	704	307	236	172	244
Hong Kong	374	391	400	372	344	346	359	339	315	327	309
Japan	18	17	17	107	786	–	–	–	–	664	655

Source: FAO *Trade Yearbooks*.

DOI: 10.4324/9781003492917-7

In January 1990, there was talk of Burma making exports (*London Rice Brokers' Association Circular* (*LRBAC)* 31st January 1990 1). There were a tender in February for 20,000 tons of *Emata* 25 per cent brokens but it was not clear if this was concluded (*LRBAC* 28th February 1990 1). Rice was available for export but not at competitive prices (*LRBAC* 31st March 1990 1). Efforts were made to find buyers for *Zeera* and *Emata*, but prices were not competitive (*LRBAC* 30th April 1990 1). Prices fell for high-quality rice in Thailand making Burma *Zeera* and *Emata* 100 per cent even less competitive (*LRBAC* 30th June 1990 1). In October, business was done for one cargo of 5 per cent brokens of *Emata* and *Zeera* mixed, and it was thought more was available (*LRBAC* 31st October 1990 1). Rice was still available in November, but little business had been done (*LRBAC* 30th November 1990 1).

In January 1991, it was reported that 100,000 tons of *Emata* 25 per cent and *Emata* Super 5 per cent had been traded by barter, although there was no confirmation of the higher grade. There were unconfirmed reports of an additional 50,000 tons bartered for urea (Ed. a fertiliser) (*LRBAC* 9th January 1991 1). More *Emata* 25 per cent was possibly available and other qualities by barter, but there were few offers (*LRBAC* 5th February 1991 1). The lack of oil and oil products meant transport in Burma was difficult. This prevented stocks from arriving at the port of Yangon (Rangoon) and some shipments had been delayed from February into March. Those holding rice bartered against fertiliser were controlling prices and demanding more than buyers would pay. The export target for Burma from the current crop could be 500,000 tons (*LRBAC* 1st March 1991 1). By April, loading of vessels was now going smoothly, but it was difficult to get offers except from re-sellers. Exports to the end of February were 32,540 tons, against 2,900 tons in 1990 (*LRBAC* 1st April 1991 1). 25 per cent brokens were available and some *Emata* Super 5 per cent, prices varying for barter or straight sales (*LRBAC* 30th April 1991 1). *Emata* Super 5 per cent and *Emata* 25 per cent were quoted for barter, with a price reduction if converted into straight offers (*LRBAC* 7th June 1991 1). The planting of the new crop was only just coming to an end in June and was expected to be greater than the 1990 crop (*LRBAC* 28th June 1991 1). *Emata* 25 per cent was still on offer for September and October shipment, and also some broken rice (*LRBAC* 31st July 1991 1). In September, there were quotes for *Emata* 25 per cent and also 35 per cent, the lower offers linked to barter. No business was reported. Floods in the southern Irrawaddy region damaged some crops, and the overall Burma crop was reduced (*LRBAC* 30th September 1991 1). (Ed. From this date, the *Circular* refers to Burma as Myanmar. It became Myanmar in June 1989, see Andrews 2002 122). Although there was no more news of floods, the final crop was expected to be down in 1990. Paddy production was likely to be 13,800,000–14,000,000 tons, about average for the period 1989/1990 (*LRBAC* 31st October 1991 2). In December, Super 25 per cent was traded, including barter discount for shipment December/January, but the quantity was limited (*LRBAC* 31st December 1991 2).

In 1992, *Emata* Super 25 per cent was offered for shipment in February/March but offers were not widespread (*LRBAC* 31st January 1992). Because estimates for the main crop had been lowered it was difficult to predict the exportable surplus for the season (*LRBAC* 28th February 1992 2). *Emata* Super 25 per cent was on offer but how much was not clear (*LRBAC* 31st March 1992 2). *Emata* 25 per cent was still quoted but not at competitive prices (*LRBAC* 31st May 1992 2). Although *Emata* 25 per cent long grain was still talked about in August for 1 or 2 cargoes below the quoted price, there was no business (*LRBAC* 31st August 1992 2). Prices for this quality were reduced (*LRBAC* 30th September 1992 2). In the World Food Programme tender on 7th October, 17,500 tons of *Emata* 25 per cent was sold to West Africa at a price well above previously quoted levels (*LRBAC* 31st October 1992 2).

In March 1993, the *Circular* commented that few people could remember when so many countries were offering rice and so few buying. Even countries like Burma, China and Indonesia which sometimes did not offer rice were back on the market, but attracting little interest (*LRBAC* 31st March 1993 1). Burma's new season offers had begun with *Emata* 25 per cent said to be of better quality this year, with prices reduced for barter (*LRBAC* 31st March 1993 1). (Ed. Note the *Circular* had reverted to using the term Burma!). Shipments of contracted *Emata* 25 per cent were taking place. Due to favourable tidal conditions, there were no problems with the size of vessels or the loading rate, which averaged 2,000 tons a day for recent vessels (*LRBAC* 30th April 1993 1). Shipments of previous contracts continued, mainly *Emata* Super 25 per cent (*LRBAC* 28th May 1993 2). *Emata* Super 25 per cent continued to be available, and fairly regular shipments of this quality were taking place (*LRBAC* 30th June 1993 1). Re-sellers were offering *Emata* 25 per cent for West Africa, with an additional discount for a full cargo. Prices were falling (*LRBAC* 30th July 1993 1). The situation remained the same in August (*LRBAC* 31st August 1993 1).

There was no further news from Burma until July 1994 when it was reported that Burma was expected to have a good crop. But the Myanmar Export Import Company (MEIC) were not offering rice although there was some available for barter. There were big delays due to heavy rains, and loading was very slow and difficult. The Government had announced that no vessel nominations would be accepted for a month (*LRBAC* 31st July 1994 1). Because Burma was one of the cheapest origins of low-quality rice, there were many shipments of *Emata* 25 per cent to Africa, Madagascar and Indonesia, although there were fears about the quality of recent shipments. Earlier in the year, however, quality had been acceptable. Due partly to delays in inland transportation and loading caused by the rains, there were restrictions to vessel nominations during August. This upset the shipping intentions of some operators. A significant amount of Burmese rice had been traded, but there were rumours that some 25,000–30,000 tons of contracts had been cancelled for various reasons. Some *Emata* 25 per cent which had been bartered was sold by a Singapore intermediary to Indonesia. The cancelled rice had also probably been resold government to government to Indonesia (*LRBAC* 31st August 1994 1–2). Changes seemed to be taking place in Burma, and it appeared that the Myanmar Export Import Services (MEIS) (Sic. Company? See MEIC 31st July 1994 1 above) no longer had overall control over exports. More rice was becoming available for barter, and Burma had a much better year than usual for exports, and this was continuing. *Emata* 25 per cent was being offered, and as in Pakistan loading problems were easing with the passing of the rains (*LRBAC* 30th September 1994 2). The changes in Burma seemed to have accelerated, and large quantities of rice for November and December shipments were sold by ex-patriot Burmese, particularly to buyers in Indonesia. This included 20,000 tons of *Emata* 25 per cent for November/December shipment. Extensive sales for January/February/March 1995 were rumoured. The quantity for the New Year was not clear, but it seemed not less than 100,000 tons had already been committed (*LRBAC* lst November 1994 2). (Ed.) Exports in 1994 at 933,000 tons were the best year of the decade (see Table 6.2 above).

At a tender in December substantial quantities of *Emata*, 25 per cent brokens from the 1994/95 crop was sold for shipment in February/April. Burma clearly intended to export 1,000,000 tons this year, mainly new crops but including some old crops (*LRBAC* 1st December 1994 2). In February 1995 there were reports of extensive government-to-government trade with China, possibly 150,000 tons, although the signed protocol might have been for 300,000 tons. But there were shipment problems. Consequently offers of Burmese *Emata* 25 per cent were confined to resale hands, but buyers were not interested (*LRBAC* 1st February 1995 2). In March it was reported that Burma had nothing left to sell, having committed itself to exporting a possible 1,000,000 tons, which if shipped would be a new record for them (Ed. In recent times, but not in comparison to pre-war figures which ran at over 3,000,000 tons! see *Table 1.1*) (*LRBAC* 31st March 1995 1). In May it was noted that there had been very poor loading performance, and a string of vessels were waiting to load rice in Yangon (Rangoon) (*LRBAC* 1st May 1995 1). Burma was shipping what was left of old contracts to Indonesia, and so were Vietnam and India, with smaller quantities from Pakistan and Thailand (*LRBAC* lst May 1995 2). Burma had sold in excess of 1,000,000 tons from their current crop, but the question was how much rice could the country actually mobilise to clear the backlog? Loadings were difficult and a number of vessels were waiting in port. State sellers were not taking vessel nominations in May. Some business was reported by resale of *Emata* 25 per cent (*LRBAC* lst May 1995 2). By the end of May, it was reported that the line of vessels was not getting any less, and only a trickle of rice was arriving at the port. Several vessels had left because of no rice availability (*LRBAC* 31st May 1995 1). The main problem was the slowness with which rice was being delivered to Yangon (Rangoon), and the consequent delay in loading. But there had been a recent improvement and vessels were now achieving 800–900 tons a day, with 2 ships being loaded simultaneously (*LRBAC* 31st May 1995 2). However, the lack of loading ability in Burma continued (*LRBAC* 30th June 1995 1). Few shipments were made in June, and an impressive number of vessels were waiting for berths. Rain was complicating matters, and there was a long way to go to catch up on back shipments. Renegotiated contracts were being reconfirmed and stowed Yangon for *Emata* 35 per cent, but there were no first-hand offers (*LRBAC* 30th June 1995 2). The *Circular* commented that lack of supply from Burma, Thailand, Vietnam and Pakistan continued, and sustained demand from Indonesia in particular was only counterbalanced by the large volumes of rice available from the Food Corporation stock in India (*LRBAC* 1st August 1995 1). In Burma loading remained slow and they had nothing to sell (*LRBAC* 1st August 1995 3). Loading continued slow

(*LRBAC* 1st September 1995 2). Lack of shipment continued in October (*LRBAC* 2nd October 1995 1). There was still a considerable tonnage of unshipped rice contracts, but the authorities were waiting for the new crop to make up the shortfall. 70,000 – 80,000 tons were thought to be three months late. September shipments were few with only 2 vessels loaded (*LRBAC* 2nd October 1995 3). India stepped into the breach in the world market particularly (but not exclusively) for lower quality rice requirements, caused by reduced exports from Myanmar (Burma), Thailand and Vietnam (*LRBAC* 1st November 1995 1). No crop forecast was available from Myanmar, but there was a 10 per cent increase in planting. Some 750,000 tons committed from the previous crop remained unshipped, and it was expected these contracts would be executed first on the resumption of shipments in November/December. Myanmar was expected to be a major supplier again in 1996 (*LRBAC* 1st November 1995 3).

In January 1996 the *Circular* commented that 1995 had been an extraordinary year. World trade had risen by about 2,500,000 tons to nearly 19,000,000 tons. China and Indonesia had imported close to 3,000,000 tons each due to domestic crop shortfalls, but Burma, Thailand Vietnam and Pakistan the normal exporting countries had also experienced shortages. The situation was only saved by India which early in the year exported from its large surplus of Government stock, and later in the year made private sales of all qualities from its good domestic crop. But they had huge logistic difficulties moving and loading this rice, made worse by the Government's increasing contract prices. Burma and Vietnam could not fulfil their commitments in the second half of the year having already sold huge volumes of rice. In the case of Vietnam, it went straight over the border into China. Pakistan also ran out of rice due to a poor crop and big sales to Bangladesh. Thailand continued to export but faced problems later in the year due to flooding. Demand from Africa however had fallen because prices were so high. But the outlook for the New Year was a little different. China had a better crop, and they had recently sold one or two cargoes. Indonesia had increased production and was not expected to import so much rice. The Philippines would need to import, but only about 500,000 tons and Bangladesh would probably take 1,000,000 tons again (*LRBAC* 2nd January 1996 1). In Burma, the new crop was reported to be good, and higher than the previous year (*LRBAC* 2nd January 1996 3). Burma was honouring old shipments and also selling small amounts (*LRBAC* 26th February 1996 1). The Chinese Government maintained it would not need to import rice this year, but neither would it be an exporter. However, it was thought China would make direct imports over the Burma and Vietnamese borders, with high-quality rice coming to the coastal states from Thailand and Vietnam (*LRBAC* 26th February 1996 1). Vessels were loading in Burma in February, and limited amounts of *Emata* 25 per cent were available (*LRBAC* 26th February 1996 3). Availability in Burma had now tightened up (*LRBAC* 1st April 1996 2). Shipments continued in June with 25 per cent on offer (*LRBAC* 3rd June 1996 3). In August it was reported that there were some problems with disease, but the *Circular* thought it only applied to 20,000 tons of old crop paddy stored in one area and was unlikely to affect the new crop (*LRBAC* 5th August 1996 3). There was no further news from Burma until November, when it was reported that 25 per cent was available but not a competitive price (*LRBAC* 4th November 1996 1). In December came reports that the Burma crop was very poor, supply would be late, and they were not ready to sell (*LRBAC* 3rd December 1996 1).

In March 1997 there was a tender for 20,000 tons of 25 per cent, but it was cancelled (*LRBAC* 3rd March 1997 1). *Emata* 25 per cent was for sale, but over-priced (*LRBAC* 2nd April 1997 2). By May hardly any rice had been exported from Burma, and their prices were uncompetitive, particularly when taking into account the difficulties of this origin (Ed. unspecified!) *LRBAC* 2nd May 1997 1). In July at a tender for 100 per cent *Emata* all bids were turned down as too low, although close to the Thai 100 per cent level. This was unrealistic as Vietnamese 5 per cent was very cheap (*LRBAC* 2nd July 1997 1). There was no further news (*LRBAC* 4th August 1997 1). Then at the beginning of September, the *Circular* wrote:-

> "*El Nino*. From the most recent information available to us *El Nino* represents a very real danger in many areas of the world. Predictions suggest that the effect will be even greater than in 1982/83 with the same weather abnormalities but more severe. Potential droughts will effect (sic) Central and Southern Africa, Australia, Indonesia, Thailand, India and Pakistan, and in contrast abnormally cold and wet weather with possible flooding in Peru, Argentina, Uruguay and Southern Brazil.
>
> (*LRBAC* 1st September 1997 1)

Now Burma announced it would hold a tender for 15,000 tons of *Emata* 25 per cent brokens. This was held by the MEPT (a Department of the Ministry of Agriculture), not the MEIS (Myanmar Export Import Services) which normally held rice tenders. Bids were received but the outcome is unknown. The *Circular* thought this was strange as recent flooding had damaged the new crop and there were grave concerns that there would not be enough for local consumption. It commented cryptically that there were other reasons for selling rice, but did not explain what these might be! (*LRBAC* 3rd October 1997 1). In the end, this tender was not awarded (*LRBAC* 6th November 1997 1).

Burma was then absent from the *Circular* until October 1998 when it was reported under Indonesia that there had been a tender at which Myanmar was awarded 10,000 tons for September, and 10,000 tons for November. Further negotiations took place leading to another 50,000 tons from Myanmar for September/October, and 20,000 tons for December (*LRBAC* 2nd October 1998 2–3). There was no more news from Burma in 1998, and none at all in 1999, a year of very low recorded exports of 54,000 tons, one of the worst years of the decade and second only to the 28,000 tons of 1997. 1996 had also been a poor year at 92,000 tons and even 1998 had only 120,000 tons (See *Table 6.1* above). It was as if Burma was almost ceasing to be an exporter! To emphasise this, note that the *Circular* commented in August 1999 that Indonesia was to hold a tender for imports of 75,000 tons of 25 per cent brokens "all origins acceptable except for Myanmar" (*LRBAC* 3rd August 1999 1).

Vietnam had only recently returned to the world market as an exporter in 1989 with 1,420,000 tons. But by January 1990 they were running in terms of price for low-quality rice, although they also sold some high-quality rice to Iran (*LRBAC* 31st January 1990 1). They were making aggressive offers to West Africa, leaving only Angola and the Cameroons open to Thailand (*LRBAC* 31st January 1990 3). Business included 35 per cent brokens to West Africa, and Senegal bought 60,000 tons of broken rice delivery to Dakar. They also sold 50,000 tons of 35 per cent to Sri Lanka for March/July including 180 days credit (*LRBAC* 31st January 1990 3). The *Circular* commented that the quantities available in Vietnam seemed very large, and 2,000,000 tons for export looked possible, even probable. The range of qualities from this origin was widening all the time, but prices were weak (*LRBAC* 28th February 1990 1). Even Thailand was losing trade to Vietnam (*LRBAC* 28th February 1990 3). The shift from Thailand to Vietnam as a source of middle quality rice continued because of Thailand's high prices. In February Vietnam sold 200,000 tons of 10 per cent brokens to Iran and 500,000 tons to Russia. 300,000 tons of this was by barter, and the rest for cash, with the best offers being for barter (*LRBAC* 28th February 1990 3). There were rumours of negotiations between Vietnam and China for 200,000 – 300,000 tons (*LRBAC* 28th February 1990 1). This deal was clarified as 200,000 tons, but whether a fixed price or outline contract was not clear (*LRBAC* 31st March 1990 1). Russia negotiated a purchase of 100,000 tons 25 per cent brokens from Vietnam to be shipped to India in exchange for 140,000 tons of Indian high-grade white rice to be shipped to Russia (*LRBAC* 31st March 1990 2). Rice shipped and committed to be shipped in 1990 now amounted to about 1,500,000 tons out of Vietnam's target of 2,000,000 tons for the year. But this included some questionable contracts, particularly 200,000 tons of 10 per cent to Iran, 200,000 tons to China and 300,000 tons to Russia. Vietnam continued to dominate the West African lower quality market (*LRBAC* 31st March 1990 3). Iran purchased some 10 per cent from Vietnam, whereas previously they only took the highest grades such as Thai 100 per cent whole grain or 5 per cent brokens (*LRBAC* 30th April 1990 1). Contracts with China continued to be executed, and also shipments to Cuba were arranged through China (*LRBAC* 30th April 1990 1). Virtually, all low-grade sales from Thailand to Africa had been displaced by aggressive Vietnamese marketing (*LRBAC* 30th April 1990 3). Vietnam was now offering 5 per cent, 10 per cent, 15 per cent, 25 per cent and 35 per cent in 50 kilo jute sacks. Exports since lst January were around 500,000–600,000 tons with commitments for future shipments of 500,000 tons to the U.S.S.R., 200,000 tons to China, 132,000 tons 10 per cent to Iran, 140,000 tons of 35 per cent to the Philippines via Indonesia, and deals to traders of lower quality for West Africa (*LRBAC* 30th April 1990 3). However, Vietnam's pre-eminence in the lower quality market faded due to competition from Pakistan and Thailand (*LRBAC* 30th June 1990 1). Export commitments were now about 2,250,000 tons including government-to-government sales of 500,000 tons of 35 per cent to the Philippines, and 100,000 tons of 5 per cent and 10 per cent to Iran, which were receiving priority. However, there were problems in North Vietnam requiring 600,000–800,000 tons due to low production there (*LRBAC* 30th June 1990 3). In July, it was reported that there would be no more shipments that year except to complete the Government contracts with Iran and the Philippines (*LRBAC* 31st July 1990 1). Yet in October, licences were granted for 143,000 tons and taken up by traders for November/December, mostly 5 per cent and 10 per cent brokens. Crop prospects were about the average for the last few years, some 18,000,000 tons of paddy (*LRBAC* 31st October 1990 3). But loadings were slow and more and more vessels were accumulating in port, making Vietnam a very uncertain origin (*LRBAC* 30th November 1990 3).

There was no news from Vietnam until January 1991 when it was reported that shipping conditions had eased, and the backlog of vessels had gone. However, prospects of new business were remote until the Government decided what quotas to give (*LRBAC* 9th January 1991 3). Vietnam remained out of the market (*LRBAC* 5th February 1991 1). The situation was very confused (*LRBAC* 5th February 1991 3). Vessels had been arriving in port for loading and staying for several weeks without loading (*LRBAC* lst March 1991 3). Difficulties continued (*LRBAC* 1st April 1991 1). 5 per cent, 10 per cent, 15 per cent, 20 per cent, 25 per cent and 35 per cent were available but difficult to buy and vessels were waiting weeks to load (*LRBAC* 1st April 1991 3). Some shipments were made in April against outstanding barter business for last year's urea (fertiliser) imports. For the first time in some months, valid offers were made basis of free trade. It was said, but not confirmed, that Vietnam wished to allocate about 1,000,000 tons of 10 per cent for export this season (*LRBAC* 30th April 1991 3). Shipment of private business continued with 50,000 tons of 10 per cent contracted for June/August shipment shipped to Hochiminh (Saigon). There were offers of 10 per cent, 25 per cent and 35 per cent for June/July (*LRBAC* 7th June 1991 3). Political changes were taking place in Vietnam with rumours of 40/50 per cent changes in the higher levels of the ruling Congress Party. Shipments continued with talk of the purchase of 100,000 tons of 10 per cent broken. The usual range of brokens remained available in 50-kilo bags (*LRBAC* 28th June 1991 3). The political situation remained confusing, but rice shipments continued with 15 per cent and 25 per cent on offer in 50-kilo bags (*LR-BAC* 31st July 1991 3). Loadings in September were lower, with one or two vessels held up by the absence of cargo. There were fears that recent floods had caused the greatest devastation to food supplies in the history of Vietnam, with 70,000 hectares of paddy fields and 40,000 hectares of other cultivated areas under water. Floods are not necessarily destructive to paddy crops, but 60,000 hectares awaiting harvest would be lost, some 300,000 – 350,000 tons of paddy. Cambodia was suffering from the flooding of the Mekong River and the city of Phnom Penh and was seeking rice from Vietnam. An additional 20,000 tons had been sold to Cambodia from the Southern Provinces of Vietnam (*LRBAC* 30th September 1991 3). In October Vietnam was quiet with old contracts being shipped, including vessels with 5 per cent and 10 per cent for Brazil and Peru, and 25 per cent and 35 per cent for West Africa. There were unconfirmed reports of 100,000 – 200,000 tons being sold to Indonesia, of which 100,000 tons were old debts and 100,000 tons were new government-to-government business. 15 per cent, 25 per cent and 35 per cent was available (*LRBAC* 31st October 1991 3). Later reports suggested that Indonesia had actually bought 150,000 tons (*LRBAC* 30th November 1991 1). Sales of 35 per cent had been made to North Korea, and the 150,000 tons to Indonesia were thought to be correct (*LRBAC* 30th November 1991 3). Prices fell in December with the new crop, and there were sales of 10 per cent to Peru, and shipments of old contracts to Brazil (*LRBAC* 31st December 1991 3).

In January shipments slowed as shipments to Brazil and Peru were completed. However, the market was thrown into confusion because of an apparent agreement between Vietnam and Thailand about marketing rice, causing an increase in export prices fixed by Vietnam. Markets in West Africa and South America were quiet, and there was not much business at the new levels. There were unconfirmed reports of 30,000 tons of 5 per cent to Iran, and 30,000–40,000 tons to Malaysia (*LRBAC* 31st January 1992 3). Otherwise, markets were quiet (*LRBAC* 28th February 1992 1). It seemed definite that 100,000 tons of 10 per cent had been sold to Iran, and 50,000 tons of 5 per cent to Malaysia, keeping the mills busy for these higher qualities. 8,000 tons of 20 per cent brokens were sold in a recent Zimbabwe tender. There was the usual unofficial cross-border trading with China of low-quality local rice (*LRBAC* 28th February 1992 3). In March Vietnam was the only Asian country to show decreasing prices, and they were the most aggressive sellers of low-quality rice (*LRBAC* 31st March 1992 1). In the World Food tender in March for 35,761 tons of 35 per cent, Vietnamese rice was sold at an extremely low level (*LRBAC* 31st March 1992 3). In April, there were exports to Peru and Mexico with additional vessels loading to both destinations and reports of an increased tonnage of 5 per cent and 10 per cent to Iran (*LRBAC* 30th April 1992 3). Vietnam continued to be the most aggressive seller of low-quality rice, with several vessels on their way to West Africa with unsold rice. 15,000 tons of 35 per cent was sold to Mozambique in an EEC Food Aid tender. Also, 4000 tons of 15 per cent, which would probably be Vietnamese, was sold to Cape Verde with 90 days payment (*LRBAC* 31st May 1992 3). The market was steady but there were rumours of 200,000 tons of 35 per cent being sold to India government to government to boost their stocks (*LRBAC* 31st July 1992 1). The market continued steady (*LRBAC* 31st July 1992 3). Prices fell in August (*LRBAC* 31st August 1992 1). There were reports that Vietnam had sold 100,000 tons of 5 per cent white rice to Malaysia in the face of Thai competition for 100 per cent Grade B (*LRBAC* 31st August 1992 3). In September 5 per cent, 10 per cent, 15 per cent, 25 per cent, 35 per cent and "broken rice" was being quoted, all in 50-kilo polypropylene or jute bags (*LRBAC* 30th September 1992 3). Because of attractive price levels Vietnam had been securing sales to Aqaba (Jordan) previously supplied from Pakistan, in particular 90,000 tons 10 per cent free out Aqaba. Elsewhere 35 per cent had been traded against urea imports. In other business quotations for all qualities were for 50 kilo polypropylene or jute bags (*LRBAC* 31st October 1992 3). Sales from Vietnam to Aqaba now totalled 150,000 tons, mostly scheduled before the end of December. Despite the large number of vessels in port, loading was progressing efficiently. Export levels were being dictated by barters for urea and other fertilisers at low prices, including a sale to Peru for a mixed cargo of 10 per cent, 15 per cent and 25 per cent at a composite price and very extended payment schedule (*LRBAC* 30th November 1992 1. *LRBAC* 30th November 1992 3). Total sales to Aqaba were now about 200,000 – 250,000 tons and shipments would be brisk through to the end of January. Some of the larger vessels were loading over 2000 tons a day. However, there were quality problems for rice bought for Peru and Brazil, with rejection at loading for sub-standard rice, and consequent slow loading. Quotations were for the usual grades in 50-kilo polypropylene bags. There were premiums for South American destinations for improved quality (*LRBAC* 31st December 1992 3).

Chinese New Year holidays in Vietnam in 1993 coincided with a hardening of the market. There was unconfirmed business in 10 per cent and 15 per cent in Peru. Vietnam was looking for exports in 1993 of around 1,900,000 tons to match 1992. All the usual qualities were quoted in 50 kilo new polypropylene bags (*LRBAC* 29th January 1993 3). Vietnam and Pakistan continued to make the running for the middle grades of rice (*LRBAC* 28th February 1993 1). The December/January crop was good, if slightly below last year in volume, and there was more high-quality rice available which seemed to be a continuing trend. Exports in 1993 were expected between 1,500,000 – 2,000,000 tons, similar to last year's record of 1,900,000 tons (*LRBAC* 28th February 1993). Activity in the rice market picked up but at low prices which hit the profitability of farmers and millers. Prices in South East Asia were at a 13 or 14-year low (*LRBAC* 30th April 1993 1). Barter trade was currently banned (*LRBAC* 30th April 1993 3). There was an increase in the price of 35 per cent brokens, but reduced availability for export due to rice being moved from the South to the North and the appreciation of the Dong against the U.S.$Dollar (*LRBAC* 28th May 1993 4). Since the end of April there has been a big drop in exports (*LRBAC* 30th June 1993 4). A cargo of mixed qualities including 15 per cent and 20 per cent was sold to Peru, and 100,000 tons of 5 per cent to Iran (*LRBAC* 30th July 1993 4). The sale to Iran was confirmed, and there were shipments to Malaysia of 5 per cent. 100,000 – 140,000 tons of white rice was said to have been sold to Yemen. Quality rice was not available in large quantities, and stringent attitudes were being imposed on export licences. There were forward sales to Iran, and demand from Yemen and Malaysia was expected (*LRBAC* 31st August 1993 3–4). There were exports to Mexico and Peru by private trade, and Government deals to Cuba, Indonesia and Iran. But buyer's inspectors had been rejecting considerable quantities of 5 per cent and 10 per cent tendered for shipment, causing loading delays (*LRBAC* 1st October 1993 4). By October, 125,000 tons of shipping was waiting in Hochiminh to load, and an additional 275,000 tons of private trade was committed for November/December shipment. This was leading to offers being withdrawn and difficulty in executing old contracts (*LRBAC* 31st October 1993 4). In October/November, Vietnamese prices moved up as a consequence of Japanese buying in Thailand, leading to many pre-contracted sales being defaulted or significantly adjusted in price (*LRBAC* 30th November 1993 4). Following these widespread defaults, the situation quietened down. Exports for 1993 were likely to be about 2,000,000 tons. A new crop was expected in the second half of January with availability of 22,000,000 tons (Ed. of paddy?). Vietnam remained a cheap seller of quality rice such as 5 per cent and 10 per cent, especially for Peru and Brazil, to which shipments continued apace (*LRBAC* 31st December 1993 4).

In February 1994 significant loadings were made to Columbia, Haiti, Peru and Brazil, although the new crop was over a month late. Most of this business was 5 per cent and 10 per cent. Iran bought 100,000 tons of 5 per cent and an American company bought 75,000 tons of 5 per cent, probably intended for Haiti. 5 or 6 cargoes of Vietnamese 5 per cent were committed or on the water for Peru/Columbia/Haiti/Brazil and it was thought that Columbia and Peru would continue to take respectable quantities (*LRBAC* 28th February 1994 1. *LRBAC* 28th February 1994 4). The world market was now more or less at a standstill (*LRBAC* 31st March 1994 1).

Shipments to Central and South America had slowed down, and although Government sales to Iran continued to be shipped, few other vessels were arriving. However, March 1994 was the first time American companies had bought directly in Vietnam, and one American company signed a long-term agreement for joint collaborations from paddy purchase through to milling and shipment (*LRBAC* 31st March 1994 4). In a surprising development, it was reported that China had bought 350,000 tons 35 per cent from Vietnam. This was possibly 100,000 tons for direct shipment and the remaining 250,000 tons an estimate of cross-border movement from North Vietnam over the next quarter (*LRBAC* 30th April 1994 1). Very high quality 5 per cent was trading depending on shipment, but there was a shortage of low-quality rice due to the China sale (*LRBAC* 30th April 1994 3). Because of the active export programme, there were at one stage some 18–20 vessels loading or waiting to load for various destinations (*LRBAC* 31st May 1994 1). Most ships were loading 5 per cent brokens for Central America, but 60,000 tons of 20 per cent brokens were being loaded for Cuba, 1 vessel for Tanzania, and at least 2 vessels loading high-quality rice for China (*LRBAC* 31st May 1994 4). China was taking high-quality rice from Vietnam where small vessels ranging from 6,000 – 8,000 tons had been loading 10 per cent brokens (*LRBAC* 30th June 1994 1). Congestion at Hochiminh eased with debt settlement rice (?) being available at discounted prices. Shipments of 10 per cent brokens had been taking place to China, 20 per cent brokens to Cuba, and 5 per cent, 10 per cent and 15 per cent to Central/South America. A mixed cargo of 12,000–13,000 tons of 15 per cent and 35 per cent were sold to Tanzania (*LRBAC* 30th June 1994 3). Prices rose in Vietnam and Thailand owing to Indonesia coming into the market seeking 700,000–1,000,000 tons for shipment to February 1995. China too was having a poor crop due to large-scale flooding in the south, and the wealthier coastal states were purchasing high-quality rice privately from Vietnam and Thailand, possibly 200,000–300,000 tons already. A purchase from Vietnam of 48,000 tons of 5 per cent and 10 per cent was confirmed and shipment was near completion (*LRBAC* 31st July 1994 1. Also, *LRBAC* 31st July 1). There was a government-to-government sale of 250,000–300,000 tons to Indonesia for shipment by the end of February 1995. However, vessels were arriving in port to find their cargoes not ready, and considerable delays in loading (*LRBAC* 31st July 1994 3). Following the significant government-to-government sales to Indonesia, shipment activity to China, and continuing shipments to Central and South America, shipping congestion and subsequent delays were widespread at Hochiminh City. The official position was that there was a shortage of 15 per cent, 35 per cent and "brokens", and a circular from the Ministry of Agriculture and Food stated that only contracts registered by 18th August would be allowed to be exported. This was not a prohibition on export but was used by some to default or renegotiate prices. Heavy rains were slowing loading rates (*LRBAC* 31st August

1994 4). Fuelled by the demands from Indonesia and China, all export origins other than the United States saw considerable firming of prices, and negotiations were taking place for private business for 5 per cent and 10 per cent from Vietnam for prompt shipment. However, there was extreme flooding in the North of Vietnam, causing the movement of rice from the South which was bound to affect new crop prices (*LRBAC* 30th September 1994 1). In Vietnam, some sellers were unwilling to deliver against old contracts, and there were some retrospective controls on export licences. There was even talk of a full export ban for the last quarter of the year. It seemed unlikely that there would be any new licences issued for 25 per cent or 35 per cent broken rice (*LRBAC* 30th September 1994 4). There was further deterioration in the availability of export licences (*LRBAC* 1st November 1994 1). Below normal temperatures and heavy rains beyond the usual dates led to a loss of around 300,000 tons, but the main crop due early in 1995 was likely to be about 23,500,000 tons (Ed. of paddy?), which was not significantly different from 1994. However, the movement of rice to the North to cover flood damage was causing supply problems (*LRBAC* 1st November 1994 1–2). Business was halted probably until the end of the year, or even the arrival of the new crop in February/March 1994 (*LRBAC* 1st November 1994 4). There was an interruption in supply to Indonesia over the past few months (*LRBAC* 1st December 1994 2). In December, the only shipments were to Cuba (*LRBAC* 1st December 1994 4).

Originally, there were hopes that exports would resume after the Tet holidays, but that optimism was misplaced. During December and January, some old licences were re-activated, approaching 200,000 tons. However, the government was considering paying a subsidy to local haulage companies to move rice from the South to the North where it was needed, which would take away part of the new crop surplus (*LRBAC* lst February 1995 4). The government announced they would allow exports of 1,200,000 – 1,400,000 tons of main crop rice and 800,000 tons second crop rice, but export licences were few (*LRBAC* 28th February 1995 1). There were reports that 700,000–1,000,000 tons had already been sold, but some of this might have been old commitments. Business for March was thought to be 250,000 tons, and for April 250,000 tons, all for 5 per cent, 10 per cent and 15 per cent. However, the government had only sanctioned 130,000 tons for March (*LRBAC* 28th February 1995 3). Vietnam continued to be a seller of 35 per cent but loading remained slow with only 22,000 tons loaded between the 11th and 27th March. There were 14 vessels in port including 5 for Indonesia, 1 for Mombassa, 1 for Dar es Salaam, and 1 for Cuba. 7 vessels were to complete loading in the last week of March. There were reports of a new government-to-government sale of 200,000 tons of 15 per cent brokens to China (*LRBAC* 31st March 1995 4). In May it was reported that despite a world shortage of vessels, Hochiminh had hosted more than 24 vessels in recent weeks (*LRBAC* 1st May 1995 1). There was still brisk demand in China and prompt cargoes from Vietnam of 5 per cent and 10 per cent were snapped up if prices were about the market level (*LRBAC* 1st May 1995 2). What remained of old contracts were being shipped from Vietnam to Indonesia (*LRBAC* 1st May 1995 2). However, the market was thrown into confusion by a Government statement that no more export licences would be granted for the time being. There were a number of vessels in port suffering from various problems leading to slow loading (*LRBAC* 1st May 1995 4). Despite the stop-go export licence situation and unofficial movements over the border, shipments were to take place but at a reduced level. Government sales and debt repayment contracts were being given preference (*LRBAC* 31st May 1995 1). China was frustrated by irregular Vietnamese deliveries (*LRBAC* 31st May 1995 1). The Vietnamese authorities were scaling down their export intentions, and apparently limiting exports in July and August to 100,000 tons per month. But even this figure might not be reached because of loading difficulties, and lack of rice and/or export licences (*LRBAC* 31st May 1995 4). The lack of export licences continued (*LRBAC* 30th June 1995 1). The authorities were trying to curtail the unofficial cross-border trade, but exports for the year were well ahead of last year, although loading was sporadic (*LRBAC* 30th June 1995 3). The *Circular* commented that the lack of supply from Vietnam, Thailand, Pakistan and Burma and continuing demand from Indonesia was only counterbalanced by large volumes of rice available from the Food Corporation stock in India which made up for shortfalls elsewhere in the world (*LRBAC* lst August 1995 1). Vietnam continued to have little to sell before the new crop, although occasional cargoes of rice did become available. 5 per cent had been offered but was expensive (*LRBAC* 1st August 1995 4). In September, Vietnam was still not a seller (*LRBAC* 1st September 1995 1). The government announced it would allow exports of 170,000 tons government to government, which included 23,000 tons to Cuba, 15,000 tons to Russia, 10,000 tons to Malaysia and 30,000 tons to the Philippines, but it was unlikely this could be shipped in September. A severe tropical storm in North Vietnam had caused severe flooding (*LRBAC* 1st September 1995 4). In October, some shipments took place, and some Vietnamese 5 per cent was committed to Indonesia for shipment in October/November/December (*LRBAC* 2nd October 1995 4). India again stepped into the breach in the world market to fulfil lower quality rice requirements, but not exclusively lower quality. This was because of reduced exports from Vietnam, Thailand and Myanmar in recent months (*LRBAC* 1st November 1995 1). Conditions remained confused in Vietnam for export licences, and there were only occasional shipments (*LRBAC* 1st November 1995 4). At the beginning of December, there was no mention of rice for export (*LRBAC* 1st December 1995 4). The *Circular* commented that over the past year, both Vietnam and Burma had been unable to fulfil their commitments due to having already sold large volumes of rice, in Vietnam's case straight over the border into China (*LRBAC* 2nd January 1996 1).

Prices were lower in Vietnam by 5 per cent and 25 per cent for January shipment. But these were for small shipments, and Vietnam was not likely to be a serious seller for another month or two (*LRBAC* 2nd January 1996 4). The Philippines then made commitments for 884,000 tons for import, mainly 25 per cent, including 362,000 tons from Vietnam, 225,000 tons from China, 150,000 tons from Thailand, 125,000 tons from India and 20,000 tons from the United States (*LRBAC* 26th February 1996 1). But in general, Vietnam remained an unknown factor (*LRBAC* 26th February 1996 1). At the end of February, they were on holiday (*LRBAC* 26th February 1996 4). By April, they were back from holiday and had new crops to sell (*LRBAC* 1st April 1996 1). The *Circular* believed the Vietnamese Government was going to control exports this year by not issuing export licences if prices were too low (*LRBAC* 1st April 1996 4). By May, prices in Vietnam had dropped and they were the most competitive origin for most qualities (*LRBAC* 1st May 1996 1). The Philippines were negotiating for another 100,000 tons of 25 per cent from Vietnam (*LRBAC* 1st May 1996 2). There were also said to be negotiations for 50,000 tons to Brazil, and shipments were taking place to Iran (*LRBAC* lst May 1996 3). Three cargoes of Vietnamese 5 per cent were reported as sold to Brazil (*LRBAC* 3rd June 1996 1). There were sales of broken rice to Africa from Vietnam and Thailand, thought to be to Senegal (*LRBAC* 3rd June 1996 1). The Philippines were said to be in negotiation with Vietnam for 200,000 tons of 25 per cent (*LRBAC* 3rd June 1996 3). Prices fell in June by 5 per cent and 25 per cent, and there were sales of 30,000 tons of "brokens". Offers were now unavailable for "brokens" and 25 per cent was also unavailable probably due to the deal with the Philippines. Shipments were taking place to Iran and there were reports of delays in loading (*LRBAC* 2rd June 1996 4). The deal for 200,000 tons to the Philippines was still not concluded (*LR-BAC* 4th July 1996 3). Exports from Vietnam were very large in June and would continue high into August. 90,000 tons of 5 per cent were reported as sold to Iraq, and 150,000 tons of 25 per cent to the Philippines, but neither deal was confirmed. Exports for June were 250,000 tons and July was also likely to be 250,000 tons. 5 per cent 'water polished', 5 per cent, 10 per cent, 15 per cent, 25 per cent and 35 per cent were quoted (*LRBAC* 4th July 1996 4). Prices fell and new customers were sought (*LRBAC* 5th August 1996 1). There was still no confirmation of the 90,000 tons to Iraq or the 25 per cent to the Philippines. 7,000 tons of "brokens" were sold, and 17,000 tons of 35 per cent to the World Food Programme (*LRBAC* 5th August 1996 4). Prices dropped but quality was poor as it was a wet season crop (*LRBAC* 3rd September 1996 1). Prices fell as demand slowed (*LRBAC* 3rd September 1996 4). Sri Lanka bought 3 cargoes of rice from Vietnam and India in 2 different tenders (*LRBAC* 3rd October 1996 1). There would be no more purchasing from the Philippines until next year (*LRBAC* 3rd October 1996 3). Shipments in September continued solidly, and there were about 20 vessels in port waiting to load (*LRBAC* 3rd October 1996 4). Vietnam had been the cheapest supplier for most of the year but was now challenged by Pakistan. Vietnam sold 5 per cent to Iran on Iranian terms. Five or six cargoes of 25 per cent were also sold to unspecified destinations (*LRBAC* 4th November 1996 4). Then Vietnamese prices increased substantially particularly for low-quality rice, because floods had delayed loading. The planting of the main crop was also delayed, and was now due end of February or early March (*LRBAC* 3rd December 1996 1. *LRBAC* 3rd December 1996 4). The U.N. oil for food and medicine deal for Iraq held a tender for 60,000 tons of 10 per cent, asking for offers from Vietnam, Thailand, Pakistan and India, but not Burma (*LR-BAC* 31st December 1996 1). Vietnam was relatively quiet in December, although there were 6 vessels in port loading 64,000 tons of 20 per cent and 25 per cent for Malaysia, North Korea and Cuba. It was rumoured 40,000 tons of 10 per cent had been sold to the Austrian Government for Iraq (*LRBAC* 31st December 1996 4).

The first Iraqi tender was held and purchases included 90,000 tons of Vietnamese 10 per cent (*LRBAC* 3rd February 1997 1). The market was active and over

140,000 tons of 5 per cent and 10 per cent were sold for March/April shipment. Price ideas for Hochiminh were for 5 per cent "double polished", 5 per cent, 10 per cent, 15 per cent and 25 per cent (*LRBAC* 3rd February 1997 4). The Philippines bought 100,000 tons of 25 per cent from Vietnam. There were also considerable sales to the private trade, destinations unknown (*LRBAC* 3rd March 1997 1). There were reports in Vietnam in February of more sales, including 2 cargoes of 10 per cent, 1 cargo of 25 per cent, and 1 cargo of 35 per cent, as well as 3 cargoes of optional origin 5 per cent, 10 per cent and 15 per cent and one additional cargo of 5 per cent. The 25 per cent market firmed up as a result of the Philippines sale, and it was thought that Iran was due to purchase up to 300,000 tons of 5 per cent. But there were only 3 vessels in port loading rice (*LRBAC* 3rd March 1997 4). The Government of Vietnam protected their government-to-government relationships, particularly with the Philippines, making it difficult for traders to cover their commitments. The ports were busy with shipments to the Philippines (*LRBAC* 2nd April 1997 4). But prices dropped in Vietnam because they missed out on sales to Iran and the Philippines by asking for higher prices. Yet Vietnam was a large seller of "broken rice", and over 100,000 tons were sold, although in the past Vietnam was only a limited exporter of this grade. Shipments and loadings were going ahead (*LRBAC* 2nd May 1997 1). Prices fell with the arrival of the new crop, and farmers sold enough rice to cover expenses, whilst beginning to store rice in the hope of better prices later. 25 per cent and 35 per cent were sold by traders for shipment to West Africa, and quantities to the Philippines. Some old sales were also covered in the Philippines. There were large sales of "brokens". At a World Food tender, a trader sold 29,000 tons of Vietnamese 35 per cent broken rice for April/May shipment to North Korea. There were 12 vessels in port with 8 due shortly (*LRBAC* 2nd May 1997 4). Trade was brisk with 25 per cent and 35 per cent for June/July, mostly for West Africa. A large number of vessels arrived to load. It was rumoured North Korea had purchased 100,000 tons from Vietnam, and they certainly needed to buy (*LRBAC* 3rd June 1997 1). Vietnam dominated Asian rice exports with reduced prices of 5 per cent and 35 per cent. Rains were hampering deliveries to the ports and loading. North Korea was desperate for rice, and there was talk of them buying 100,000 tons of 25 per cent or 35 per cent, but their problem was how to pay for it (*LRBAC* 3rd June 1997 4). Large volumes of rice were shipped from Vietnam to West Africa. 1 shipment of Vietnamese rice was made to Brazil (*LRBAC* 2nd July 1997 1). Vietnam continued to be an aggressive supplier of high-quality rice, and there were about 20 vessels in port loading low-quality rice. Loading rates were high, though slightly down due to rain. Letters of credit for 60,000 tons of 10 per cent for Iraq had arrived under UN oil for food business. 2 vessels had been nominated for this and a further 2 expected shortly. Vietnam was talking of an exportable surplus of 4,000,000 tons this year. So far 1,641,141 tons have been exported, with vessels loading or nominated for another 300,000 tons (*LRBAC* 2nd July 1997 4). In August there was a drop in volumes being shipped to West Africa, but an increase for Iran and East Africa. Loading was hampered by heavy rains (*LRBAC* 4th August 1997 1). The main wet season crop was a little later than expected. From now on, all exporters would mix an amount of wet crop with their rice giving a slightly inferior appearance to rice shipped earlier in the year. Most exporters were now asking for contracts to allow a minimum of 14.5 per cent moisture. Vessels were taking longer to load because of rain, and about 20 were loading. Vessels recently loaded included 5 with a total of 76,000 tons for Iraq, and others loaded 12,000 tons for North Korea, 16,000 tons for Cuba, and 47,000 tons for East Africa. Exports for June totalled 413,233 tons, but only 218,371 tons for the first 21 days of July due to rain (*LRBAC* 4th August 1997 4). Flooding in Vietnam then caused major logistical problems. But the *Circular* warned of the impending *EN*SO event which would bring drought to many parts of Asia, including Indonesia, Thailand, India and Pakistan although it did not mention Vietnam or Burma. It was predicted to be worse than the 1982/83 event (*LRBAC* 1st September 1997 1). Meanwhile, there was a terrible famine situation facing North Korea. A European Union tender was held to purchase 41,275 tons of 35 per cent as aid and looked to Vietnam as a possible source of supplies. But Vietnam basically withdrew from the market (*LRBAC* 1st September 1997 2). Severe flooding in many parts of the Mekong Delta was damaging rice in the fields, and making it difficult to dry. It was also causing serious logistical problems with transportation due to high water levels in many of the rivers and canals. Only 10 vessels were in port loading (*LRBAC* 1st September 1997 4). However, the Philippines made large purchases of rice of which Vietnam supplied 100,000 tons (*LRBAC* 3rd October 1997 1. *LRBAC* 3rd October 1997 2). During August, Vietnam had shipped 284,373 tons, bringing the total for the year so far to 2,414,849 tons. On 29th September, 274,400 tons had been shipped that month, with 10 vessels in port expected to load a further 123,069 tons (*LRBAC* 3rd October 1997 4). On 16th October there was a small currency devaluation of the Dong from 11,700 to 12,000 to the U.S.$Dollar, approximately 1.5 per cent. For most of the month, there had been 6 or 7 vessels in port, but this went up to 15. This included 4 for Iraq, 1 for Iran, 4 for West Africa, 1 for East Africa, 1 for Algeria, 1 for Central America, 1 for Cuba, 1 for Malaysia and 1 for North Korea, loading a total of 180,000 tons. In September 24 vessels had loaded 307,890 tons, but in October only 17 vessels completed 144,007 tons, bringing the total for the year to 2,866,746 tons. Typhoon Linda hit the southern tip of Vietnam killing many people and destroying houses and rice fields with torrential rains. Fortunately, this was between crops and unlikely to have any impact on production (*LRBAC* 6th November 1997 4). However, the typhoon brought floods to the Mekong Delta, delaying planting and more than 50 per cent of the crop would be harvested a month late. There was also disruption to the transportation of rice, and the loading of vessels. The total quantity loaded in November reached 191,419 tons (*LRBAC* 4th December 1997 4).

In January 1998, the world rice market was driven by heavy purchases from Indonesia and the Philippines. Vietnam supplied 100,000 tons to the Philippines with an option for another 100,000 tons (*LRBAC* 6th January 1998 1). Vietnam also sold rice to Indonesia and had commitments to supply Iran, Iraq, and Malaysia (*LRBAC* 6th January 1998 4). In February, the *Circular* wished its readers a happy and prosperous year of the Tiger and noted the holidays were well underway in the Far East.

In Vietnam, the holidays lasted longer than elsewhere, and would not be over until about the 10th of the month (*LRBAC* 2nd February 1998 1). However, from early January offers of Vietnamese rice had come in giving international merchants an opportunity to cover their sales to Indonesia where demand was great. By the middle of the month commitments for the first quarter had reached 1,400,000 tons. Commitments for February were thought to be 450,000 tons and for March 400,000 tons. By 26th January, a total of 197,534 tons had been loaded, with 5 vessels under loading for 65,368 tons (*LRBAC* 2nd February 1998 3–4). The *Circular* then gave the export figures for 1997.

Table 6.3 Vietnamese export figures for the year 1997 (metric tons)

January	72,898.149
February	67,552.500
March	318,189.666
April	228,200.054
May	481,068.062
June	512,778.991
July	389,787.878
August	284,373.708
September	307,890.128
October	144,007.316
November	191,419.678
December	91,062.194

Total Exports for the year were 3,149,228.324 MTS (*LRBAC* 2nd February 1998 3–4).

In Vietnam the armada of vessels which was expected to arrive immediately after Chinese New Year did not come, to the shock of the Vietnamese exporters who had been frantically preparing their cargoes. Payment difficulties on shipments to Indonesia had led to a severe lack of confidence. Traders stopped nominating new vessels until payment had been received on vessels already discharged in Indonesia. After negotiations with Indonesia confidence returned and vessels started to arrive in large numbers. One large purchase was 100,000 tons of 5 per cent for the Philippines, and there was a purchase of 150,000 tons of 5 per cent for Indonesia, all March/April. Estimates of Vietnamese commitments were over 2,200,000 tons, all to be shipped by the end of May. These were new crops, and shipments could only start in February. On 16th February the Vietnamese Government devalued their currency by 5 per cent. Hochiminh was very busy, and local barge charges increased between mills and ports, and from farm to mill. Last year's exports were about 3,100,000 tons and so far commitments in 1998 were over 2,200,000 tons. Although the main crop had not yet been harvested and was not expected until mid-March, 138,000 tons were loaded in the first 22 days of February, with vessels in port for another 313,000 tons. It was believed that the final figure for vessels loading in February would be between 270,000 and 300,000 tons. Commitments for March/April/May were around 1,900,000 tons, just over 600,000 tons per month, an enormous challenge (*LRBAC* 4th March 1998 4). But in

April, there were large defaults in Vietnam (*LRBAC* 5th April 1998 3). The Vietnamese government reported that commitments might have reached 3,000,000 tons, but the exportable amount from the winter/spring crop could be as low as 1,500,000 tons. After a meeting between government ministers and the Vietnamese Southern Food Corporation, it was announced that prices on all new contracts would have to be approved by the Steering Committee before business was concluded. The pressure to export was great with huge numbers of vessels arriving and exporters having to prepare cargo. But the winter/spring crop was smaller than anticipated. The first phase of the harvest went smoothly in February, but that harvested in March suffered from hot and dry conditions with low field and milling yields. Exporters were cancelling contracts and refusing to ship because they could not obtain rice. During March, approximately 70 vessels loaded a total of 753,828 tons, the largest total ever in one month. More than half of this was for Indonesia, the next largest destination being the Philippines. That left 25 vessels in port, 4 were waiting for a berth or cargo, and 10 vessels were to arrive shortly. These vessels were expected to load another 441,000 tons (*LRBAC* 6th April 1998 4). World demand for rice remained enormous, with the largest requirement being for Indonesia (Ed. The *EN*SO effect!). The Philippines were still buying (Ed. Also *EN*SO related), and there were suggestions that due to drought Malaysia would have to increase purchases. Bangladesh was set to increase its imports too on top of the usual traditional demand. But in Vietnam, the crop would be delayed between 30 and 40 days, and more if the rains did not come (*LRBAC* 30th April 1998 1). Final figures for exports from Vietnam in March were outstanding, with Hochiminh loading 74 vessels with 794,923 tons. Adding quantities shipped by container and other methods the figure was 840,000 tons, showing the ability of the Vietnamese to work at a rate never seen before. April shipments were expected to be close to 650,000 tons bringing the total for the year so far to just under 2,000,000 tons. However, shipments in May would be sharply reduced, down perhaps to 300,000 tons. Most of this was loaded in April but completed in May. There were reports that from the 1st June, the Vietnamese Government would ban further exports until it was seen how the second crop developed. 500,000 tons of commitments were thought to be still in hand, so cancellations or renegotiations were expected. The weather in Vietnam was exceptionally hot and dry for the time of year. Dry weather in the North suggested shipments of 400,000–500,000 tons might be required from the South. At the end of April, it was impossible to buy rice from Vietnam (*LRBAC* 30th April 1998 4). The Vietnamese government were still not considering export licences in May, and no further sales were concluded. However, there had been rain, and second crop planting was taking place, but the harvest would not be in before the beginning of September (*LRBAC* 29th May 1998 1). No further export licences were issued. May shipments were cut substantially and only expected to be 350,000 tons, with the June figure even less. Rain was now falling and it was hoped that the monsoon would develop. Although delayed, planting had now begun, with hopes of a harvest at the beginning of September. During April 63 vessels loaded 665,000 tons. Vietnamese exports for the first 23 days of May totalled 314,507 tons, leaving another 5 vessels in port expected to load 58,000 tons. Two of these were loading 22,000 tons to be completed in early June. Over the month there was an increase in vessels for destinations other than Indonesia and the Philippines. There were 11 for Indonesia, 4 for the Philippines, 1 for Malaysia, 5 for Iraq, 1 for Iran, 5 for Africa, 2 for Baltic ports and 1 for South America (*LRBAC* 29th May 1998 4). The new crop seemed a long way off and most of the Mekong Delta would not be harvested until the beginning of September. As there were occasional interim crops the government relaxed its stance and allowed an export licence for 50,000 tons. Other exporters used existing licences to conclude the occasional cargo. There was a government-to-government sale of 200,000 tons of 10 per cent brokens to Iraq shipment in July/August/September and some private sales of 25 per cent for July shipment. Up to 24th June, only 12 vessels were completed, loading a total of 98,167 tons. Five were for the Philippines, 1 for Indonesia, 1 for Brazil, 1 for Iraq, 1 for West Africa and 3 smaller vessels for Malaysia. There were a further six vessels in port expected to load another 65,000 tons, 3 for the Philippines, 1 for Iraq and 2 smaller vessels for Malaysia. Almost all shipments in June were made by the government through the Southern Food Company (*LRBAC* 3rd July 1998 4). There was a severe shortage of rice in Cambodia following recent drought conditions blamed on *EN*SO together with the high level of exports to Vietnam. These were driven by the enormous demand for Vietnamese rice exports earlier in the year (*LRBAC* 31st July 1998 1). In Vietnam, exports were down to a mere trickle. The final quantity loaded for June was 96,167 tons. Up to 24th July, 15 vessels had completed a total of 139,180 tons, bringing the total for the year to 2,536,959 tons. During July there were 7 vessels for the Philippines, 2 for Indonesia, 4 for Malaysia, 1 for Iraq and 1 for South America. Currently, there were 3 vessels in port to load 23,239 tons, 1 for the Philippines, 1 for Indonesia, and 1 for Iraq (*LRBAC* 31st July 1998 4). Weather patterns in the Far East continued to cause great concern, with serious flooding in China. Vietnam was also hit by the weather and stopped selling. They did not expect to resume until the New Year. Meanwhile, Indonesia bought some quantities from Vietnam and Thailand (*LRBAC* 28th August 1998 1). It was thought that the Indonesian Government had purchased 100,000 tons of Vietnamese 25 per cent brokens. The Indonesian Government also announced a tender for 600,000 tons of rice with origins restricted to Vietnam, Thailand and China (*LRBAC* 28th August 1998 2–3). As most exporters were aware of the flooding in China, and that Vietnam had withdrawn as a supplier, the only viable option for this tender was Thailand (*LRBAC* 28th August 1998 3). In August the Vietnamese Government announced that they would not allow any more sales of Vietnamese rice, but contracts already in place and registered with the Government would be executed. Prior to this, there had already been a substantial reduction in shipments from Vietnam. The government was concerned initially about drought in Central Vietnam, and later about flooding in the South. They were not expected to allow further sales until January. Vietnamese commitments were mainly for Indonesia, the Philippines, Malaysia and Iraq. In August about 14 vessels had completed loading, 7 for Indonesia, 2 for Iraq, 3 for West Africa, 1 for Brazil and 1 for Cuba. Exports for August were expected to be about 135,000 tons. In July 16 vessels had completed loading 144,895 tons (*LRBAC* 28th August 1998 4). In Indonesia, a government tender was held on 16th September and 24,000 tons were awarded to Vietnam for November delivery. Further negotiations with Indonesia led to a deal for another 200,000–300,000 tons of 25 per cent (*LRBAC* 2nd October 1998 2–3). As noted, the

Vietnamese government continued to try to make government-to-government sales to Indonesia and the Philippines, leading to a deal for a further 300,000 tons. Any private sales by Vietnamese companies to Indonesia, the Philippines, Iran, Iraq and Malaysia had to have prior Government approval, and the price had to be higher than sales on government-to-government business. During August, the Vietnamese actually loaded 12 vessels with a total of 118,635 tons, most of which were for the Philippines. Up to 25th September, 15 vessels had loaded 152,815 tons, of which 6 were for Indonesia, 3 for the Philippines, 3 for Iraq, 1 for Eastern Europe, 1 for East Africa and 1 for Brazil (*LRBAC* 2nd October 1998 4). At the Asia International Rice Conference on 29th/30th October, it was forecast that world import demand would reach a record 26,750,000 tons in 1998 but was expected to decline in 1999 by 3,000,000 – 7,000,000 tons. The main reductions in demand would come from Indonesia, the Philippines, Bangladesh and Brazil. Lower prices were immediately quoted in Thailand, Vietnam, India and Pakistan (*LRBAC* 6th November 1998 1). New sales of rice were now allowed by the Vietnamese Government, but prices were carefully controlled. 25 per cent was in high demand for Indonesia, including recent commitments to ship 500,000 tons. 200,000 tons had already been shipped there, leaving 300,000 tons to be shipped in November/December. There were government-to-government contracts to Indonesia, Malaysia and Iraq, but little else. During October 22 vessels loaded 184,000 tons, 13 of which were for Indonesia, 5 for Iraq, 2 for Malaysia, 1 for Algeria and 1 for Eastern Europe. In November, five vessels were loading 48,000 tons of which 4 were for Indonesia and 1 for Iraq. Planting for the new crop was underway in the Mekong Delta, but the Delta has no protection against storms coming in from the South China Sea and the situation needed watching (*LRBAC* 6th November 1998 4). Prices fell (*LRBAC* 7th December 1998 2). By December planting was complete in the Mekong Delta. Tropical storms had bypassed the Delta but hit central Vietnam with loss of life and destruction of housing and crops. November shipments would be about 160,000 tons, bringing the total for the year to 3,180,000 tons. 18 vessels were loaded of which 12 were for Indonesia, 3 for Iraq, 2 for Malaysia and 1 for Japan. In early December, there were 10 vessels in port, expecting to load 100,000 tons. There were only 3 for Indonesia and 1 for the Philippines, but 2 for Iraq, 1 for Malaysia, 1 for Japan and 2 for West Africa. Price indications were in 50 kg polypropylene bags for 5 per cent, 10 per cent, 15 per cent and 25 per cent (*LRBAC* 7th December 1998 4). In Indonesia, a long-awaited tender was announced on 16th December utilising a financial offer by the Islamic Development Bank (IDB). Vietnam was included as one of the options for origin for 25 per cent shipment January/February and made the cheapest offer for delivery to a safe Indonesian port (*LRBAC* 4th January 1999 2). Vietnamese prices were below those in Thailand (*LRBAC* 4th January 1999 3). However, the government steering committee announced it would not allow any business to be done below a certain price, and the Indonesian tender went to Pakistan. The final export figures for November 1998 were 160,376 tons. Exports for the first 28 days of December were 205,654 tons, bringing the total for 1998 to 3,390,000 tons with a further four vessels in port to load 52,200 tons. The final total for 1998 was expected to be close to 3,500,000 tons. The main destinations during December were again the Philippines and Indonesia, with three vessels for Malaysia with 5 per cent, two vessels of 10 per cent for Iraq, one vessel of 10 per cent for Japan, and two for West Africa, one of which was carrying 5 per cent and 1 carrying 5 per cent and 15 per cent (*LRBAC* 4th January 1999 4). The *Circular* then compared the export figures for Vietnam for 1998 with those of 1997, both years of exceptionally high exports due to high demand from Indonesia, the Philippines and elsewhere, linked to the *EN*SO incident of these years:

Table 6.4 Rice export figures for Vietnam 1997 and 1999 (metric tons)

	1997	*1998*
January	72,898.149	243,359.689
February	67,552.500	257,535.342
March	318,189.666	794,923.616
April	288,200.054	664,828.754
May	481,068.062	338,964.016
June	512,778.991	98,167.923
July	389,787.878	144,895.038
August	284,373.708	118,635.507
September	307,890.128	175,876.139
October	144,007.316	184,185.280
November	191,419.678	160,376.830
December	91,062.194	229,711.768
Total	3,149,228.324	3,411,459.902

(*LRBAC* 2nd February 1999 inserted between 2 and 3).

In January 1999, 25 per cent was traded at low prices, but the government announced they would limit exports for the first quarter of the year to 1,000,000 tons. Commitments had already been registered for 600,000 tons and were currently believed to be over 800,000 tons. The *Circular* commented that February was always a strange month in Vietnam, as during the New Year celebrations from 13th to 22nd February, the country came to a halt. So after a quiet February, a busy March was expected (*LRBAC* 2nd February 1999 4). The government then announced they would allow 1,000,000 tons to be exported in the first quarter of the year, 2,000,000 tons in the second quarter and 1,000,000 tons in the last half of the year. Shipments for February totalled 241,418 tons, bringing the total for the year so far to 408,464 tons. There were eight vessels in port to load 102,891 tons for destinations, including the Philippines, West Africa, Iraq, Syria and Northern Europe (*LRBAC* 3rd March 1999 4). During March, exports were expected to total 347,000 tons, bringing the total for the year so far to 756,000 tons, well below the government limit of 1,000,000 tons for the first quarter. Only five vessels were underloading. The largest buyer in March was the Philippines, although this contract was coming to an end, and the next largest was Iraq. The quantity shipped to West Africa was disappointing (*LRBAC* 6th April 1999 4). In April, Vietnam experienced heavy rains, which delayed the drying and preparation of rice and also loading. Local barge and transportation costs increased. There were about 26 vessels in port, some of them having been there since the beginning of the month. Demand was mainly for low-quality rice. Exports for April were likely to be 360,000 tons, much less than expected due to the poor weather. Exports for the year so far were 1,100,000–1,200,000 tons (*LRBAC* 30th April 1999 4). The *Circular* commented that heavy rains in Vietnam and Thailand led many to think this was the direct result of *La Nina* linked to the recent *El Nino* (Ed. *EN*SO) event of 1997/98 (*LRBAC* lst June 1999 1). There were regular shipments from Vietnam to Indonesia (*LRBAC* 1st June 1999 2). In early May, heavy rains continued to disrupt the preparation and loading of cargo. Exports during April reached 399,947 tons, and in May, it was 499,081 tons. Commitments for June were believed to be 350,000 tons (*LRBAC* lst June 1999 4). However, only 280,000 tons were loaded. There was a regular flow of business by private traders to Indonesia for lots of 2000–5000 tons. The government announced it intended to buy 500,000 tons of paddy to support paddy prices and as security stock in case of flood damage. There was speculation in the local press that heavy flooding might affect the Mekong Delta in the next few months (*LRBAC* 9th July 1999 4).

Table 6.5 Rice shipments from Vietnam from January to June 1999 compared with 1998 (metric tons)

	1998	*1999*
January	240,000	160,000
February	250,000	240,000
March	800,000	360,000
April	660,000	400,000
May	330,000	460,000
June	100,000	280,000

(*LRBAC* 9th July 1999 4. Figures from histogram).

The second crop arrived in both Vietnam and Thailand (*LRBAC* 3rd August 1999 1). There was active trade to Indonesia for 25 per cent, but most of the enquiries were for small lots of 2000–3000 tons for which exporters generally received a slight premium for selling in these small amounts. Commitments for August and September were about 600,000 tons. Exports for July were about 308,170 tons, bringing the total for the year to date to 2,221,600 tons (*LRBAC* 3rd August 1999 4). In Vietnam, in August, there was heavy rain and flooding in the Red River Delta in the north, but little in the Mekong Delta in the south. Crops were likely to benefit from this rain (*LRBAC* 26th August 1999 1). Exports by the end of August were expected to be 3,200,000 tons, with the government target for the year at 4,000,000 tons, leaving about 800,000 tons to be shipped in the next four months. The government raised the minimum price by 25 per cent, but this was probably only a guide price. Recent shipments were mostly to Indonesia (*LRBAC* 25th August 1999 4). Then came the news that Indonesia would ban all private imports of rice except for high quality 5 per cent or better. The price for 5 per cent double polished fell sharply and so did 25 per cent (*LRBAC* 1st October 1999 4). At the beginning of November, the Vietnamese government again intervened to support prices by financing exporters and millers to purchase around 300,000 tons of rice, with no interest payments for six months. Heavy rains made drying, milling and transportation difficult. In central Vietnam, floods displaced large numbers of people and left vast areas of land under water. However, in the long run, this was probably good news for future crops. During October, exports from Hochiminh totalled about 200,000 tons, mostly for Africa. At the end of September, exports were 3,800,000 tons, substantially ahead of the previous year's figures. By the end of October, exports were thought to be just over 4,000,000 tons (*LRBAC* 5th November 1999 4). The small harvest at the end of November into early December would increase the exportable surplus by 100,000 tons. Main crop planting was close to completion. 5 per cent were double polished, and 10 per cent, 15 per cent and 25 per cent were quoted in 50-kg polypropylene bags (*LRBAC* 3rd December 1999 4).

In Thailand, in January 1990, prices were firmer due to government purchasing (*LRBAC* 31st January 1990 1). The Thai market was controlled by demand for high-grade rice in Iran, Iraq, Malaysia and to a lesser extent Peru. Business was reported for Thai 15 per cent to Callao in Peru, and negotiations were taking place for Iraq. In West Africa, only Angola and Cameroons were open to Thailand, because of aggressive offers from Vietnam. There were offers basis 100 kilo new single bags for 100 per cent B, 5 per cent, 10 per cent, 15 per cent, 25 per cent, 35 per cent and Parboiled 100 per cent, 5 per cent and 10 per cent. Also, Brokens A1 Super and A1 Specials were priced well below 35 per cent (*LRBAC* 31st January 1990 3). Government policy was to purchase 1,000,000 tons this year to support prices and give 3 per cent loans to farmers. They had already bought 500,000 tons leaving another 500,000 tons to purchase. Much trade was being lost to Vietnam. Exports in the first two months had been very low, totalling 600,000 tons. The only major trade last month was 130,000 tons A1 Specials sold government to government to Senegal (*LRBAC* 28th February 1990 3). In March, a delegation in China was thought to be putting together a deal for 100,000 tons to be paid for with cement (*LRBAC* 31st March 1990 1). Export prices fell because of continued competition from Vietnam. Exports for the first two months of the year were 653,600 tons, some 36 per cent down on 1989. To provide support, the government intended to buy 100,000 tons to add to the 500,000 tons they had already purchased (*LRBAC* 31st March 1990 2). Iran, one of the world's largest importers, recently bought 10 per cent from both Thailand and Vietnam, whereas previously they had only bought the highest quality such as Thai 100 per cent, and other origins with top-quality milling and 4 per cent (Ed. 5 per cent?) brokens (*LRBAC* 30th April 1990 1). Total exports to 31st March were only 1,000,626 tons compared with 1,669,840 last year. Exports were dominated by high-quality shipments to the Middle East, but other major shipments included Cuba with 25 per cent brokens. Vietnam had taken nearly all the low-grade sales to Africa. Current quotations were in 100 kilo jute bags and reflected high moisture second crop material. There were 10,000 tons long grain white rice 10 per cent for China and six cargoes for Iran, split equally between 5 per cent and 10 per cent brokens for May/June/July. There were also six cargoes of 100 per cent B to Iraq (*LRBAC* 30th April 1990 3). Prices continued to fall. The business was confined generally to the higher grades, but there were unconfirmed reports of one or two cargoes of 35 per cent being traded at low prices. May exports were 279,240 tons, giving a total for the year so far of 1,525,840 tons, indicating a possible annual figure of 3,500,000 tons. This was compared with last year's 6,000,000 tons (*LRBAC* 30th June 1990 3). There was an increase in demand partly due to the suspension of exports from Vietnam. The government sold 100,000 tons 35 per cent brokens at a low price to the Philippines for July shipment. There was an additional option for 300,000 tons, which it was believed the Philippines would take up. Iran bought 14 cargoes of 100 per cent Grade B loaded Bangkok for shipment to the end of the year. The government announced they would be buying 100,000 tons of rice to support the market (*LRBAC* 31st July 1990 3). Freight rates rose by about 10 per cent due to political problems in the Middle East (*LRBAC* 31st August 1990 1). The situation in Iraq affected the market, and two cargoes afloat were diverted to Malaysia and sold at a loss. An additional 85,000 tons of 100 per cent B was sold to Malaysia for October/January shipment. 80,000 tons of brokens were sold to Senegal, which the sellers were trying to cover in Thailand. Parboiled prices firmed as a result of sales to Saudi Arabia and Yemen. Whilst the government talked of buying 100,000 tons to support prices, this had so far not occurred (*LRBAC* 31st August 1990 2–3). The market firmed in Thailand due to purchases from Russia (*LRBAC* 31st October 1990 1). This was 200,000 tons of 15 per cent (*LRBAC* 31st October 1990 2). It was a government-to-government deal for shipment in November/December with payment over 2 years at an interest rate of 7 per cent per annum. The buyers had nominated vessels for the initial 60,000 tons to load during the first half of November. Average monthly reports from January to August were 300,000 tons, but September was 371,330 tons, giving an accumulated figure of 2,881,070 tons. This was down some 2,000,000 tons on last year's figure of 4,997,570 tons. The market situation was aggravated by bad weather, causing flooding and disruption to loading. But crop forecasts for 1990 were only 500,000 tons down on last year at 20,500,000 tons basis paddy. Crop damage particularly from insects was thought to be not greater than last year at 12–14 per cent (*LRBAC* 31st October 1990 2–3). Up to the end of November, 3,570,000 tons had been exported, and it was expected the figure for the year would be close to 4,000,000 tons. Almost 40 per cent of this was high-quality 100 per cent Grade B. Letters of credit had been opened by the Russians, but they were not in order, and five or six vessels arriving to load were turned away and went to Vietnam to load. It was thought the letters of credit would be in order in the near future. Expected shipments in December included 24,000 tons of white rice 100 per cent for Syria, 15,000 tons white rice 35 per cent for Madagascar, 54,000 tons white rice 100 per cent for Iran, 14,000 tons of white rice 100 per cent for Malaysia, 8000 tons of parboiled 100 per cent for Benin and 20,000 tons A1 Specials (Ed. a low-quality grade) for Mauritania (*LRBAC* 30th November 1990 3).

From Russia, it was reported that letters of credit to the Thai government were still not in order, and vessels which had arrived to load had left and gone to other ports (*LRBAC* 9th January 1991 2). Thailand only exported 3,926,760 tons in calendar year 1990, which was the lowest figure for five years. There was a recent sale of 250,000 tons of 100 per cent B to Malaysia with extended payment. Also, the Thai government declared its intention to buy 200,000 tons of 100 per cent B from exporters to support prices (*LRBAC* 9th January 1991 3). With the outbreak of the Gulf War in January 1991, there was a sharp increase in rice prices in Thailand and throughout the world. But Vietnam was out of the market (*LRBAC* 5th February 1991 1). Doubts continued about Russia's ability to fulfil broken rice contracts, but 7000 tons were traded from the Black Sea (*LRBAC* 5th February 1991 2). The crop in Thailand this year was thought to be 16,000,000 tons of paddy as opposed to 18,000,000 tons last year. Export figures for January would be about 350,000 tons. In February, 276,000 tons was sold to Malaysia, comprising 250,000 tons 100 per cent B, 20,000 tons glutinous 10 per cent, and 6000 tons A1 Super for delivery first half of 1991. The government attempted to buy 100,000 tons 100 per cent B but only received offers of 36,000 tons (*LRBAC* 5th February 1991 2). Hostilities ceased in the Gulf bringing relief (*LRBAC* 1st March 1991 1). From Russia came news that there was no finalisation on the business being discussed with Thailand (*LRBAC* 1st March 1991 2). There was a military coup in Thailand on the weekend of 23/24th February, and it was not clear what the new government support programme for rice farmers might be (*LRBAC* 1st March 1991 3). This was the National Peace-Keeping Council (NPKC; Andrews 2002 199). There were no new large sales from Thailand but exports continued at a reasonable rate. There were reports of difficulties with top-quality sortexed parboiled causing premiums for sortexed and top quality to be increased (*LRBAC* 1st March 1991 3). Prices dropped a little, and exports up to the end of February were 670,000 tons as opposed to 654,000 tons last year. Current predictions were that exports for the year would be similar to last year at 4,000,000 tons. 100,000 tons were to be shipped to Africa and North Korea during April (*LRBAC* 1st April 1991 3). Thai New Year Holidays were 12th–15th April, and prices recovered afterwards (*LRBAC* 30th April 1991 1). Business was reported to Jordan for four cargoes of Thai 10 per cent. One or two cargoes amounting to a total of 20,000–25,000 tons of 100 per cent Grade B were reported to Chile. Additional business by barter for 40,000–50,000 tons of 100 per cent Grade B was done, with shipment in June/July/August. This might also go to Chile. Exports in March were 346,442 tons, bringing the total for the first quarter to 1,017,096 tons. Only 95,000–100,000 tons were exported in the first half of April (*LRBAC* 30th April 1991 2–3). The market was controlled by demand for higher quality rice, both white and parboiled. Significant quantities of 100 per cent B down to 10 per cent brokens were traded to Jordan. There were also five cargoes of 100 per cent Grade B to Brazil, 12,000–14,000 tons of 5 per cent to Dubai, and a significant quantity of high-quality parboiled shipped to Benin. Towards the end of May, the Thai government announced they would release 280,000 tons of 25 per cent previously bought and stored under their market support programme. It would be released back to the Thai exporters who provided it at a price ex-warehouse. May exports totalled 404,700 tons, giving a total of 1,713,593 tons exported in the first five months of 1991. More than 200,000 tons were already expected to be shipped in June, so the final figure for the month could be good. 11,000 tons of broken rice A1 Specials (Ed. a cheap grade) was sold to Mauritania (*LRBAC* 7th

June 1991 3). In June, Iran refused to accept high prices. But with shipments expected in July, and shipments remaining from June to Aqaba in the Gulf, Malaysia, Brazil and Syria for 100 per cent Grade B and some 5 per cent brokens, prices were underpinned. 50,000–100,000 tons of broken rice was contracted for July/August for Gambia, Dakar (in Senegal) and other West African destinations. Also, 50,000–70,000 tons of parboiled rice was sold to Benin to be shipped by the third week of July. As a direct result, very high-quality paddy for top-quality parboiled dark golden sortexed rice was in short supply (*LRBAC* 28th June 1991 3). During July, there was a reasonable volume of trade, but an exceptional sale was 245,000 tons of 15 per cent brokens to Aqaba for shipment in August/December, with an agreement for a further 400,000 tons next year. This raised prices and priced Thailand out of much of the world market. Exports for the month to 29th July were 324,503 tons, making a total figure for the year of 2,401,293 tons (*LRBAC* 31st July 1991 2). Thailand was now suffering competition from India for upper-quality rice (*LRBAC* 31st August 1991 1). At the other end of the market, there was a recent sale to Senegal of 25,000 tons of broken rice (Ed. per cent unspecified) for arrival by the end of October and another 25,000 tons of the same to arrive by mid-November, including 90 days interest. Some previous Senegal sales had been covered short when vessels came to load. Exports for the first three weeks of August were about 270,000 tons (*LRBAC* 31st August 1991 2–3). Up to 23rd September, 256,986 tons had been exported for the month, giving a total for the year of 2,985,153 tons. Broken rice was in demand for vessels nominated for Senegal and Mali, causing exporters to rush to cover their requirements. Besides this, there were sales on a regular basis for good quality mature broken rice for the pasta trade and a strong demand for low quality for animal feed. A letter of credit for 30,000 tons of 15 per cent had been opened as part of the old Iraq contract (*LRBAC* 30th September 1991 3). There was a sale of 300,000 tons of 25 per cent, and 25,000 tons of 10 per cent by one of the major Thai exporters. The shipping programme to Senegal had come to an end. There was a sale to Indonesia of 25,000 tons of 10 per cent and 25 per cent. There were rumours of 210,000 tons of 100 per cent Grade B to Iran (*LRBAC* 31st October 1991 3). There was an old sale of 80,000 tons of Thai rice to Indonesia bringing the total from Thailand to 405,000 tons (*LRBAC* 30th November 1991 1). The new crop was now being harvested. Russia was enquiring for 200,000–500,000 tons of 25 per cent, although the Thai Government had agreed on special credit terms of two years, Russia still had to find a way of paying for it. There were sales to Iran and Indonesia, and the Government would be supporting paddy prices again this year (*LRBAC* 30th November 1991 2–3). Broken rice was sold to Senegal. Two cargoes had been concluded with one vessel having completed loading 30,000 tons, and an additional 25,000 tons had been bought. Malaysia bought 25,000 tons of fragrant rice and 15,000 tons of glutinous rice (*LRBAC* 31st December 1991 3)

There were good shipments during January, and discussions with Russia, China, Iran and possibly Indonesia (*LRBAC* 31st January 1992 1). The incoming new crop was expected to be up 10 per cent to around 17,600,000 tons of paddy. There was business to Peru, and it was thought a contract would soon be confirmed for 300,000 tons of 15 per cent to Russia for shipment of 75,000 tons per month from February to May, including two year's credit. Thai exporters expected to secure sales for a further 200,000 tons to be shipped in the second half of the year. At the end of January Thailand expected to have exported over 400,000 tons. The final figure for 1991 was 3,993,460 tons which was 2 per cent higher than 1990 and the December figure alone was 373,000 tons, showing good shipping activity. There was potential business to Indonesia, and the annual "friendship" contract to China was expected to be about 250,000 tons. There was also a sale of 50,000 tons of high-grade rice to Malaysia (*LRBAC* 31st January 1992 2–3). The Russian purchase of 500,000 tons was now confirmed (*LRBAC* 28th February 1992 1). Shipments to Indonesia against old contracts continued from Thailand (*LRBAC* 28th February 1992 2). Total exports from Thailand in January were 493,725 tons, but with the reduction in movement early in February due to the Chinese New Year celebrations, the expectation of 400,000–450,000 tons for February was unlikely to be met. The government sale of 500,000 tons of 15 per cent (Ed. for Russia) was now confirmed as noted above. It was for 2 years credit at 7¾ per cent per annum, although the credit was unconfirmed. The rice would be tendered by the Government probably at 100,000 tons per tender to match shipment requirements for March/April/May and then September/October. There were reports of a military purchase of 70,000 tons of parboiled 100 per cent sortexed to Yemen, plus an additional one or two cargoes possibly amounting to 30,000 tons to the private trade (*LRBAC* 28th February 1992 2–3). In Thailand, exports so far had averaged around 450,000 tons per month, and for April they looked good again (*LRBAC* 31st March 1992 1). As noted total exports in March were expected to be over 450,000 tons, and were expected to be heavy to Iran and Iraq. A sale was thought to have been made to Indonesia of 200,000 tons of 25 per cent, but this was not confirmed (*LRBAC* 31st March 1992 2–3). There was new business from Thailand to Iran and shipments of existing business from Thailand to Aqaba and Indonesia. There was also buying from Peru and Mexico, mostly from Vietnam but also from Thailand (*LRBAC* 30th April 1992 1). Exports for the first quarter reached 1,329,000 tons, which was 30 per cent greater than the same period last year. On 27th April, exports reached 443,000 tons, and were expected to reach 500,000 tons by the end of the month. So Thailand was on target to exceed 5,000,000 tons for the year. 195,000 tons of 100 per cent Grade B was concluded for Iran for May/July (*LRBAC* 30th April 1992 2–3). The market came to a virtual halt during the week of May 18th/22nd due to political demonstrations, but exports continued much as normal (*LRBAC* 31st May 1991 1. *LRBAC* 31st May 1992 3). May exports did not look to be much higher than 300,000 tons. In April, there was a sale of 10,000–12,000 tons of A1 Specials for June/July shipment (*LRBAC* 31st May 1992 3). Exports for July were expected to be 450,000 tons. This was helped by the government purchasing 150,000 tons of 25 per cent and 50,000 tons of 15 per cent. There were reports that the government was asking rice millers to purchase 500,000 tons of second crop at a premium of 150,000 Baht over current prices, with the Government reimbursing the millers for the premium. A government delegation sold 60,000–100,000 tons to Senegal for October/November/December shipment including 180 days of finance but this was not confirmed. There was steady loading of rice and arrival of vessels for Iran which caused a shortage of 100 per cent B. 2

vessels arrived to load brokens, causing the broken market to rice dramatically. This was made worse by a shortage of maize for which broken rice is a substitute for animal feed (*LRBAC* 31st July 1992 3). Prices fell in Thailand and to a lesser extent in Vietnam. This was partly because Indonesia had started to sell rice, whereas previously they had been major buyers from Thailand (*LRBAC* 31st August 1992 1). One of the factors behind the collapse of prices in Thailand was that the remainder of the Russian purchase of 15 per cent was not being shipped due to heavy congestion in the discharge ports, and therefore lack of vessel designation from buyers. Also, the government support programme which purchased 150,000 tons of 25 per cent and 50,000 tons of 15 per cent had now ended and was in store, and there was no further Government support. In addition, there were difficulties in payment on some shipments to Iran, so exporters were not accepting new vessel nominations. Exports for August were only 301,490 tons, well down on the recent figures of 500,000 tons per month. Despite this, exports for the 8 months of the year so far were 3,454,792 metric tons. To make matters worse, as noted, Indonesia had sold 200,000 tons of white rice 35 per cent brokens, although normally they were buyers not sellers. Thailand had also missed out on sales of 100,000 tons of 100 per cent B to Malaysia, which had gone to Vietnam (*LRBAC* 31st August 1992 2–3). In September, there were effective devaluations of Sterling and the Italian Lire, causing a disturbance in the world rice market where prices were usually denominated in U.S. dollars. The U.S. dollar had also seen a drastic reduction in its purchasing power (*LRBAC* 30th September 1992 1). In September 240,000 tons were sold by a leading exporter to Iran on Iranian terms. Regular small quantities of 10 per cent brokens were being sold to Dubai in double 45 kilo bags. Current quotations were for 100 kilo single jute bags, 100 per cent Grade B, 5 per cent, 10 per cent, 25 per cent, 35 per cent and A1 Specials. Also parboiled 100 per cent, 5 per cent and 10 per cent (*LRBAC* 30th September 1992 2–3). The final figure for September was 303,533 tons giving a total for the first 9 months of the year of 3,758,373 tons. But shipments had slowed and only 245,605 tons were reported for export up to 27th October. The largest single shipment was a repeat sale of 240,000 tons to Iran by a Thai exporter, and this as in the original business was 100 per cent Grade B white rice. Official forecasts of the new crop were reduced by 1,500,000 tons to 19,000,000 tons basis paddy. Meanwhile, there had been larger than usual shipments to Benin over the last few months (*LRBAC* 31st October 1992 2–3). The final figure for October was a little higher than expected at 305,027 tons, giving a total for the year of 4,063,400 tons. In the first three weeks of November, exports were running at a similar level at 268,113 tons. Iran and the Gulf were major buyers. To support the market, the government apparently decided to buy 150,000 tons from exporters, and 50,000 tons from millers, basis 15 per cent brokens, at above the market price. Funds were announced to underpin the price of paddy at about 10 per cent above the current market level, raising the price per ton from 3,800 Baht to 4,100 Baht (*LRBAC* 30th November 1992 2–3). By the end of November, total exports for the 11 months were 4,395,150 tons, and it was expected 250,000–300,000 tons would be shipped in December, much the same as the 331,750 tons exported in November. As reported in November, the Government bought 80,000 tons of 100 per cent Grade B, and 60,000 tons of broken rice for delivery by the end of December. The price was U.S. Dollars $7 over the current export price. There was another announcement asking for offers for 140,000 tons of 100 per cent Grade B and 60,000 tons of broken rice also at a premium over the normal export price. There was also business in broken rice to Senegal and a high volume of parboiled to Benin December/early January. It was thought that Nigerian import restrictions might be lifted or eased, and there was a wish to have stocks nearby should this happen (*LRBAC* 31st December 1992 2–3).

In January, the market was affected by the Chinese New Year holidays, and Government buying activity (*LRBAC* 29th January 1993 1). Total exports for calendar year 1992 were 4,779,871 tons, which was just under a 20 per cent improvement in 1991. It was thought the main crop might be reduced to 16,900,000 tons. The government had been actively buying 15 per cent brokens and quantities of "broken rice" were bought in early January, with a tender on the 27th for 100,000 tons of 100 per cent Grade B, and possibly the same quantity of 15 per cent. 95,000 tons of "broken rice" were bought in the last few days of December and early January, intended for Senegal and Mauritania. The government were anticipating Government-to-government business including 40,000 tons of A1 brokens to Mauritania, 10,000 tons of A1 brokens to North Korea on deferred payment, 200,000 tons 100 per cent Grade B to Malaysia exchanged for urea and 500,000 tons 15 per cent brokens to Russia on deferred payment combined with renegotiations for outstanding payment. Whilst the Government buying was intended to help farmers, the consequence was to make Thailand even less competitive with Vietnam and Pakistan (*LRBAC* 29th January 1993 1–2). The Government continued to purchase large volumes of rice to support the market but to no avail. They were under pressure to sell the rice they had purchased, and there were reports of sales of 100,000 tons to Hong Kong, 100,000 tons to Yemen, and 250,000 tons to the Philippines. There were unconfirmed rumours of 250,000–400,000 tons being sold by the Government to Iran. There were also reports of 3 lots of 100,000 tons of various qualities being sold to private purchasers abroad based on 15 per cent brokens. During February the Government was believed to have bought 100,000 tons of 100 per cent B, 200,000 tons of parboiled 100 per cent, and 200,000 tons of brokens, bringing the total bought this year to 1,400,000 tons already (*LRBAC* 28th February 1993 2–3). Trade expectations for the year were 2,200,000 – 2,300,000 tons. But prices were at a 10-year low in Thailand, despite the Government buying more than 1,000,000 tons earlier in the year at higher than market levels. Thai exports were down on last year with February exports at 247,666 tons and 315,976 tons for the first 29 days of March. April would be even worse as the Thai New Year holidays would halt work for 4 or five days in the middle of the month. 3 vessels were nominated to lift a total of 71,000 tons of 15 per cent for Aqaba, but there was no other activity for white rice. Parboiled sales continued to Cotonou in Benin for 100 per cent sortexed dark gold quality, and 5 per cent and 10 per cent were available at a discount (*LRBAC* 31st March 1993 3). Activity picked up in the world rice market. But this was at a tremendous cost to farmers' and millers' profitability in Thailand, Vietnam and Burma, as prices were running at a 13/14 year low. The United States continued to be an aggressive exporter (*LRBAC* 30th April 1993 1).

Prices in Thailand have been amongst the lowest since 1980. Exports for the first 26 days of April amounted to 275,307 tons, following the March figure of 364,275 tons. So in aggregate, the first quarter of the year was just over 967,000 tons, down 27 per cent from the first quarter of 1992. Estimates for the world rice trade for 1993 were now put at 1,000,000 tons less than in 1992, so it was difficult to see how Thailand could attain the 4,200,000 tons it had hoped for, even though this was 500,000 tons down in 1992 (*LRBAC* 30th April 1993 3). The May edition of the *Circular* began with a focus on Thailand. It believed Thailand held the key to future price movements in the world rice market. The world price decline had had a drastic effect on the farming community in Thailand. The Thai milling industry and Thai exporters had also suffered, because of greater participation on the world scene from Vietnam, China and the United States. However, during May there were reports that the Thai Government had given some price support by subsidising exports and/or supporting prices. They had certainly bought some parboiled, 15 per cent white rice, and broken rice. The authorities were to hold a series of tenders in June, the first for two lots of 10,000 tons of each grade, namely parboiled 100 per cent, white rice 25 per cent Super, and broken rice A1 Super. But if these tenders continued, traditional Thai exporters could be sidelines as international traders bid for the tenders. Unfortunately, Government support buying, which should have put 850,000–1,000,000 tons in store from buying earlier in the year, had not succeeded in safeguarding farmers' incomes by supporting paddy prices (*LRBAC* 28th May 1993 1). As noted above, the first quarter exports were only 967,077 tons, down 27 per cent on last year. With the April export figures at 349,077 tons and the first 24 days of May at 311,986 tons, the total for the year to the 24th May was a little over 1,600,000 tons which if maintained would give a total for the full year of under 4,000,000 tons. Some reports suggested it might be as low as 3,500,000 tons, which would be the lowest for the last 12 years. Official sources were now expecting a normal crop year, which would give even more price support problems for the government. There was continuing business to Dubai, where prices moved down for 10 per cent brokens, and some broken rice was bought for Banjul in the Gambia, and also Mauritania. 8000–10,000 tons of 35 per cent were also sold destination not given. Two cargoes of mixed qualities were contracted for Peru, consisting of 100 per cent Grade B, 5 per cent brokens, 10 per cent brokens and 15 per cent brokens. Current quotations basis 100-kilo new single jute bags stowed were for 100 per cent B, 5 per cent, 10 per cent, 15 per cent, 25 per cent and 35 per cent. Also, A1 Super brokens, parboiled 100 per cent, 5 per cent and 10 per cent (*LRBAC* 28th May 1993 3). Nigeria suddenly announced import licences were available for direct import of rice, which stimulated Thai parboiled prices. However, in Thailand, when the new rice tenders mentioned above were announced, the minimum prices set by the Thai Government were substantially above the bids received, and no business was done (*LRBAC* 30th June 1993 1). There was no attempt to re-schedule the tender, as a solution to payment problems with Russia was likely to lead to a shipment there of 300,000 tons of 15 per cent brokens. There were also said to be 100,000 tons of "broken" rice and 15 per cent brokens for North Korea, 150,000 tons of 35 per cent brokens to the Philippines in exchange for fertiliser, and 160,000 – 180,000 tons of! 00 per cent B to Iran. The reports for Iran, Russia and North Korea were not new, but if shipment took place prices would be affected. The movement of the Philippines sales had already started with 65,000–70,000 tons of freight having been nominated. As for Nigeria, 15,000 tons had been traded of parboiled 5 per cent for a vessel loading in early July. Continuing trades to Dubai were the mainstay of the market apart from Government business. But there was talk of a contract for 200,000 tons, also reported as 400,000 tons, for Iraq, for 10 per cent or 15 per cent or a combination of both. But payment was to be made from blocked accounts which had not worked previously. Exports for the month to the 28th June were 365,860 tons, bringing the total for the year to just under 2,000,000 tons. Current quotations were for 100-kilo new single jute bags (Ed. This was the last reference to single jute bags and 100-kilo bags) (*LRBAC* 30th June 1993 3). 50,000 tons of Thai parboiled 5 per cent was transacted for Nigeria based on 15,000 tons cargo size (*LRBAC* 30th July 1993 1). Government buying kept prices steady. At a tender in July 100,000 tons of parboiled 100 per cent, 20,000 tons of 15 per cent and 20,000 tons of A1 Super brokens were made available, but the only bid accepted was for 15,000 tons of 15 per cent white rice. The government also sold to Iran 200,000 tons of 100 per cent Grade B for October 1993/January 1994. The price reflected the premium needed to get quality top-grade white rice during the second crop season. There were difficulties in loading current Iranian vessels because of sub-standard rice. Official estimates indicated a final crop for the 1992/93 year of 20,000,000 tons (Ed. presumably paddy), made up of 17,500,000 tons of main crop, and 2,500,000 tons of second crop. This was almost 3,000,000 tons higher than the 1991 crop and showed the problem the government was faced with in trying to maintain price levels to farmers. Thailand exported 437,898 tons in the first 26 days of July, mostly from government-sponsored contracts. Total exports for the year to 26th July were 2,241,267 tons. Government price support purchasing continued with the Public Warehouse Authorities and the MOF (Farmers' Co-op) taking 100,000 tons each, made up of 50,000 tons each 100 per cent B, and 5 per cent/15 per cent broken rice (*LRBAC* 30th July 1993 3). Six cargoes had been contracted for Nigeria, adding up to 70,000 tons, and all but 1 was for Thai parboiled 5 per cent non-sortexed, the remaining cargo being 100 per cent non-sortexed. With a change in power in Nigeria scheduled, it was questionable whether these vessels would be discharged without difficulty on arrival in Lagos. The first vessel, M/V *Silver Chariot* was due to arrive in the first week of September, having been delayed by a week to ten days whilst political events were assessed (*LRBAC* 31st August 1993 1). Total exports for July were 533,000 tons, bringing the total for the first 7 months of 1993 to 2,648,855 tons. Exports for August were likely to be 500,000 tons, with 353,683 tons loaded to 23rd August. The major activity was to Iran, the United Arab Republic, Iraq and Benin/Nigeria. Thai Government sales for Iran, Korea and Russia made up a good part of exports this year. There was some state business and some loadings of broken rice for Senegal. Current quotations were stowed in 50-kilo polypropylene bags (Ed. This was the first time polypropylene bags were quoted rather than jute, and 50-kilo bags instead of 100 kilo). (*LRBAC* 31st August 1993 3). At the beginning of October, the

Circular drew attention to the serious situation in Japan which had experienced the worst rice crops for almost 50 years, due to extreme wet and cold weather. Already Thailand had contracted to supply Japan with 100,000 tons of 100 per cent Grade B, together with 30,000 tons of glutinous rice. 1,400,000 tons could be required by Japan over the next 12 months, from all origins including Thailand (*LRBAC* 1st October 1993 1. An additional 459,743 tons were exported from Thailand in August to various destinations, and 170,000 tons to the 20th September. Business in September was mainly for parboiled rice and 10 per cent/15 per cent broken white rice to the Gulf. Quotations were for 50-kilo polypropylene bags for all the usual grades, but in addition, there were new categories of parboiled sortexed 100 per cent, and parboiled sortexed 5 per cent all at a premium (*LRBAC* lst October 1993 3). There was hardly any free trade business except in 10 per cent and 15 per cent to Dubai and parboiled to Benin/Nigeria. This was because Thai rice was overpriced compared with Vietnam. But now the government was operating an export incentive programme, which had already sold some 50,000 tons of broken rice at below the market rate. It hoped lower quality white rice could also be sold if suitable offers were given. Exports were sustained by Government sales, and up to 25th October, some 326,558 tons had been exported compared to an estimated 250,000 tons in September. Parboiled prices had risen due to increased demand (*LRBAC* 31st October 1993 3). In November, prices around the world rocketed for top-quality rice including 100 per cent Grade B from Thailand. There had been heavy buying from Japan. Little business was reported from Thailand except to Japan, Iran and Dubai. The rice policy of the new military leader in Nigeria had yet to be defined. But some of the old direct import licences for parboiled rice from Thailand had been utilised (*LRBAC* 30th November 1993 1). The *Circular* commented that in some quarters the Bangkok rice market was being likened to the casinos of Las Vegas or Atlantic City, which did not do justice to the difficult situation the Thai rice market was facing. For most of the year, the problem was supporting farmers with Government buying. The prices surged by 50 per cent due to Japanese buying. In November 100,000 tons were sold to Japanese traders for prompt shipment. A few weeks later but still in November, an additional 60,000 – 80,000 tons of 100 per cent B was bought at an excessive price by Japan. These purchases caused the Bangkok market to rise, fall, rise again and then fall again. Crop prospects were originally for 20,000,000 tons (Ed. of paddy?), slightly above the 1992 crop, but then projections were reduced by 1,500,000–2,000,000 tons. Exports for October were 429,529 tons and 286,300 for the first three weeks of November. There were healthy movements of parboiled to Benin, and an increase in shipments to South Africa (*LRBAC* 30th November 1993 1. *LRBAC* 30th November 1993 3). Following all the excitement in the rice market in November, December was rather similar with occasional purchases from Japan at high prices (*LRBAC* 31st December 1992 1). Thai exports had performed well during 1993, partly as a result of the Japanese purchases. It looked as though a total of 4,700,000–4,800,000 tons would be reached, which looked unlikely at the beginning of the year. The main buyers from Thailand were Iran, United Arab Emirates, Benin, South Africa, Sudan, the Philippines and Hong Kong, all of whom took over

200,000 tons each per annum. They were followed by Singapore, Malaysia, and the United States, each of which took between 150,000 and 200,000 tons annually. At the end of November, there was concern about very low water levels which might affect second crop plantings (*LRBAC* 31st December 1993 3).

Table 6.6 Thailand rice exports 1993 (metric tons)

	Month	*Total*
January	355,158.52	355,158.52
February	247,666.30	602,824.82
March	364,275.43	967,100.25
April	349,076.56	1,316,176.81
May	425,868.31	1,742,045.12
June	409,752.42	2,151,797.54
July	533,088.69	2,684,886.23
August	459,743.45	3,144,629.68
September	297,150.65	3,441,780.33
October	429,529.44	3,871,309.77
November	415,225.88	4,286,535.65
December	450,000.00[a]	4,736,535.65
Total exports	4,736,535.65	

[a] Estimate

(*LRBAC* 31st December 1993 3).

There was a 50 per cent devaluation of the CFA (Communaute Financiere Africaine) Franc which effectively doubled overnight the price of exports to major Francophone destinations such as Mauretania, Senegal, Ivory Coast, Benin, Cameroon, Mali and Burkina Faso (*LRBAC* 31st January 1994 1). Between 190,000 and 200,000 tons were negotiated for Japan for delivery in February/March, with strict quality standards, particularly concerning chemical residue (*LRBAC* 31st January 1994 2). Thai exports for December 1993 reached just under 516,000 tons which invalidated the estimate in the December report. So the figure for the calendar year 1993 was a total of 4,802,000 tons. As previously mentioned 200,000 tons of Thai 100 per cent B had been sold to Japan for shipment by the end of March. An Iranian delegation had been seeking 100,000 tons, and it was reported that there was a possible sale by one exporter of 100,000 tons 100 per cent Grade B basis Iran terms. As a result of the devaluation of the CFA, demand for parboiled rice declined. The Thai government held a tender for 68,000 tons in 5000-ton lots for parboiled rice 100 per cent non-sortexed, and a total of 40,000–50,000 tons was awarded divided between three Thai exporters. Japanese shipments continued, and by 24th January 350,000 tons had been exported (*LRBAC* 31st January 1994 3). Demand from Japan had dominated the world rice market since October 1993 but was now fading from the headlines (*LRBAC* 28th February 1994 1). From China, it was reported that Japan had stated that they preferred the Chinese quality of rice, which might affect Thai exports in due course (*LRBAC* 28th February 1994 1. *LRBAC* 28th February 1994 2). Exports for January 1994 reached 477,430 tons. There was a drop off during

February due to Chinese New Year and local Thai holidays, but exports in the first three weeks of the month were nonetheless 311,000 tons. There was a discussion over a contract for North Korea for 200,000 tons, but it was never executed and it seemed there would be a new contract for only 50,000 tons 15 per cent brokens. Thailand was suffering from a lack of demand for 100 per cent B as a result of reduced interest from Japan, and also for 5 per cent and 10 per cent due to competition from Vietnam for both Iran and Middle East markets in general. The market for parboiled rice to Cotonou in Benin was effectively closed, but there were hopes that the Philippines would finalise a contract. There was considerable concern within Thailand about available water for the second crop. Vietnam was still a cheaper quality supplier for the middle grades. Current quotations were for 50-kilo polypropylene or 100-kilo jute bags (Ed. Note that both polypropylene and jute bags are available) (*LRBAC* 28th February 1994 3). The lst of April was the start of the new financial year in Japan, and it was rumoured they would make more purchases as they would need to have imported 2,700,000 tons from October 1993 to September 1994. So far 685,000 tons had been sold to Japan from Thailand, and 590,000 tons had already been shipped leaving 95,000 tons yet to come. Of this, 570,000 tons were 100 per cent B, and 50,000 tons glutinous rice (*LRBAC* 31st March 1994 2). Exports from Thailand in February were 416,888 tons, which was high considering the holiday interruptions including Chinese New Year. During the first 28 days of March, 379,000 tons were shipped (*LRBAC* 31st March 1994 3). There were some sales of parboiled and parboiled *loonzain* from Thailand, and some activity in Central and South America. There was no significant increase in demand from Africa where Francophone countries were struggling to cope with the drastic devaluation of the CFA, although there were signs that things were picking up for the Nigerian market via Cotonou in Benin (*LRBAC* 30th April 1994 1). From Japan, it was reported that 100,000 tons of 100 per cent Grade B had been bought from Thailand at a premium over main crop prices. So far, over 500,000 tons had been shipped from Thailand to Japan with 150,000–200,000 tons yet to come (*LRBAC* 30th April 1994 2). In April, exports from Thailand to the 25th were 211,000 tons, significantly down on March, due to the Thai New Year holidays. Similar figures were expected for the next few months for Japan and the Middle East, plus regular container exports (Ed. This is the first reference to containers in Thailand). There would also be some parboiled exports. Plantings for wet crops were larger than originally expected because farmers were attracted by the high prices caused by Japanese purchases (*LRBAC* 30th April 1994 2). Whilst there was congestion in Vietnam, with at one stage 18–20 vessels loading or waiting to load, in Thailand there was a downturn in activity now the Japanese sales were completed (*LRBAC* 31st May 1994 1). Japan had apparently decided to take no more rice from Thailand for the time being. Exports for the month of April were only 285,619 tons, and May would be a little better with 244,600 tons for the first 24 days. The main crop was being specifically held for Japan (*LRBAC* 31st May 1994 3). The figure for May was 277,815 tons, considerably down on previous months due to a lack of Japanese shipments. June would probably be about 250,000 tons with 234,000 tons reached by the 27th. There were unconfirmed rumours of 100,000–150,000 tons of ordinary milled rice becoming possible government to government to Indonesia. To promote exports the Thai Rice Committee invited bids from Thai rice exporters at below market prices for 10 per cent brokens down to 35 per cent brokens, just to stimulate milling activity and subsequent export. There was considerable activity in parboiled, and there were commitments for parboiled 100 per cent sortexed down to ordinary 10 per cent non-sortexed. These included 1 vessel for North Yemen, 1 for South Africa, 1 for Somalia, 1 for Djibouti, 1 for Cotonou in Benin taking 22,000 tons, and one loading 16,000 tons for Nigeria, making prompt total shipments of 90,000–100,000 tons (*LRBAC* 30th June 1994 3). There was excitement as Indonesia came into the world rice market to buy 700,000–1,000,000 tons of 25 per cent for shipment by the end of February 1995. This was at a time when China had a poor crop due to large-scale flooding and was not expected to be an exporter of low-quality rice. The Chinese coastal states had been purchasing high-quality rice from Thailand and Vietnam, possibly some 200,000–300,000 tons. However, China was a noodle and rice-eating country, and would normally buy the cheaper commodity, which was wheat for noodles (*LRBAC* 31st July 1994 1). In August, the major shipments from Thailand were of parboiled rice, including 1 vessel for Yemen, 1 for South Africa, 1 for Somalia, 2 for Cotonou in Benin and 1 for Nigeria, making a volume of at least 100,000 tons. There were reports that the Thai Government had sold 200,000 tons of white rice 25 per cent brokens to Indonesia, and a further sale of 100,000 tons had been made to Indonesia by a group of private exporters. There were rumours of sales to China of various qualities. The supply of brokens was extremely short as a result of low sales of high-quality rice, and therefore a limited amount of brokens was available. The market for fragrant rice remained steady. Exports for the period 1st–25th July were 203,990 tons, and for June the total export figure was 270,972 tons (*LRBAC* 31st July 1994 3). Despite the extensive demand from Indonesia for low-quality rice, Thailand's prices were uncompetitive (*LRBAC* 31st August 1994 1). The loadings of 5 per cent, 10 per cent and 15 per cent to China from Thailand and Vietnam were not followed by further sales (*LRBAC* 31st August 1994 2). Demand for Thai parboiled remained strong with extensive shipments, and heavy rainfall which caused production problems for the parboiled industry. There were good prices for parboiled 100 per cent sortexed light golden colour, with discounts for lower qualities. Rice loadings up to the 29th August were 324,775 tons, compared to July's figure of 272,000 tons. But reasonably priced brokens or 35 per cent brokens were absent from the Bangkok market because of good demand, and lack of milling in the months when Thailand was uncompetitive against other origins, particularly Vietnam. But now shipments were taking place to Indonesia following government to government and private sales. Expectations were of a good new crop following very heavy rainfall which made water available to farmers after three or four years of low water stocks (*LRBAC* 31st August 1994 3). There was continued demand from Indonesia on world markets, and also from China where there had been central buying and buying from private purchasers. The Thai crop was expected at the usual time but was not significantly greater than last year (*LRBAC* 30th September 1994 1). There was some activity in Thailand with 5 per cent and 10 per cent for China (*LRBAC* 30th September 1994 2). The main action in the Thai marketplace was broken rice for West Africa, and smaller shipments to Indonesia, as well as vessels loading 25 per cent brokens for the government-to-government contract to Indonesia. Also, some 5 per cent and 10 per cent shipments to China are already referred to. There were rumours of a Thai Government contract for 20,000 tons 100 per cent Grade B for Iran for shipment in November/December, and 100,000 tons 100 per cent Grade B government-to-government to Malaysia, also November/December. In addition, there was a possible 100,000 tons of 25 per cent for Indonesia. Exports for August were 384,807 tons, which was an improvement in July, and 330,000 tons had already been moved in the first 26 days of September (*LRBAC* 30th September 1994 3). In Thailand, the main crop was expected to reach 18,000,000 tons (Ed. paddy?) some 9 per cent greater than the previous year, and the highest crop since 1989. It was the first year for several years that Thailand would move into the second crop with more than adequate water supplies. The total crop was expected to be about 19,800,000 tons (*LRBAC* 1st November 1994 1–2). Indonesia was the key to world market movements in September and October and had suffered a well-publicised drought with resulting crop damage. Their 1994 crop season was likely to be only 46,500,000 tons, some 2,000,000 tons down on a normal year, which explained how they had contracted an import figure of 1,500,000 tons (*LRBAC* 1st November 1994 1–2). In China, limited shipments continued from Thailand against old contracts (*LRBAC* 1st November 1994 2). In Thailand, in November the major news was the possibility of the Government allowing a U.S. Dollar $10 per ton export subsidy on any rice of 10 per cent brokens or lower including broken rice for individual shipments or orders of a minimum of 10,000 tons for shipment 1st December through to 28th February 1995. Government ratification was awaited. Meanwhile, there were shipments to China and Indonesia, as well as more traditional business, and exports reached 421,955 tons, the highest monthly figure since January. Final exports for September were 390,312 tons. Accumulated exports for the first ten months of 1994 were 3,563,519 tons. At an abortive tender run by the government, only 2000 (Ed 20,000?) tons of 100 per cent Grade B were offered against a requirement of 100,000 tons. This was an attempt by the Government to cover the first part of their sale to Iran of 230,000 tons. It was expected that the tender would be run again with possibly the very early new crop, or an increase in price the government was prepared to pay. The future price trend in Thailand was going to be controlled by the possibility of a Government export subsidy, the sale to Iran, and the prospect of further shipments to Indonesia. Also by new sales of high quality rice to Malaysia (*LRBAC* 1st November 1994 3). In China, old contracts were being shipped out of Thailand, and a new business was reported during November of some 5 per cent brokens from Thailand and also some 25 per cent. Shipment was prompt, and the Thai market expected regular small orders from China from 25,000 tons to 40,000 tons at a time. But there were also rumours that China was ready to start exporting again, particularly 35 per cent long shape (*LRBAC* 1st December 1994 1). Indonesia still controlled the market, and Thailand was expecting a delegation from there looking for possibly 300,000–400,000 tons (*LRBAC* 1st December 1994 2). Thai exports in October were 421,955 tons bringing the 10-month export figure to 3,500,000 tons. The first 28 days of November indicated an export figure of 490,000 tons, putting a figure for the calendar year of 4,500,000 tons within reach. There had been sales to China of lots of around 25,000 tons each, and letters of credit had arrived from Iran followed rapidly by vessel nominations to lift rice against a Government contract for 230,000 tons. There was an expectation of more demand from China and Indonesia. There was also demand for broken rice for small shipments of 6000–8000 tons per vessel for Indonesia, and an extensive demand for West Africa where some 80,000–90,000 tons had been contracted, much for shipment in December, but some for January. There was interest in the market in Bangkok's ability to load five or six vessels scheduled from about 25th November to the middle of December. The parboiled market was in the doldrums in recent weeks because of significant stocks in Cotonou in Benin (*LRBAC* 1st December 1994 3).

In February 1995, the *Circular* commented that just after everyone had forgotten the Japanese influence from the latter half of 1993 through to the first quarter of 1994, a drastic reduction of crops in Indonesia had turned that country from being a small exporter to being a major importer. The vagaries of the weather pattern had also delayed crops in Thailand and Pakistan, and severely reduced crops in China (*LRBAC* 1st February 1995 1). In China, the Central Buying Agency was buying large quantities of rice of all grades from Thailand and Vietnam, and there was also private business to provincial coastal buyers for high-quality Thai 100 per cent Grade B and 5 per cent broken rice (*LRBAC* 1st February 1995 2). Indonesia continued to receive shipments from Thailand, and other sources including Pakistan, Vietnam and Burma (*LRBAC* 1st February 1995 2). In Thailand, the Chinese New Year holidays intervened, but port facilities in Bangkok were stretched to the full with a whole line of vessels waiting to berth and load rice. Indications were that January would achieve exports of 600,000 tons and the same was expected for February. China and Indonesia were regularly buying from Thailand and there was an Iranian sale in the background. There was also demand for 100 per cent broken rice which had driven up the price, making the difference in price between 100 per cent broken rice (Ed. the lowest grade) and 100 per cent Grade B (Ed. the highest grade) the least for very many years. (*LRBAC* 1st February 1995 3).

Table 6.7 Thailand rice exports 1994 (metric tons)

January	477,430
February	416,888
March	380,000
April	285,619
May	277,815
June	270,972
July	272,000
August	384,807
September	390,312
October	421,955
November	518,025
December	651,525
Total exports	4,711,348

(*LRBAC* 1st February 1995 3).

Worldwide there was demand from Bangladesh, and China was thought to need about 1,500,000 tons. Bangladesh was reported to have bought in February 120,000 tons of parboiled from Thailand and India, and North Korea was thought to have made a barter trade with the Thai government for 300,000 tons of rice (*LR-BAC* 28th February 1995 1). This turned out to be true, and the agreement by North Korea with the Thai Government was for 300,000 tons of 35 per cent brokens by barter, of which 100,000 tons were to be shipped in March. But some of these terms were still in doubt. Indonesia bought 40,000 tons of 25 per cent broken rice from the Public Warehouse organisation. Bangladesh bought 50,000 tons of a maximum of 20 per cent (Ed. 25 per cent?) brokens from the Thai government and 37,500 tons of parboiled rice from private exporters. There was a forthcoming purchase in the domestic market by the Thai Government for shipment to Iran. The last shipments under the government export subsidy programme had to be made by the end of February. Loading had speeded up in the last few weeks to meet the deadline, with export figures during the last week of February of 182,362 tons, about 54,000 tons more than the previous week. January shipments reached a record of 680,321 tons and the delivered quantity for 1st–27th February was 619,560 tons, another enormous quantity (*LRBAC* 28th February 1995 3). The government introduced a new export subsidy scheme on 1st April to give a U.S. Dollar $10 per ton reduction in price for 400,000 tons of rice with 10 per cent and higher broken content. The 300,000 tons deal between the Thai government and North Korea was confirmed (*LRBAC* 31st March 1995 1). Export levels continued high in March with 512,219 tons shipped from 1st - to17th March. The North Korean government finally made their purchase of 300,000 tons of 35 per cent and the Thai Government started purchasing to cover this. The Thai government subsidy mentioned above was to run from 1st April to 31st July. The Government also entered the market to cover 150,000 tons of 100 per cent Grade B for its sale to Iran. It also offered exporters the opportunity to sell 87 tons of 35 per cent to North Korea for each 100 tons of 100 per cent B sold to Iran, at a price above the market. China and Indonesia were the major customers of Thailand this year (*LRBAC* 31st March 1995 2–3).

Table 6.8 Thailand rice exports to China and Indonesia 1995 (metric tons)

	China	*Indonesia*
January	187,430	156,980
February	213,470	129,360
March[a]	169,940	42,690

[a] 1st–20th.
(*LRBAC* 31st March 1995 2–3).

China's requirements could only be guessed, although prompt shipments from Vietnam of 5 per cent and 10 per cent were snapped up, and there was also trade from Thailand in all grades down to 100 per cent brokens (*LRBAC* 1st May 1995 2). Small quantities of rice were being shipped from Thailand to Indonesia (*LRBAC*

1st May 1995 2). Total figures for Thailand for March were 580,865 tons, but April was only likely to reach 360,000 tons because of the holidays at the beginning of the month. This was the first month that Thailand had not exported 500,000 tons since October 1994. The Government announced they would make available up to 400,000 tons of export subsidy at U.S. Dollars $10 per ton, with a U.S. Dollars $5 penalty on defaulted contracts. There were purchases by the Government for its 100 per cent Grade B sales to Iran and for its sales of 35 per cent brokens to North Korea. 1st May was a public holiday in Thailand (*LRBAC* 1st May 1995 3). In China, there was a slowdown in spot trading from Thailand due to a drastic price increase there (*LRBAC* 31st May 1995 1). Thai exports had been running at high levels from October 1994 with 550,000 tons per month being shipped, and sometimes over 600,000 tons. The exception was in April 1995 when there were several Thai holidays and only 374,147 tons were exported. The figure for the first 21 days of May was 351,000 tons. But Thailand was hit by a shortage of lighters which caused problems moving rice down to the port. The situation would not improve soon as lighters were also required to discharge corn and soybean meal which the Government had allowed to be imported in significant quantities. There were rumours of sales to the Philippines of 75,000–80,000 tons of 35 per cent broken grain in exchange for fertiliser, with the balance in cash. Non-government buyers in Iran bought 60,000–70,000 tons of 100 per cent Grade B standard Thai terms (*LRBAC* 31st May 1995 3). The extensive export commitments from Thailand were likely to cause problems unless the wet crop was greater than previously seen (*LRBAC* 30th June 1995 1). But demand from China for Thai rice was considerably reduced because of high prices (*LRBAC* 30th June 1995 1). There was congestion in Bangkok with a shortage of barges to move the rice downriver adding to slow loading conditions and general shipping delays. Exports for May were 526,393 tons and 456,830 tons up to 27th June despite rains. Rumours continued about a sale of 100,000 tons of 35 per cent brokens to the Philippines, as well as additional business to Iran for 100 per cent B (*LRBAC* 30th June 1995 3). There were reports of a sale of one cargo of 100 per cent B to an Iranian private buyer, as well as 3 cargoes to the Iranian Government on non-Iranian terms for shipment in August/September. Iranian vessels continued to load and new vessels were nominated. Loading had been slow as a clamp down on illegal immigrants resulted in a shortage of stevedores and lighters. But after elections the situation eased (*LRBAC* 1st August 1955 3). Five or six cargoes of 5 per cent rice, a high quality, were purchased for China. Malaysia had requested offers of lots of 10,000 tons of 100 per cent B for prompt shipment. The weather was very poor, and there continued to be a shortage of stevedores due to tight controls on illegal immigrants. Three vessels were expected to arrive in Iran at the beginning of September, but it was difficult to buy 100 per cent B to load them. 2 or 3 vessels were expected to load white and parboiled rice for South and West Africa. But it was always difficult to produce parboiled at this time of year as the rice could not be dried outside because of the rain. Export figures for 1st–28th August were 332,265 tons (*LRBAC* 1st September 1995 3). There was widespread flooding in China and the general availability of rice in the international market was limited to quantities previously contracted from Thailand and potentially India

(*LRBAC* 2nd October 1995 1). Stocks in the Bangkok area were almost exhausted, and there was widespread flooding affecting large areas of the major rice-growing paddy fields. These were the worst floods for more than a decade, but rice is more resilient to flood than drought and it was not clear how much damage would result. However, transportation of paddy or anything else from up-country was severely disrupted. For the month of August exports were 376,875 tons and 354,656 tons up to the 25th of September (*LRBAC* 2nd October 1995 3). There was a continued lack of stock in Bangkok due to the weather, and heavy flooding in some areas, although the floods were confined to the north, north-eastern and central provinces. Exports in September reached 435,854 tons, giving a total for the first 9 months of the year of 4,554,344 tons. Exports in October were expected to be over 315,000 tons, despite the weather. There had been significant sales to Malaysia, said to be replacing previously defaulted sales, and new business to Indonesia for 100,000 tons 25 per cent brokens (*LRBAC* 1st November 1995 3–4). In November, Thai prices were well above Indian prices for comparable grades (*LRBAC* 1st December 1995 1). Five or 6 cargoes of 25 per cent were traded for December/January shipment, as well as 100 per cent Grade B thought to be for South America. October exports were 337,186 tons, bringing the total for the first 10 months up to 4,891,530 tons. Crop damage from the floods was raised from 600,000 tons to 1,100,000 tons basis paddy. But the second crop could produce 3,400,000–3,500,000 tons, which would be 1,000,000 tons more than previous good years, compensating for the losses (*LRBAC* 1st December 1995 3).

In January, the *Circular* commented that 1995 had been an extraordinary year with a huge increase in world trade in rice to nearly 19,000,000 tons, an increase of 2,500,000 tons over the previous year. China and Indonesia had imported nearly 3,000,000 tons each due to large shortfalls in their domestic crops. But there were shortages in supply from the usual exporters like Thailand, Vietnam, Burma and Pakistan. The situation was only saved by the emergence of India as an exporter, which had a large surplus of government stock to sell at the beginning of the year, and later in the year private rice to sell after a good harvest. But this was marred by India's huge logistical problems, and by the FCI (government) increasing the price of contracts. Burma and Vietnam could not fulfil commitments later in the year because they had already sold so much, in Vietnam's case straight over the border into China. Thailand continued to export despite being affected later in the year by flooding (*LRBAC* 2nd January 1996 2). China would probably be a large importer in the coming year, particularly to the coastal states which would buy high-quality milled rice from Thailand and Vietnam (*LRBAC* 2nd January 1996 2). In December 1995, the Philippines had bought from the Thai government 150,000 tons of 25 per cent, with an option for a further 50,000 tons. The Thai government continued to purchase 100 per cent B for their sale to Iran. So far 100,000 tons had been sold. Sales of high quality rice continued to be made to the Chinese coastal states, and there was a 5,000 tons sale of glutinous rice to Laos under German aid. In January, new sales of 25 per cent brokens were reported to Indonesia, including significantly 20,000–30,000 tons of fragrant rice. Malaysia bought 30,000 tons of 100 per cent B and 10,000 tons of 10 per cent. The estimated main crop for 1996 was 17,500,000 tons, down 1,000,000 tons on 1995. But the second crop was estimated at 3,500,000 tons, an increase of 1,000,000 tons on 1995. About 1,000,000 tons of the second crop would be rice re-planted to replace that lost in the floods, to be harvested in February 1996. The export figure for the first eleven months of 1995 was 5,317,192 tons (*LRBAC* 2nd January 1996 4). The Philippines committed themselves to importing 884,000 tons, mainly 25 per cent brokens. Of this Thailand was to supply 150,000 tons, Vietnam 362,000 tons, China 225,000 tons, India 125,000 tons and the United States 20,000 tons (*LRBAC* 26th February 1996 1). Although China had declared it would not be an importer or an exporter this year, the *Circular* thought there would be rice imported directly over the Burmese and Vietnamese borders, and regular high quality rice imports from Thailand and Vietnam to coastal states (*LRBAC* 26th February 1996 1). Thailand was on holiday in the third week of February. In January, the Thai government had continued to cover their commitments to Iran by purchasing 83,000 tons of 100 per cent B. The main shipments so far this year had been to Iran, the Philippines, China, Malaysia, and Indonesia as well as parboiled to South Africa and Cotonou in Benin. There were rumours of a further 200,000 tons to the Philippines, and 300,000 tons to North Korea. However, North Korea had payment problems and had not yet paid for rice shipped 4 years ago. 150,000 tons bought last year would not be shipped until the government had received barter commodities from North Korea to the value of the rice. There were 50,000 tons for Russia, of which 1 cargo had been sold but payment remained a problem. Also 150,000–200,000 tons for Iran, although the price was still under negotiation (*LRBAC* 26th February 1996 3–4). Commitments included 150,000 tons to the Philippines to be shipped by the end of April, and 110,000 tons to Malaysia by tender for April/May/June. Also, 2–3 cargoes for Iran to be shipped April/May, one cargo of 100 per cent B for Syria, and 15,500 tons of brokens for Mauritania. There were small lots of business going continually to Hong Kong, Malaysia and China. Exports for February were 430,991 tons, which was substantially down on the December and January figures which were close to 600,000 tons for each month (*LRBAC* 1st April 1996 3). The Philippines had so far imported 150,000 tons from Thailand this year (*LRBAC* 1st May 1996 2). In Thailand, the government gave a U.S. Dollar $10 per ton subsidy for 10 per cent brokens and less exported between April 15th and May 15 per cent. This appears to have resulted in 300,000 tons of business over and above normal business. Export figures for March 1996 totalled 492,731 tons, bringing the total for the year so far to 1,486,550 tons (*LRBAC* lst May 1996 2). The U.S. Dollar $10 subsidy was extended until 15th June, stimulating another flurry of low quality rice sales (*LRBAC* 3rd June 1996 1). Recent purchasing in Thailand and Vietnam suggested Senegal was buying (*LRBAC* 3rd June 1996 1). The second crop was poorer than usual. Early rains had slowed loading, causing a shortage of lighters and transport difficulties to Bangkok. Production of parboiled rice was also affected, because although mechanical dryers did exist, most parboiled rice was still sun dried. There was strong demand for parboiled from Nigeria. Export figures for April totalled 417,076 tons, and 444,505 tons up to the 28th May (*LRBAC* 3rd June 1996 3–4). On the 15th June, the last rice under the government subsidy scheme was shipped, but due to heavy rains delaying delivery of rice and loading, up to 20 ships missed the deadline and did not qualify for the subsidy. A backlog of vessels continued to create congestion at the port. Some A1 special was sold. (Ed. a low grade of brokens). There was a tender for 35,000 tons of 100 per cent B for Japan, of which 4500 tons was sold for prompt shipment, and 5000–6000 tons for August shipment. Prices for high-quality rice such as this were encouraged by vessels for 35,000 tons and 12,000 tons loading for Iran. A Thai government delegation was in China hoping to persuade the Chinese government to purchase 30,000 tons of rice under their official protocol agreement. The delegation was then going on to Indonesia to try to persuade them also to buy. Sales of note during the month included 40,000 tons of 15 per cent to Malaysia. Export figures for May totalled 518,324 tons, and 274,276 tons from 1st to 18th June (*LRBAC* 4th July 1996 3). In the Philippines, talks about purchases of rice from Thailand and Vietnam had not resulted in business (*LRBAC* 5th August 1996 3). In August, several cargoes of A1 Special were sold. There were rumours of purchasing by North Korea, but payment remained a problem. Export figures for June were 422,298 tons, making a total of 2,847,244 tons for the first half of the year. The figure for 1st - 30th July was 399,268 tons (*LRBAC* 5th August 1996 3). Of particular interest in August were the first sales to the EEC under the free quota system compensating non-EEC countries for the loss of market in Sweden, Austria and Finland. The Thai quota was 21,500 tons with 60 per cent to the Public Warehouse Organisation, and 40 per cent to private exporters. Both parboiled rice and fragrant rice was included (*LRBAC* 3rd September 1996 1). China continued to buy some high-quality rice from Thailand (*LRBAC* 3rd September 1996 1). Indonesia had discussion with Thailand for the purchase of 200,000 tons of rice in exchange for military equipment, but it was not clear whether this had been concluded (*LRBAC* 3rd September 1996 3). Fragrant rice prices rose due to the implementation of the quota system for Europe. The quota of 21,455 tons of wholly milled rice, 1812 tons of brown rice and 31,200 tons of broken rice would normally have been spread over the whole year, but because of the delay in deciding implementation it had all been sold at once this year. Prices were very high for fragrant milled and parboiled milled, and the fragrant price had risen by about 10 per cent. Malaysia was to tender for 30,000 tons Thai white rice 100 per cent Grade B, and it was rumoured that Iran had bought 3 or 4 cargoes of 100 per cent B on private basis. Export figures for July were 415,273 tons (*LRBAC* 3rd September 1996 3). In Thailand, there were reports of floods in the North. Prices in general were falling but in fragrant rice they were booming. Parboiled shipments were being made to Nigeria. 12,000 tons of 100 per cent B were made to Syria by tender, but prices were high because Syria regularly rejected cargoes after arrival. Fragrant rice appeared for the first time in the list of quoted prices, and so did glutinous rice (*LRBAC* 3rd October 1996 3). Harvest time in South East Asia was nearing (*LRBAC* 4th November 1996 1). At a tender in Japan, Thailand sold 28,000 tons of 100 per cent B and 5000 tons of glutinous brokens, 1700 tons of Al Super and 600 tons of glutinous 10 per cent. Another tender was expected late November/early December (*LRBAC* 4th November 1996 3). There was to be an election in Thailand on 17th November. New crop fragrant was already becoming available but ordinary quality not until mid-December. There were large purchases of parboiled by Nigeria for arrival before Christmas. Exports during October were to Iran, Malaysia and Nigeria. Exports up to October

28th were 308,662 tons (*LRBAC* 4th November 1996 3–4). Japan held another tender, and purchased 130,000 tons of mainly medium grain including 30,000 tons from Thailand, 10,000 tons from China, 12,000 tons from Australia, and 70,000 tons from the United States (*LRBAC* 3rd December 1996 1. *LRBAC* 3rd December 1996 3). The elections took place on the 17th November but the new coalition government had still not been formed. Reports were that the main crop harvest would be 5–10 per cent below original forecasts, but still better than the previous year. In the Japanese tender, five lots of 100 per cent B were sold for shipment December/January 15th. Also 5000 tons of glutinous brokens at good prices, reflecting the high quality required for Japan (*LRBAC* 3rd December 1996 3–4). Despite the fact that harvest time had arrived, prices rose, particularly for fragrant rice. This was because the crop was late, and exporters having sold large volumes short were finding themselves squeezed. Prices for fragrant rice were reaching new records because the crop was 10 per cent less than last year, and China was purchasing large quantities to arrive before their New Year. A United Nations food and medicine deal for Iraq had arrived, and Iraq had since held a tender for 60,000 tons of 10 per cent brokens with offers invited from Thailand, Vietnam, Pakistan and India (*LRBAC* 31st December 1996 1). New crop would not arrive before January, and field and milling yields were low making it difficult to obtain 100 per cent B, and increasing the availability of broken rice. There were several sales of parboiled 100 per cent sortexed to Nigeria. In a recent Malaysia tender 8000 tons of 100 per cent B were sold, 8000 tons of fragrant and 4000 tons of glutinous rice. There was strong demand from China for milled fragrant rice, and prices of fragrant had risen sharply. The Thai levy free quota for the EEC was announced, and it would be channelled entirely through private exporters. It would be sold in three lots and would amount to 21,455 tons. Prices would be high as exporters had to pay a levy of U.S. Dollars $200 for every ton to the Government (*LRBAC* 31st December 1996 3–4).

The new rice year began in a surprising fashion with the Thai rice market strong, although it normally fell with the arrival of the harvest. The Philippines bought 50,000 tons from Thailand, and it was thought they would buy 500,000 tons for shipment during the first half of the year (*LRBAC* 3rd February 1997 1). Prices for fragrant continued to increase as demand was high for this quality. The Philippines bought 50,000 tons of 25 per cent or 35 per cent for shipment February/March, with a further 150,000 tons concluded subject to approval. Exports for the first 27 days of January were 327,062 tons. The export volume for 1996 totalled 5,250,533 tons (*LRBAC* 3rd February 1997 3–4). The only sizeable new demand in the world was from the Philippines, which bought 205,000 tons of 25 per cent from Thailand and 100,000 tons of 25 per cent from Vietnam, with an option for a further 100,000 tons and 100,000 tons of optional origin of 25 per cent with another 100,000 tons buyers' option (*LRBAC* 3rd March 1997 1) (Ed. Clearly there were problems in the Philippines.). The Philippines purchase of 205,000 tons were for shipment March to June. 80,000 tons of fragrant brokens were sold to the trade. Malaysia bought 5000 tons of glutinous and 10,000 tons of 100 per cent B. There were no signs of the harvest of the late planted new crop. The fragrant market remained firm with strong demand. The volume of vessels to load was extremely low. Total exports for

January were 377,948 tons, and for the first 24 days of February, they were 235,551 tons (*LRBAC* 3rd March 1997 3). On the international rice market, China re-emerged as a rice exporter, selling 25 per cent broken rice. Meanwhile, the Philippines had purchased 655,000 tons from various sources, and might buy more (*LRBAC* 2nd April 1997 1). An Iranian delegation to Thailand left empty-handed as suppliers would not accept Iranian payment terms. But in a Malaysian tender, 10,000 tons of 100 per cent B were sold, and also 10,000 tons of fragrant rice, and 3000 tons of glutinous rice, all for April shipment. Fragrant rice was in good demand. Total rice exports for February were 287,334 tons, and for the first 24 days of March, 283,450 tons (*LRBAC* 2nd April 1997 3). Thailand sold 250,000–300,000 tons of 100 per cent B to Iran for May/June/July/August shipment and large volumes of parboiled to Nigeria for May/June shipment. Large quantities of fragrant brokens were also sold for export. 80,000 tons of unspecified brokens were sold mainly to West Africa (*LRBAC* 2nd May 1997 1). The 250,000–300,000 tons of 100 per cent B to Iran mentioned above were purchased mainly through international traders, but some directly, for May/June/July/August shipment. Much of this rice was covered in Thailand, but some traders had options to supply Vietnamese rice which they did for at least two cargoes. Nigeria had been purchasing heavily for May/June/July shipment, and including shipments in April could be committed to as much as 200,000 tons of parboiled rice. There was a tender for Malaysia for 90,000 tons of 100 per cent B, 10 per cent and 15 per cent, with shipments of 30,000 tons per month for May/June/July. A large number of vessels were loading A1 super fragrant brokens, and vessels were also loading 50,000 tons of 25 per cent for the Philippines. The newspapers said that rice millers and exporters would be entitled to incentives as part of a government scheme to push up second crop paddy prices. There would be loans of 5 per cent to traders who agreed to buy 1,000,000 tons of paddy, and loans of 5 per cent to exporters who exported at least 500,000 tons during the qualifying period. Export figures for March totalled 374,835 tons, and from lst April to 31st April 247,608 tons. At the end of May, Thailand was on holiday for a few days (*LRBAC* 2nd May 1997 3). Prices in Thailand increased sharply in May as a result of vessels coming to load high quality white and parboiled for Iran and Nigeria. There were problems with the Iranian inspectors over grain length, so loading was very slow. Nine vessels loaded 25 per cent for the Philippines, and others loaded for Malaysia and China. Total exports for April were 418,655 tons and up to 26th May were 307,060 tons. As of 18th April 1997 new standard export specifications were agreed between the Rice Exporters' Association, the Ministry of Commerce, the Ministry of Agriculture, the Rice Millers' Association and the SGS (Ed. the inspection, verification and certification company). Most changes were minimal except for the amount of black and partially black kernels allowed in parboiled rice (*LRBAC* 3rd June 1997 1. *LRBAC* 3rd June 1997 3). There were heavy loadings in Thailand for the Philippines, Iran and Nigeria (*LRBAC* 2nd July 1997 1). Prices increased due to the heavy loadings of 100 per cent B for Iran, 25 per cent for the Philippines, and parboiled 100 per cent sortexed for Nigeria. There was also a tender for Japan for 28,500 tons of Thai 100 per cent B, and 10,500 tons of broken rice A1 super (Ed. a low grade). Exports for May were 395,834 tons, with total exports for the first 5 months at 1,855,028 tons, a reduction of 23.4 per cent on last year. Exports for June were 473,184 tons (*LRBAC* 2nd July 1997 3). At the beginning of August the Thai government devalued the Thai Baht by as much as 26 per cent. Prices of parboiled however were unchanged because of substantial demand from Nigeria and West Africa (*LRBAC* 4th August 1997 1). The Baht had been in a basket of currencies trading in a narrow range with the U.S. Dollar, but for political and economic reasons the Government had now allowed it to float and find its own level. The monsoon had been disappointing with particular danger for fragrant rice which is normally planted in August and harvested in November. Exports for June reached 473,184 tons, bringing the total for the year to 2,328,212 tons. Exports for the first 21 days of July came to 274,707 tons (*LRBAC* 4th August 1997 3). There was severe flooding in Vietnam. In Thailand the currency devalued a further 10 per cent against the U.S. Dollar, sending shock waves through the world rice market. But other Asian economies had also suffered substantial devaluations, reducing the importing powers of countries such as the Philippines, Indonesia and Malaysia. The *Circular* then commented that *El Nino* (in bold) represented a real danger in many areas of the world, and predictions suggested that the effect would be even greater than in 1982/83 with the same weather abnormalities but more severe. Potential droughts would affect Central and Southern Africa, Australia, Indonesia, Thailand, India and Pakistan, with abnormally cold and wet weather and possible floods in Peru, Argentina, Uruguay and Southern Brazil (*LRBAC* 1st September 1997 1). The *Circular* also reported on the terrible situation in North Korea, and the European Union held a tender to buy 41,275 tons of 35 per cent broken long grain to arrive in Korea within 45 days. Acceptable origins were Vietnam or Thailand. But Vietnam withdrew and it seemed the business would go to Thailand (*LRBAC* 1st September 1997 2). Thailand was now the cheapest origin for almost all grades. The Baht fell further against the U.S. Dollar, and was down about 35 per cent over the past few months. The Government had taken steps to stabilise the currency but without success. An agreement was reached between the Thai Government and the IMF for a package of loans with tough terms attached, including increasing VAT from 7 per cent to 10 per cent, sharp increases on business taxes, and government projects cut. Further money had been lent to the Thai Government by Japan and Brunei. Malaysia, Indonesia and the Philippines were in a similar predicament regarding their currencies. Because of a general lack of confidence, little business had been concluded. In Thailand the fall in the value of the Baht had led to imported materials like fertiliser and pesticides for the coming crop increasing in cost. Some purchases of rice were made by international traders for broken rice, and Iraq purchased 30,000 tons of Thai 10 per cent brokens through the UN oil for food agreement, shipment October/November. 2 cargoes had been sold to Iran on Iranian terms for September/October shipment. Exports for July were 425,212 tons, bringing the total for the first 7 months of the year to 2,753,773 tons. During the first 25 days of August a total of 329,469 tons were exported (*LRBAC* lst September 1997 3). From the United States, it was reported that the huge differential between prices in Thailand and prices in the United States was not sustainable. U.S. prices were expected to fall, but did have support from the advantage the United States had in selling rice to Southern and Central America. But if the differential continued so large there was every chance that exemption would be given allowing imports of Asian rice to these markets (*LRBAC* 1st September 1997 3–4). Prices in Thailand increased sharply. The Philippines made an international purchase of 350,000 tons, but Thailand received no direct business, and Vietnam only 100,000 tons (*LRBAC* 3rd October 1997 1). The 100,000 tons from Vietnam for the Philippines was 25 per cent brokens for arrival January/February 1998, and other origins were being considered for the remaining 200,000 tons (*LRBAC* 3rd October 1997 2). From North Korea it was reported that the European Union tender for 41,275 tons of 35 per cent brokens long grain white rice to arrive with 45 days did go to Thailand. Destinations were Nampo (on the Yellow Sea on the south-west of the Korea just south of Pyongyang), and Chongjin (on the north-east of the Korean peninsula on the Sea of Japan, just south of Vladivostok in Russia) (*LRBAC* 3rd October 1997 3). In Thailand the market was volatile in September due to economic uncertainty, and it was rumoured that the Prime Minister would be forced to step down, but on 26th September he was still in power and survived a vote of no confidence. The Baht continued to weaken. The Prime Minister changed the Ministers of Commerce and Finance. The Baht fell again. Recent business included 5 cargoes of 100 per cent Grade B, 4 of which were destined for Brazil and some 25 per cent destination unspecified covered by merchants. There was a tender held in Japan under the GATT minimum access agreement for 28,000 tons of 100 per cent B, 1,000 tons of glutinous, and 6,000 tons of A1 Super for shipment 20th October/30th November 1997. The prices agreed were high but included difficult requirements for Japan regarding pesticides and toxins, and 30 kilo packing with marks printed on sticky labels. In a World Food Programme tender 4,500 tons of Thai 35 per cent brokens were sold for Rwanda. In a round of business done by the Philippines, Thailand was not successful. Parboiled shipments continued to Nigeria and South America. Exports for August were 412,916 tons bringing the total for the first 8 months of the year to 3,166,645 tons. During the first 29 days of September 447,437 tons were loaded (*LRBAC* 3rd October 1997 3). The Baht weakened again, and was only saved by an announcement by the Prime Minister that he intended to resign on 6th November. The Baht stabilised. The Prime Minister's resignation would not mean a new election but a re-organisation of the coalition Government. It was not clear who would be next Prime Minister. There had been a severe decline in the Thai economy. Many smaller companies had had their trade finance withdrawn by some of the smaller banks, and even the larger banks were only offering trade finance on stricter terms. In the North East where fragrant rice was grown conditions had been excellent. Acreage had increased due to the previous year's high prices. Both fragrant and glutinous were expected to be harvested mid-November, with the other varieties in December. On 23rd October, Japan held another tender for 30,000 tons of 100 per cent Grade B, 5000 tons of broken rice A1 Super, and 5,000 tons of 10 per cent brokens. The prices were high as they had to comply with Japan's tough phytosanitary requirements including limits on pesticides and insecticides. Exports for October were 465,349 tons, bringing the total for the year to 4,094,425 tons. During the first 3 days of November, a total of 34,634 tons had been shipped (*LRBAC*

6th November 1997 4). Prices rose in the Far East, particularly in Thailand, due to the early entry of Indonesia into the market as a buyer, possibly for as much as 500,000 tons. There were concerns about the drought being faced by Indonesia, and it seemed they would need more than 2,000,000 tons (*LRBAC* 4th December 1997 1). This reflected the comments made in September of the effects of the current *El Nino* (*EN*SO), comparing it with that of 1982/83 (*LRBAC* lst September 1997 1). The Prime Minister resigned on 6th November and Mr Chuan Leekpai agreed to be the new Prime Minister. The Baht rose. On or about 15th November Indonesian buyers came into the market for 400,000 tons, including many private buyers rather than the usual government buyer. This seems to have been for 25 per cent brokens and traders were also covering commitments to the Philippines for 25 per cent brokens concluded about two months previously. The Indonesian shipments were for December/January with the major emphasis on December, whereas the Philippines shipments were for January/February/March. The fragrant harvest was a little early but there was only one fragrant crop in the year. Much of the fragrant crop was stored and released slowly during the year to avoid too great an impact on prices at harvest time, and to ensure fragrant was available over the year.

Table 6.9 Thailand Ministry of Agriculture estimate for production of rice varieties 1998 (metric tons 000)

	1996	*per cent*	*1997*	*per cent*	*1998*[a]	*per cent*
Total	17,728	100.00	17,781	100.00	17,839	100.00 + 0.32 per cent
White rice	12,146	68.51	12,323	69.30	12,552	70.36 + 1.85 per cent
Glutinous rice	5,581	31.48	5,458	30.69	5,286	29.63 – 3.15 per cent
Fragrant rice	4,530	25.55	3,976	22.36	4,662	26.13 + 17.00 per cent

Note:

a Fragrant rice is included in the overall figures for white rice and also listed separately (*LRBAC* 4th December 1997 2–3).

Further purchases by Indonesia and the Philippines caused excitement in the international rice market. Indonesia initially bought 1,000,000 tons, and then sanctioned another 500,000 tons bringing the total to 1,500,000 tons. The Philippines also returned to purchase a further 200,000 tons with options for another 200,000 tons of which 100,000 tons plus a 100,000 tons option was from the Vietnamese Government. This brought the total bought by the Philippines to 550,000 or 750,000 tons depending on whether the options were included or not (*LRBAC* 6th January 1998 1). The Baht fell yet again, and was fluctuating wildly causing great uncertainty to exporters. Exports were expected to reach 600,000 tons for December, and about 600,000 tons in January so there was not much rice left for other sales. Exporters were finding it difficult to cover commitments they had already made. Most of the Indonesian business mentioned above would come from Thailand, with much of the business concluded without the involvement of international merchants. An Iranian delegation was offered 100 per cent B on standard terms but rejected the prices as too high. Discussions continued with individual exporters, and there were rumours of eight cargoes having been concluded, but no further details were known. The Philippines were discussing the purchase of 150,000 tons of 25 per cent brokens. In a recent World Food Programme tender for Iraq, 6700 tons of 10 per cent brokens shipment 20th January to 20th February was awarded to Thailand and Vietnam at the suppliers' option. There was an increase in demand for fragrant rice from China, and the next tranche of TRQ (Tariff Rate Quota) for Europe caused fragrant prices to jump sharply, particularly fragrant 100 per cent Grade B Hong Kong quality, with African quality somewhat less. Thai rice looked cheap compared to other suppliers. Traditionally Thai rice had loyal followers who would buy it at a premium over other origins. 100 per cent B continued to sell. Because of the fall in the currency, farmers were getting high prices. But the price also took into account the higher cost of imported goods like fertiliser and insecticides. In contrast, A1 Super brokens (Ed. a low quality) looked expensive. Exports in December were 742,667 tons, a record for one month. This brought the total for 1997 to 5,272,211 tons, well beyond earlier expectations of only 4,600,000–4,800,000 tons (*LRBAC* 6th January 1998 3).

It was the year of the Tiger, and in February the holidays were under way in the Far East. The Thai Baht fell further but was less volatile. Demand from Indonesia and the Philippines continued to drive the international rice market (*LRBAC* 2nd February 1998 1). Over the Christmas holidays and early January, Iran officials made a tour of the Far East, including Thailand, Vietnam and Pakistan, and they bought nine cargoes of Thai rice via international traders. This was on partial Iranian terms for shipment from February through April. The millers, already heavily committed, raised their prices sharply and even with the Baht weakening, prices rose 100 per cent B. A U.S. delegation that had previously been in Indonesia arrived in Bangkok in the middle of January, and was encouraged by the improved economic situation in Thailand and the steps the Thai government had taken to tackle the economy. They expressed their hope that the United States would be able to give some direct support to Thailand. This helped the Baht recover. The Philippines, in negotiation with the Thai government, bought 100,000 tons of 5 per cent (Ed. 25 per cent?) brokens for shipment in March, April and May, with an option for another 50,000 tons. Exports for the first 25 days in January totalled 556,106 tons but slowed in the last week of January due to holidays (*LRBAC* 2nd February 1996 2–3).

Table 6.10 Thailand exports 1997 (metric tons 000)

January	377,948
February	287,899
March	374,835
April	418,655
May	395,834
June	473,184
July	425,212
August	412,916
September	462,718
October	465,349
November	435,277
December	742,677

Note: Total 5,272,494.
(*LRBAC* 2nd February 1998 2–3).

The *Circular* commented that the international market was aware that Indonesia needed upwards of 5,000,000 tons and that the Philippines intended to buy a further 600,000 tons from June. But concerns were growing about availability from exporting countries with Pakistan close to sold out, and the Vietnamese Government expected to slow the pace of sales by insisting all new contracts be approved for price and shipment date (*LRBAC* 4th March 1998 1). In Thailand, the Baht had been very volatile making it difficult for exporters to calculate their prices. However, on the whole, it had strengthened against the U.S. Dollar. But there was also lack of demand for rice. Having exported heavily in December, January and February, commitments for March/April shipment were small. The Vietnamese new crop had arrived and was attracting rival interest. Some exporters who had made shipments direct to Indonesia and accepted letters of credit opened by Indonesian banks found payment was not forthcoming. A general agreement was made that no further shipments would be made to Indonesia until these payments had been received. But some payments were still outstanding. January exports were 683,276 tons, up by about 80 per cent on January 1997. Although large it was not as high as December's figure of 742,677 tons. February exports were 562,426 tons, bringing the total for the first two months of 1998 to 1,244,678 tons (*LRBAC* 4th March 1998 2–3). In March, the Baht continued to rise for most of the month, then fell back. Large defaults were being experienced in Vietnam. Despite the weaker currency and few vessels loading, the market was showing little sign of weakness. This was not surprising when taking into account just how much rice had already been shipped from the new crop and reports that the local market was tight and short of rice. There were concerns the second crop would be smaller than usual. The weather was hot and dry for the time of year, and with weather patterns in the whole region in turmoil, Thailand could not be sure the rains would appear as usual about the middle of May. The Thai New Year was approaching and most companies would close down from the 10th to the 15th April. Official holidays in Thailand were the 6th, 13th, 14th and 15th. Exports during March reached 565,332 tons bringing the total for the first quarter of the year to just over 1,800,000 tons. This compared with the first quarter of the previous year when 1,040,683 tons were shipped (*LRBAC* 6th April 1998 3). The *Circular* commented that demand for rice remained enormous, led by Indonesia. The Philippines remained a buyer and there were suggestions that due to drought Malaysia would have to substantially increase its purchases. Bangladesh too was to increase its imports to 700,000 tons, all on top of traditional yearly demand. In the past, when there was a sharp increase in demand it always coincided with increased supply from one origin or another. In 1995, when demand rose due to Japanese requirements, India exported record quantities and kept the lower end of the market supplied. But this year, supply might tighten. In the North of India, poor weather had caused considerable damage limiting availability, and recent news from Thailand and Vietnam increased concerns the second crop could be badly affected by very hot and dry conditions. In Vietnam the crop would be 30–40 days late, and there would be further delays if the rains did not come soon. China, however, was expected to increase its exports to as much as 2,000,000 tons, compared with 939,000 tons the previous year. Even this would not be enough for world demand (*LRBAC* 30th April 1998 1). Exports from Thailand in April were expected to be 500,000 tons, bringing the total for the first 4 months of the year to 2,300,000 tons and putting Thailand on close to a record year for exports. But they would need a good second crop to achieve this. The area planted for second crop had been expanded by 20 per cent this year, although last year's crop was historically one of the largest second crops. The Government warned farmers that if the rains did not come soon there would not be enough water to irrigate this area. Most of the second crop was for export and so had a greater effect on export availability than fluctuations in the main crop. The closing down of Vietnam as a supplier was likely to increase demand from Thailand (*LRBAC* 30th April 1998 3). World markets in general tightened considerably. China had sold 2,000,000 tons but had now withdrawn. The Vietnamese Government were not considering new export licences, so no sales had been concluded. There had been rain, and second crop was being planted, but would not be ready before September. Thailand was still selling, and new crop ought to be available from the second half of June. The rains had improved and saved the second crop but the earlier dry weather would mean field yields would be lower than usual, and the quality of the rice affected. Pakistan had sold out, although the occasional vessel still loaded. An increasing number of vessels were loading in India, but this was pushing up prices in the local markets and a number of exporters were having trouble covering their commitments. So exports of white rice from India would be much less than expected. The tightness in supply was not helped by Iran purchasing close to 200,000 tons of rice from Thailand. It was expected Brazil would be a substantial buyer, mainly of U.S. paddy, but also low quality rice for the north, and Thai 100 per cent B or equivalent for the south. The temporary ban on shipments and sales to Indonesia was helping to reduce demand (*LRBAC* 29th May 1998 1). In Thailand, the market was quiet for most of May. Then the Iranians decided to buy and there were rumours of purchases from Brazil. The Iranian business was thought to be 14 cargoes totalling 200,000 tons on Iranian terms, shipment July to August. To crackdown on illegal immigrants working in Thailand, the government changed the law so that employers could be prosecuted for knowingly employing illegal immigrants. This caused an uproar as the rice mills and stevedore companies relied heavily on this cheap labour. A large number of mills had stopped working, making it difficult for exporters to cover their sales to Iran and Brazil. Prices of parboiled fell after the loading of a number of vessels which had arrived for Nigeria. Rainfall had increased hopes for the second crop, which ought to be available towards the end of June. Although the area planted was more than 10 per cent over the previous year, this would not be enough to compensate for the damage caused by the earlier hot and dry weather. It was expected the weather conditions would have caused a higher chalky content, and that the general appearance of the rice would be poorer than the previous year. This would not be good news for exporters with sales to Iran or Brazil. Exports for April totalled 541,108 tons. Up to 25th May 340,560 tons were exported from Thailand (*LRBAC* 29th May 1998 3). Supplies of rice from

Asian origins remained tight, and would remain so until the new crops came in at the end of the year. China was not selling, but had substantial commitments to ship, hampered by poor weather and localised flooding. There were some offers from Vietnam, but exporters were cautious as most of the summer/autumn crop would not be harvested until September. The quality of the rice available was poor. Exports of Thai rice increased as new crop became available, but problems with poor weather and lack of labour had kept the market tight. Indian exporters were facing substantial difficulties with a tidal wave hitting Kandla on the West Coast, and strikes on the East Coast. The quantity loaded this month from India was small compared to expectations. But the market had some respite because political upheavals in Indonesia had reduced demand from there, and the market in West Africa had slowed because of increased prices in the Far East. There was still enormous world demand for rice, but supplies were limited (*LRBAC* 3rd July 1998 1). It was reported that China had become a large exporter, second only to Thailand, with shipments close to 300,000 tons per month (*LRBAC* 3rd July 1998 1). The move by the Thai government to crack down on illegal immigrants met strong objections from exporters because of the effect on the availability of stevedores in the port, but the strongest reaction was from the rice mills which relied heavily on this source of cheap labour. Most of the mills were working slowly because of lack of labour and poor weather, and in an attempt to get the support of the farmers the mills had reduced their purchases of new crop paddy. The situation was difficult for exporters as they had made sales of high quality rice to Brazil and Iran last month at substantially below current levels, and now the vessels had arrived to load these contracts. For both destinations, good quality was required, which was in short supply as the second crop was of poor quality compared to the first crop. The resumption of World Bank lending to Indonesia meant new letters of credit were being opened for business concluded a while ago, so there was a sharp increase in the number of vessels loading for Indonesia. Sales rumoured for Indonesia were for 250,000 – 300,000 tons of 25 per cent brokens, but it was not clear whether this was new sales or renegotiation of old sales as letters of credit were opened. Total exports for May were 424,296 tons, but recovered with 474,654 tons for the first 29 days of June. This meant exports for the first half of the year had reached 3,251,096 tons, which was substantially more than for the same period in 1997 when the total was 2,328,212 tons (*LRBAC* 3rd July 1998 3–4). From Indonesia, it was reported that a delegation was being sent to Thailand to negotiate a purchase of 500,000 tons from the Government (*LRBAC* 31st July 1998 2–3). In Thailand itself millers and exporters won a reprieve from the Government on the issue of illegal immigrant workers, and the deadline was put back indefinitely. This freed up availability in the local market. There were expectations of further sales to Indonesia and the Philippines, particularly of 25 per cent brokens. Negotiations were taking place between the Philippine Government and the Thai Government for 100,000 tons. A World Food Programme tender for Indonesia took place on the 20th July for a cargo of 16,000 tons from Thailand and another 16,000 tons from Thailand or Vietnam, both going to Thailand. The delegation from Indonesia was awaited, and expected to buy 500,000 tons from government to government. The new crop was expected from the beginning of November. Five vessels were loading 85,100 tons of parboiled 100 per cent sortexed for Nigeria. There were also five Iranian vessels in port loading 75,000 tons of 100 per cent B, and there were other vessels for Indonesia, Iraq and West Africa. There were outstanding contracts for 100,000 tons to Iran. Total exports for June were 491,384 tons, bringing the total for the year to 3,289,303 tons. For the first 27 days of July, 442,263 tons were exported (*LRBAC* 31st July 1998 3–4). The *Circular* commented that severe weather patterns in the Far East were causing great concern. There had been flooding in China in August, which was expected to reduce the rice crop substantially, although reports that China would have to buy huge quantities of rice seemed overdone. The seasonal floods in Bangladesh had lasted longer than usual causing economic damage and fears for the rice crop. The Vietnamese had also suffered with the weather and had stopped selling until the New Year. Meanwhile, Indonesia had bought quantities of rice from Vietnam and Thailand and was expected to buy more, either by tender or government to government. However, discussions had been put back due to the resignation of Beddu Amang, the President of BULOG (Ed. Badan Urusan Logistic or the National Logistics Agency, which was responsible for food security and the stability of rice prices) (*LRBAC* 28th August 1998 1). In China, there were severe problems caused by terrible flooding in the Yangtze River area. Demand from the more affluent areas of China for fragrant rice and Thai 100 per cent Grade B were expected to be larger in the coming year (*LRBAC* 28th August 1998 1). It was thought that the Indonesian Government had bought 100,000 tons of Vietnamese 25 per cent, but talks of increasing this to 300,000–400,000 tons ended without success. The Indonesian government then turned to Thailand where the Thai government offered 100,000 tons on a year's credit and an additional 400,000 tons for cash. The 100,000 tons were definitely concluded stowed Bangkok, for Thai long-grain, white rice 25 per cent Super. The balance of 400,000 tons was not concluded. The Indonesian Government then announced a tender for 600,000 tons of rice with origins restricted to China, Vietnam and Thailand. The tender was to be held on 26th August but was delayed to the 27th. Then the Indonesian President insisted on the resignation of the Chairman of BULOG as mentioned above. The tender was postponed to the 10th September. Indonesia also asked for an extension of the offer from Thailand for 400,000 tons for reply on lst September (*LRBAC* 28th August 1998 2–3). In Thailand, the Indonesian delegation only purchased 100,000 tons on one year's credit. The Indonesian tender was postponed to 10th September which came as a complete surprise, and so did their request for an extension on the offer of 400,000 tons from the Thai Government to the lst September. Prices for 25 per cent brokens remained firm on expectations of sales to Indonesia. Brokens would be in large demand for mixing to create the quality required by the Indonesian market. Exports for July were 523,862 tons, bringing the total for the first 7 months of the year to 3,813,155 tons. For the first 25 days of August, 401,122 tons were exported from Thailand (*LRBAC* 28th August 1998 3). The Indonesian Government announced a tender for 600,000 tons limited to

Thailand, Vietnam, China and Burma. This was postponed on several occasions and eventually held on 16th September. The figures allotted to Thailand were September (20,000 tons), October (40,000 tons), November (20,000 tons) and December (140,000 tons). Subsequently, further negotiations took place for additional lots from different origins, concluding another 190,000 tons, none of which went to Thailand. This brought the total from all origins to 716,000 tons. Thailand made a further offer for 400,000 ton of Thai 25 per cent Super stowed Bangkok. But there was a lack of confidence in business with Indonesia and the 100,000 tons sold by the Thai government in September still had no letter of credit. Indonesia needed to import 500,000 tons a month right up to their new crop in March, a total of 2,500,000 tons (*LRBAC* 2nd October 1998 2–3). In Thailand, the only real point of interest was Indonesia. In the recent tender, many offers were made, and finally, a total of 220,000 tons was confirmed as accepted. Subsequent to this, a further 400,000 tons was concluded outside the tender. But there were concerns whether Indonesia would be able to open letters of credit promptly for these contracts. The new Thai crop was expected in December. However, the northeast had suffered from reduced rainfall and yields would be slightly reduced. Exports for August totalled 519,913 tons, bringing the total for the first 8 months of the year to 4,333,091 tons. But exports slowed in September and in the first 25 days were only 377,726 tons (*LRBAC* 2nd October 1998 3–4). The *Circular* commented that after the excitement of last month's Indonesian tenders, October was marked by disappointment as exporters found that letters of credit had been opened very slowly or not at all. So demand, in fact, was far less than originally indicated. At the Asia International Rice Conference on 29th and 30th October the stark realities of the market were laid bare, and talk during coffee breaks was of a bearish market with large new crops expected from many origins, and a reduction in demand in the coming year. World imports were expected to be a record of 26,750,000 tons in 1998, but would probably decline by 3,000,000–7,000,000 tons in 1999 with the main reductions coming from Indonesia, the Philippines, Bangladesh and Brazil. This would be about the level of 1996 and 1997. Thailand was the first affected by this news and prices fell, with the lower qualities worst hit. Vietnam, India and Pakistan followed suit (*LRBAC* 6th November 1998 1). Exporters in Thailand were hit by the uncertainty over the Indonesian business. Some of the shipment periods were very prompt, but without letters of credit nothing could be shipped. Letters of credit were opened for some of the quantities sold, but for the 400,000 tons sold after the tender there was still no letter of credit, and few believed this business now stood. As noted above, bearish messages from the Asia International Conference, which started on 29th October took their toll, and prices fell almost overnight with the lowest grades worst hit. There was a sale to Iran of 15,000 tons of Thai 100 per cent Grade B shipped Bangkok. The price included a premium for joint inspection. There were reports of further interest in another 4 or 5 cargoes. On a previous sale to Iran, letters of credit were slow to be opened arriving close to 2 months late. This delay was blamed on the poor situation in Iran. The new crop harvested in Thailand would start towards the end of the month, with the availability for shipment end of November/first half of December. It seemed likely that it would be close to a record harvest as due to high prices farmers had planted every bit of land available to them. The outlook for the second crop was not so good, with water levels in the major dams less than half normal levels due to lack of rain. The fragrant crop would be delayed because of heavy rains, and would be reduced considerably due to poor weather conditions in the northeast where as noted in October there had been low rainfall during the growing season (*LRBAC* 6th November 1998 3). There was always interest in the Thai Winter/Spring crop as this was better quality than later crops. There was a shift of emphasis from low-grade 25 per cent brokens being shipped to Indonesia, towards higher grade 5 per cent and 100 per cent B for Iran, Malaysia and Hong Kong, and smaller shipments within the region. The rains had fallen too far south and not in the catchment areas for the irrigation dams, and the second crop was almost totally reliant on irrigation. The government had given warnings they would not have enough water for the second crop. Exports for November were 523,678 tons bringing the total for the first 11 months of 1998 to 5,729,367 tons. It was expected that exports in 1998 would reach a record level of over 6,200,000 tons due to heavy commitments for December (*LRBAC* 7th December 1998 3–4). From India, it was reported that very high shipments of parboiled out of Thailand had pushed up parboiled prices leaving India a cheaper option (*LRBAC* 4th January 1992 2). From Indonesia, it was reported that the long-awaited tender for Indonesia had been announced to utilise part of the financing offered by the Islamic Development Bank (IDB). It was held on 16th December for 200,000 tons, with options for origin including India and Pakistan for 10 per cent brokens, and Egypt, China, Thailand and Vietnam for 25 per cent brokens, shipment January/February. All offers had to be for a minimum of 20,000 tons, and 68 companies put offers in, but only 38 qualified by having their documents and bid bonds in order. The tender went to Pakistan for a total of 277,000 tons (*LRBAC* 4th January 1999 2). Shipments from Thailand during December were expected to reach close to 600,000 tons, so millers and exporters had been busy. January was expected to be about 450,000 tons, with demand falling from February onwards. The government again announced that water levels in the dams were low for the time of year and insufficient for a normal second crop. Farmers were asked to reduce plantings for dry season rice by 50 per cent, and to grow crops instead like soya beans and pulses which use less water. In a normal year the dry season crop was 4,500,000–4,600,000 tons of paddy. Shipments from Thailand included 300,000 tons to Indonesia and the Philippines, and 120,000 tons of parboiled for Nigeria. Business to Indonesia might go to Vietnam where prices were lower, and some had already gone to Pakistan. This would leave Thailand with more traditional business of high quality rice and also parboiled to Nigeria. Recently, there had been enquiries from Iran, but only a few cargoes had been concluded. The quantity exported during the first 21 days of December reached 434,172 tons, well on target to reach 6,300,000 tons for the year which would be a record (*LRBAC* 4th January 1999 3).

Table 6.11 Thailand rice exports 1997 and 1998 (metric tons)

	1997	*1998*
January	377,948	683,276
February	287,899	561,426
March	374,835	565,332
April	418,655	541,108
May	395,834	424,296
June	473,184	491,384
July	425,212	523,852
August	412,916	519,913
September	462,718	412,352
October	465,349	460,266
November	435,277	523,678
December	742,667	637,821
Total	5,272,494	6,344,710 (Ed. 6,344,704?)

Comparable totals for Vietnam were 1997, 3,149,228 and 1998 3,411,459.
(*LRBAC* 2nd February 1999 inserted between 2 and 3).

During February, exports from Thailand were expected to fall and would be interrupted by Chinese New Year, although there were no official holidays scheduled in Thailand at this time. There was not enough water for the second crop and the provinces near Bangkok were already having water rationed for domestic purposes. Irrigation channels over a wide area were completely empty and many farmers were mounting a 24 hour watch on pumps they used to move water from the irrigation channels to their fields. This was so when water was released they could use it immediately, and also to ensure the pumps were not sabotaged by other farmers. Expectations were that the exportable surplus from the second crop would be reduced by about 1,000,000 tons. In the first minimum access tender to Japan 20,000 tons were sold for February shipment. On 28th January, there was another tender where four lots of 5000 tons of 100 per cent B were sold and later one lot of 5000 tons of glutinous brokens. Iran had old contracts for 100 per cent B and decided to open letters of credit and press for shipment at lower prices. With the threat of this business going to Vietnam, the letters of credit were accepted and the vessels were expected shortly for loading. A Thai delegation was to visit Indonesia to press for execution of an old contract for 100,000 tons of 25 per cent on 3 years credit. Exports during December 1998 were 637,821 tons, giving a total for the year of 6,344,710 tons. Exports for the first 25 days of January were 428,604 tons. February was expected to be much quieter (*LRBAC* 2nd February 1999 3). From India it was reported that the main interest was parboiled rice for Nigeria, but prices in Thailand fell to a level where there was only a small premium to pay for the quality and reliability of Thai parboiled, and few buyers were taking Indian rice (*LRBAC* 3rd March 1999 2). In Thailand there was some interest shown for parboiled rice, and parboiled 100 per cent sortexed was even cheaper than India. There was also business in ordinary A1 Super brokens and fragrant rice. It was expected 450,000 tons would be shipped in February, but few new buyers had come in. Shipments for the first 23 days of February totalled 330,478 tons (*LRBAC* 3rd March 1999 3). Prices fell internationally as demand reduced to more usual levels from the heady days of 1998 when international trade was believed to have reached 26,000,000 tons. There were good crops internationally with the possible exception of the second crop in Thailand which might be reduced due to lack of water, and Northern India where heavy rains after harvesting affected the quality of the rice (*LRBAC* 6th April 1999 1). In Pakistan there was a steady flow of vessels arriving to load for Indonesia. Some of the vessels were loading under letters of credit opened using the Islamic Development Bank's (IDB) credit, but it was thought that some companies with commitments to ship Pakistan rice to Indonesia had been given the option to ship from other origins, particularly Thailand and Vietnam (*LRBAC* 6th April 1999 3). Thai rice prices were the lowest since 1993. There were quality problems for low quality rice and broken rice. The greatest difficulty was the high content of weed seeds in the brokens. This affected shipments of 25 per cent brokens which had to be mixed to achieve this percentage of brokens. The problem did not affect the higher qualities with a lower percentage of brokens as it was easier to remove these small seeds by screening (Ed. i.e. sieving) when the average grain length was longer. The total quantity exported from Thailand during February reached 433,352 tons and 431,083 tons for the first 30 days of March (*LRBAC* 6th April 1999 3). Prices continued to fall in Thailand but business was minimal. Total exports during March were 465,458 tons bringing the quantity shipped in the first quarter of 1999 to 1,460,016 tons. During the first 27 days of April, only 295,943 tons were exported, partly due to the many holidays in Thailand that month (*LRBAC* 30th April 1999 3). The *Circular* commented that once again the Asian markets were being affected by bad weather, and with the memory of *El Nino* so fresh in people's minds, many were concerned that the heavy rains in Thailand and Vietnam were caused by *La Nina*. Intense rain was normally expected in Thailand and Vietnam during August and September, but not in May. But after six weeks of disruption, the weather had returned to normal in Vietnam and appeared to be doing so in Thailand (*LRBAC* lst June 1999 1). On the international market, outstanding contracts were still being shipped to Indonesia, although it was some time since the last purchases by BULOG. These included those using the Islamic Development Bank (IDB) credit line, and 400,000 tons originally done by a Bangkok company, but then taken over by a Singapore trading house. So there were regular shipments from Thailand, Vietnam and Pakistan. There were elections in Indonesia on 7th June, and it seemed unlikely more purchases would be made before then (*LRBAC* 1st June 1999 2). Heavy rains in Bangkok caused flooding and interrupted transport and cargo preparations. It was rumoured that irrigation dams were so full water might have to be released to prevent dangerously high levels. The Thai Government sold 300,000 tons 100 per cent B to the Iran Government for shipment July through to October, with two year's credit. There was also demand for 25 per cent brokens and other brokens, and demand for 25 per cent brokens for Indonesia to cover old contracts. This year because of the heavy rains the area under second crop had been increased by as much as 17 per cent. The harvest was June/July. Total exports during April 1999 were 378,465 tons and May 471,398 tons, bringing the total for the first 5 months of 1999 to 2,309,880 tons (*LRBAC* 1st June 1999 3). Early in July, more vessels were nominated to load 100 per cent B for Iran, and 25 per cent brokens for Indonesia. Private business with Indonesia was now running at 100,000 tons per month, and with shipments of brokens to Africa, this kept the price of 25 per cent firm. The market for fragrant rice remained very quiet with no new interest from China, but the Chinese Government was expected to offer some new import quotas soon. Exports in June were the highest month this year by 60,000 tons. This year's running total of 2,800,000 tons was behind last year's figure of 3,200,000 tons, but still very substantial. The area planted with second crop was the highest ever.

Table 6.12 Thailand rice exports January–June 1998 and 1999 (metric tons)

	1998	*1998*	*1999*	*1999*
January	683,276	683,276	428,604	428,604
February	561,426	1,244,703	433,352	861,957
March	565,332	1,810,036	465,458	1,327,416
April	541,108	2,351,144	378,465	1,705,881
May	424,296	2,775,441	471,398	2,177,280
June	491,384	3,266,825	535,762	2,713,042

(*LRBAC* 9th July 1999 3).

Asian markets were stable with the arrival of the second crop in Thailand and Vietnam. There was heavy demand from Iran and also Indonesia where demand from the private trade had led to shipments from various origins totalling 250,000 tons. BULOG announced a tender to be held on 10th August for 75,000 tons of 25 per cent brokens, all origins acceptable – except Myanmar! (*LRBAC* 3rd August 1999 1). In Thailand, heavy shipments to Indonesia and Iran led to exports in July of 612,236 tons, even more than June's figure of about 535,000 tons which was the record for the year to that date. Luckily this increase in exports coincided with the arrival of the second crop. Heavy rains were affecting preparation of crop and slowing down loading operations. The price of fragrant rice rose with the news that the Chinese Government had released more import quota details but fell back when the quantity was less than hoped (*LRBAC* 3rd August 1999 3). During the first half of August, heavy rains took their toll on many countries in the Far East. The flooding in the Philippines and Korea was very severe and there was flooding in China and Vietnam (*LRBAC* 26th August 1999 1). After being quiet for 2 months, Indonesia returned to the market and held a tender on 10th August for 75,000 tons of 25 per cent brokens for shipment in September/October. Origins accepted were Thailand, Vietnam, China, Pakistan and Egypt. Many offers were received, the cheapest from China. BULOG were now believed to have three contracts in hand, two of which amounted to 400,000 tons each of Thai rice 25 per cent Super, including 2 year's credit, and one lot of 75,000 tons bought in this tender, quality unspecified. There was concern that these contracts would not be delivered. The performance bond for the Thai contract had not been opened and it was thought that these contracts would be cancelled as the prices did not seem commercially viable (*LRBAC* 26th August 1999 2–3). In Thailand, seasonal rains continued over the entire country. Preparation and loading of barges and vessels was affected but exports only fell slightly. This was not helped by the low prices offered for Chinese rice in the Indonesian tender, and recent reports that BULOG had stopped buying from the private sector in Indonesia. A very substantial portion of exports over the past few months from Thailand was 25 per cent to the Indonesian private sector. Prices had also fallen with the weakness of the Thai Baht, and one of the larger Bangkok banks was reported to be in difficulties stirring up memories of the financial crisis in the Far East which began about this time in 1997. Fragrant prices rose after some new sales to China, and the parboiled market was firm due to the arrival of vessels to load 80,000 tons of parboiled. This marked Nigeria's re-entry as a buyer after a couple of months when business was minimal due to changes in import duties. Exports for the first 24 days of August were 444,412 tons, and it was expected 600,000 tons would be shipped in August (*LRBAC* 26th August 1999 3). A new President was expected to be elected in Indonesia in early November and purchases of rice seemed to be on hold (*LRBAC* 1st October 1999 1). Indonesia was still seen to be the key to the market for new crop and into the New Year. Much of the business in the August tender in Indonesia was cancelled as had been expected. The two contracts of 400,000 tons each of Thai rice were cancelled. Since then there had been no further purchases except the occasional private business, but even this was now severely restricted as the Government of Indonesia had introduced new regulations restricting private imports only to high-quality 5 per cent and better. So in essence the most important single buyer of Asian rice had withdrawn from the market (*LRBAC* 1st October 1999 3). Shipments from Thailand to Indonesia reduced quickly in September as prices in Vietnam were cheaper, and because of new import regulations in Indonesia for private sales, and the absence of new purchases by BULOG. But there was increased demand from Iran, and very heavy shipments of parboiled to Nigeria. New regulations for Nigeria caused a rush to have vessels shipped to beat a deadline before further increases in duty. Prices for fragrant were firm in the run up to the Chinese celebrations of 50 years since the Revolution. There had been heavy buying of fragrant rice to arrive before the start of the holidays, which had just about cleared stocks out. Heavy rains throughout Thailand caused some delays in loading but meant that there was no shortage of water in the growing regions, most importantly in the northeast where the fragrant rice was grown. The harvest was due to start in mid-November with availability for shipment from the end of November. Exports during August were finally 597,111 tons, and shipments up to the 27th September were 549,969 tons (*LRBAC* 1st October 1999 3). The *Circular* commented that with the end of the year and the start of the new Millennium, many companies were planning to close down for an extended period over Christmas and New Year. Companies were expressing concern about the Millennium Bug, and it was reported from Thailand that the Thai Central Bank would not do any foreign currency transactions from 15th December to 15th January in consequence. All this could seriously disrupt the normal functions of the rice industry, and anyone intending to move rice at this time was advised to take as many precautions as possible to ensure the minimum of disruptions to their shipments (*LRBAC* 5th November 1999 1). It was continuing to rain heavily in Thailand most days, although the monsoon should have been coming to an end. This had delayed the harvest of the main crop, and was delaying the harvest of the fragrant crop. It was also hampering transportation and making production of parboiled difficult. There had been a sudden shortage of rice in Vietnam, which had helped prices firm, with the exception of fragrant rice and fragrant brokens which were already strong. Fragrant brokens this year had traded at a record premium to ordinary brokens. Fragrant new crop was available, with prices at a high level due to strong demand from China. Earlier this month the Thai government agreed to a Memorandum of Understanding with the Iranian GTC (Government Trading Company?) for 300,000 tons of Thai 100 per cent B, to be shipped as soon as the contracts in hand came to an end in mid to late November. However, a delegation from Iran visited Bangkok to negotiate prices and terms but left empty handed as the Thai Government was not keen to offer three years credit. Exports during October were 558,284 tons bringing the total for the year to 5,266,864 tons. Thailand was well on target to export 6,100,000 tons this year, only 300,000 tons less than 1998's record figure (*LRBAC* 5th November 1999 3). By the second week of November the rainy season had at last come to an end. But sales had been made with the expectation of new crop arriving in the market earlier, so those with shipments had difficulty covering the rice. The crop was expected to be 20,000,000 – 20,500,000 tons basis paddy. 2000 was an election year and under normal circumstances the Government would be dissolved in April for the election in June. But it was thought there might be a vote of no confidence shortly. The farmers were an important voice in Thailand, and the Government had approved a scheme to allow the MOF (Ministry of Food?) and PWO (Public Works Organisation?) to purchase about 500,000 tons of paddy each to support prices. Greatest demand was for high quality, such as 100 per cent B for Iran and max 5 per cent for Indonesia. This was in contrast to the last two years when shipments to Indonesia and the Philippines meant high demand for 25 per cent brokens. The fragrant crop, normally 5,000,000 – 6,000,000 tons was expected to be at the upper end of this quantity. Field yields were good, but bad weather over the past month had reduced milling yields, and may have increased the percentage of chalky kernels. Significantly amongst qualities listed, Fragrant A1 Super (Ed. i.e. brokens) was listed for the first time. Exports for all rice during November totalled 623,379 tons (*LRBAC* 3rd December 1999 3).

The *Circular* did not mention Indonesia from January 1990 until October 1991 when it noted that Indonesia had negotiated purchases of around 600,000 tons (*LRBAC* 31st October 1991 1). From India it was reported that 150,000 tons of rice had been sold to Indonesia, mostly 25 per cent, but probably including 50,000 – 60,000 tons of 10 per cent (*LRBAC* 31st October 1991 2). Indonesia had indeed bought its requirements to about April 1992 with some 150,000 tons of Indian rice non-*Basmati*, 325,000 tons of Thai rice (including 25,000 tons of 10 per cent and the remainder 25 per cent), 100,000 – 200,000 tons of Vietnamese rice and 50,000 tons of undetermined origin, giving a total of 625,000 – 725,000 tons. Shipments were to start November 1991 through to March 1992 (*LRBAC* 31st October 1991 2).

From Vietnam, it was confirmed that 100,000 – 200,000 tons had been sold to Indonesia (*LRBAC* 31st October 1991 3). A further 25,000 tons of Indian 25 per cent was sold to Indonesia, making a total of 175,000 tons. There was also an old sale of 80,000 tons of Thai rice to Indonesia, bringing the total from Thailand to 405,000 tons. There was another old sale of 25,000 tons of Chinese 25 per cent to Indonesia. The exact quantity from Vietnam was not clear but thought to be 150,000 tons, bringing the total purchases by Indonesia to about 775,000 tons (*LRBAC* 30th November 1991 1). There were no new reports of business to Indonesia after the 700,000 – 750,000 tons already mentioned (*LRBAC* 31st December 1991 2).

In January 1992 shipments to Indonesia from India and Thailand progressed (*LRBAC* 31st January 1992 1). Shipments continued from Thailand (*LRBAC* 28th February 1992 2). A further sale of 200,000 tons of Thai 25 per cent to Indonesia was reported but not confirmed *LRBAC* (31st March 1992 2). Meanwhile the international market was dominated by new business to Iran, and shipments of existing business from Thailand to Aqaba and Indonesia (*LRBAC* 30th April 1992 1). Shipments from Thailand to Indonesia against old contracts were progressing (*LRBAC* 30th April 1992 1). In August, after a gap of four months, it was reported that in a change to established trading patterns, Indonesia had actually sold rice rather than imported it (*LRBAC* 31st August 1992 1). This turned out to be 200,000 tons of white rice 35 per cent brokens to an unspecified destination (*LRBAC* 31st August 1992 2–3).

There was then a gap in reporting until February 1993 when both Indonesia and Bangladesh announced they wanted to sell rice, but not at current market levels (*LRBAC* 28th February 1993 1). Despite a loss of about 250,000 tons of rice in Java recently due to floods, Indonesia still wanted to sell about 500,000 tons of rice, apparently 35 per cent, but their price was uncompetitive (*LRBAC* 28th February 1993 2). Indonesia, Burma and China were back in the market trying to sell (*LRBAC* 31st March 1993 1). Indonesia was still trying to find buyers, and there were unconfirmed reports that an additional 50,000 tons of 35 per cent had been contracted for sale by one of the participants in the last Indonesian export campaign, but this seemed unlikely (*LRBAC* 31st March 1993 2). Indonesia was now indicating expected paddy production of 47,700,000 tons for the 1993 season, a little below the 1992 record harvest. Indonesia had changed from an importer to an exporter as a result of the 1992 crop, but their prices were uncompetitive even with 2 years deferred payment (*LRBAC* 30th April 1993 2). Shipments from Indonesia of previously contracted rice slowed down, but an additional quantity thought to be 50,000 tons of 35 per cent were taken up on the same terms as previous sales, with a minimum of 2 years extended payment. Indonesia was keen to find buyers but was uncompetitive (*LRBAC* 28th May 1993 2). Indonesia continued to want to sell additional rice, although shipments from previous contracts continued to take place. As noted previously, paddy production for 1993 was forecast at 47,700,000 tons, a little less than 1992, but still leaving Indonesia needing to export (*LRBAC* 30th June 1993 2). In July Indonesia was pushing to sell 25 per cent as opposed to the original sales of 35 per cent, but no firm offers were made (*LRBAC* 30th July 1993 2). Indonesia continued to try to sell 35 per cent and possibly 25 per cent, and it was thought offers would become more numerous, particularly to West Africa (*LRBAC* 31st August 1993 2). Shipments of 35 per cent and 25 per cent continued from Indonesia to the West African market, due to the low prices (*LRBAC* 1st October 1993 2). Vietnamese exports were a little quiet as a result of competition from Indonesia and China (*LRBAC* 1st October 1993 4). The West African market took most of the unsold rice from Indonesia and China, particularly 25 per cent and 35 per cent (*LRBAC* 31st October 1993 1). But then cheap offers from Indonesia and China came to an end as most of the rice had been taken up by international traders. Negotiations between Cuba and Indonesia for a barter exchanging Cuban sugar for Indonesian rice were ongoing (*LRBAC* 31st October 1993 2). Crop estimates were now for 47,900,000 tons (Ed. of paddy), some 300,000 tons less than 1992. One result of the increased 1992 crop had been that Indonesia became an exporter of rice, having accumulated large stocks which caused storage problems. It was suggested that Indonesia would reduce its rate of increase in production from 3.5 per cent per year to 2.1 per cent per year as a result of the situation in 1993 (*LRBAC* 31st December 1993 2).

There was no further news until July 1994 when it was rumoured that Thailand was making available 100,000–150,000 tons government to government to Indonesia (*LRBAC* 30th June 1994 3). There was then excitement as Indonesia came into the market to buy 700,000 – 1,000,000 tons of 25 per cent for shipment to the end of February 1995 (*LRBAC* 31st July 1994 1). There were reports that the Thai government had sold 300,000 tons of white rice 25 per cent to Indonesia, and a further sale had been made to Indonesia by a private group of Thai exporters (*LRBAC* 31st July 1994 3). From Vietnam, it was reported there had been a government-to-government sale to Indonesia of 250,000 – 300,000 tons of 25 per cent for shipment up to the end of February (*LRBAC* 31st July 1994 3). There had been no slackening in the world market of the effects of the extensive Indonesian purchases of lower quality rice. Apart from Thailand there were extensive shipping difficulties caused by continual rain, excessive sales against available stocks, and the unwillingness of some to ship rice at the prevailing prices, which were now much higher than in the summer. Thailand and India were not involved as their prices were uncompetitive (*LRBAC* 31st August 1994 1). It was reported that a significant quantity of Burmese rice had been traded, but 25,000 – 30,000 tons were cancelled and probably resold to Indonesia on a government-to-government basis. Some Burmese *Emata* originating through barter were sold by Singapore intermediaries to Indonesia (*LRBAC* 31st August 1994 1–2). Pakistan also reported interest from Indonesia for 15 per cent – 20 per cent (*LRBAC* 31st August 1994 2–3). Thailand reported shipments to Indonesia following the government-to-government sale, and sales by private traders to Indonesia in smaller quantities (*LRBAC* 31st August 1994 3). From Vietnam, it was reported that following the significant government-to-government sales to Indonesia and shipments to China, Central and South America, congestion and delays were widespread at Hochiminh City (*LRBAC* 31st August 1994 4). Fuelled by demand and the amount of business contracted for Indonesia, all origins outside of the United States saw a firming in prices. There had also been purchase activity from central buying and private purchasers in China. Indonesia was still waiting for rain. If the rain was further delayed Indonesia would have to continue importing (*LRBAC* 30th September 1994 1). In Thailand, prices of white rice advanced in anticipation of Indonesian and Chinese demand. The main activity had been broken rice for West Africa and smaller shipments to Indonesia, as well as vessels loading 25 per cent against the government-to-government contract with Indonesia. There were rumours of possibly another 100,000 tons of 25 per cent for Indonesia, November shipment (*LRBAC* 30th September 1994 3). Prices continued to rise due to speculative views about China's possible purchases, and also the extent of demand from Indonesia (*LRBAC* 1st November 1994 1). The key to recent world market activity was Indonesia, which had suffered a well-publicised drought and consequent crop damage. The 1994 season was likely to show the availability of only 46,500,000 tons (Ed. of paddy), some 2,000,000 tons down on normal, which largely explained the currently contracted import figure of 1,500,000 tons. The rains had still not come, which raised questions about December's plantings for a February/March harvest (*LRBAC* 1st November 1994 1–2). In Myanmar (Burma), changes within the country accelerated and a lot of rice for November and December had been sold to ex-patriot Burmese who then found willing buyers in Indonesia. The most recently reported business was for 20,000 tons of *Emata* 25 per cent for November/December shipment. There were also rumours of extensive sales for January/February/March 1995. It would seem that 100,000 tons had already been committed (*LRBAC* 1st November 1994 2). From Pakistan, it was reported that new crop private trade IRRI 6 15 per cent/20 per cent brokens had been traded with a significant quantity sold to Indonesia, November/December shipment (*LRBAC* lst November 1994 3). In Thailand exports to October rallied considerably due to shipments to Indonesia and China. Further prices in Thailand would be determined by the possibility of a government export subsidy, a sale to Iran, prospects for further shipments to Indonesia, and new sales of high-quality rice to Malaysia (*LRBAC* 1st November 1994 3). Indonesia still controlled the excitement in the world rice market as they were expected to re-enter the market soon. Two-thirds of the rice that had been bought by Indonesia, of around 1,500,000 tons total purchase, had been shipped and had probably arrived. There were problems with supply for Pakistan, and supply from Vietnam was also interrupted. So Thailand was expecting purchases to be made from an Indonesian delegation, possibly 300,000–400,000 tons (*LRBAC* 1st December 1994 2). Thailand had sales to Iran and hopes of continued demand from China and Indonesia, keeping 100 per cent B firm throughout November. There was also demand for broken rice including small shipments of 6000–8,000 tons per vessel to Indonesia, and extensive demand from West Africa (*LRBAC* 1st December 1994 3).

Just when everyone had forgotten the Japanese influence from the latter half of 1993 through to the first quarter of 1994, the world rice market had to take account of drastic reductions in crops, particularly in Indonesia, which turned the country from a small exporter to a major importer. The weather patterns also delayed crops in Thailand and Pakistan and severely reduced crops in China. Fortunately, India was a safety valve and apart from *Basmati* had a good year, and considerable stocks which allowed them to step into the breach, and for the time being they were competitive in the world market (*LRBAC* 1st February 1995 1). Following a very aggressive buying campaign estimated at 1,500,000 tons, Indonesia's stated plan was to raise paddy production by 7 per cent to bring it to 49,000,000 tons. But it was difficult to see how after lengthy drought and only partial monsoon rain this could be achieved. Meanwhile shipments from Thailand and to a lesser extent Vietnam and Burma to Indonesia continued to be regular. It remained to be seen whether any Indian rice would go to the Indonesian market (*LRBAC* 1st February 1995 2). From Thailand, it was reported that China and Indonesia were buying regularly (*LRBAC* 1st February 1995 2–3). The United States sold 14,000 tons of long grain milled rice to Indonesia (*LRBAC* 1st February 1995 4). In Indonesia heavy floods followed lengthy drought and partial monsoons, causing further reductions to their crop estimates for 1995, and it was thought they might be importing close to 1,500,000 tons this year (*LRBAC* 28th February 1995 2). From Thailand, it was reported that Indonesia had bought 40,000 tons of 25 per cent from the Public Warehouse organisation (*LRBAC* 28th February 1995 3). Although Indonesia had a poor quality crop, it was not clear when they would re-enter the market (*LRBAC* 31st March 1995 1). In Indonesia, heavy rains 2 weeks before harvest were thought to have seriously damaged field yields. There was congestion in the ports which is why there was a current shortage of vessels (*LRBAC* 31st March 1995 2). From Thailand, it was reported that China and Indonesia were the major customers of Thailand this year and the export figures were as below.

Table 6.13 Thailand main rice markets January–March 1995 (metric tons)

	Jan 1995	*Feb 1995*	*March (1st-20th)*
China	187,430	213,470	169,940
Indonesia	156,980	129,360	42,690

(*LRBAC* 31st March 1995 2–3).

From Vietnam it was reported that loading remained slow with only 22,000 tons loaded 11th – 27th March. This was made worse by the fact that it was difficult to find vessels. There were 14 vessels in port, including 5 for Indonesia (*LRBAC* 31st March 1995 4). The controlling factors in the international rice trade continued to be shipments to Indonesia, China and Bangladesh. There was a shortage of vessels suitable for carrying a bagged cargo of 8000–18,000 tons due to increases in voyage times because of delays in both loading and unloading. A string of vessels was waiting to load rice at Yangon (Rangoon) in Burma, and Hochiminh (Saigon) in Vietnam had more than 24 vessels in port in recent weeks. Vessels had also been slow loading in India. As for unloading, the high levels of shipments to Indonesia and China had caused considerable delays. There were similar difficulties for bagged sugar cargoes and bulk commodities like steel and steel products, tripling round voyage times and driving up freight rates by as much as 50 per cent on some routes (*LRBAC* 1st May 1995 1). In Indonesia, the remains of old contracts were being shipped from Vietnam, India and Burma, and smaller quantities from Pakistan and

Thailand. But it was not clear what further purchases there might be as a result of the reduction in crop yields due to the weather. There was optimism there would be new buying in the last half of 1995 (*LRBAC* 1st May 1995 2). A lack of supply from Thailand, Vietnam, Pakistan and Burma but continuing demand from Indonesia was only counter-balanced by large volumes of rice available from the Food Corporation stock in India. There was also heavy flooding in China at harvest time, which was likely to make them continuing importers of rice (*LRBAC* 1st August 1995 1). Three factors currently dominated the rice market. How much would China buy? How much would Indonesia buy? How much would India export? As regards Indonesia, it was thought to have purchased 1,500,000 tons of rice, mostly from India. But there were delays from India, so Indonesia was probably a buyer for prompt shipment (*LRBAC* 1st September 1995 1). From Pakistan, it was reported that apart from old commitments by the private sector to Indonesia, there was no new crop business at the present time (*LRBAC* 2nd October 1995 3). Total world cereal production in 1995 was estimated at over 1,890,000,000 (Ed. 1.890 million) tons 57,000,000 tons less than 1994. This would affect the world rice trade in 1996. But the world rice trade in 1995 had seen an increase of 18,000,000 tons due to increased imports by China, Indonesia and Bangladesh. This was 1,750,000 tons more than the record set in calendar year 1994. India stepped in to fulfil lower quality rice requirements (although not entirely lower quality), as a result of reduced exports from Thailand, Vietnam and Myanmar (Burma), particularly in the later part of the year (*LRBAC* 1st November 1995 1). From India, it was reported there were rumours of large-scale government sales to Bangladesh, Indonesia, Malaysia and China, the latter two depending on quality trials (*LRBAC* 1st November 1995 2). From Thailand, it was reported there had been significant sales to Malaysia replacing previously defaulted sales, and new business to Indonesia for 100,000 tons of 25 per cent brokens (*LRBAC* lst November 1995 3–4).

1995 had been a most extraordinary year, with an increase in the world rice trade of nearly 19,000,000 tons, an increase of about 2,500,000 tons from 1994. Indonesia and China imported close to 3,000,000 tons each due to large shortfalls at home. This meant a strong market and a shortage of supply from the normal exporters Pakistan, Burma, Vietnam and Thailand. The market was only saved by the emergence of India as an exporter with a large surplus of government stock to sell at the beginning of the year, and later in the year after a good crop, private rice to sell of all qualities. But this was marred by huge difficulties with logistical problems, and the FCT (Government) increasing the price of their contracts. Burma and Vietnam could not fulfil commitments in the second half of the year because they had already sold large volumes of rice, in the case of Vietnam straight over the border into China. Indonesia had increased production and although they would probably continue to be an importer of rice in 1996, they were not expected to import so much. The Philippines would need to import but probably only 500,000 tons, and Bangladesh 1,000,000 tons. All this might mean that the world rice trade could be back to 1994 levels of 16,500,000 tons, although there was still uncertainty and it was difficult to know what to expect from China (*LRBAC* 2nd January 1996 1). New sales of 25 per cent brokens were reported from Thailand for Indonesia, including 20,000–30,000 tons of fragrant rice (*LRBAC* 2nd January 1996 4). It was thought Indonesia and China would not be such large buyers in 1996 (*LRBAC* 26th February 1996 1). From Thailand, it was reported that the major shipments in 1996 so far had been to Iran, the Philippines, China, Malaysia and Indonesia, and parboiled to South Africa and Cotonou in Benin (*LRBAC* 26th February 1996 3–4). From Pakistan, some unspecified shipments were continuing to Indonesia (*LRBAC* 26th February 1996 3). But at the beginning of April, it was reported that there had been changes in the market, including the fact that Indonesia was no longer a buyer but had 200,000–400,000 tons of Indian 25 per cent they wanted to resell (*LRBAC* 1st April 1996 1). From Thailand, it was reported that the government had recently sent a delegation to China hoping to get China to buy up to 30,000 tons of rice under their official protocol agreement. The delegation was then going on to Indonesia to try and persuade them also to buy (*LRBAC* 4th July 1996 3). From Indonesia, it was reported that there had been discussions with Thailand about the purchase of 200,000 tons of rice in exchange for military equipment, but it was not clear if this had been concluded (*LRBAC* 3rd September 1996 2). In November, it was reported that Indonesia and the Philippines were not in the market (*LRBAC* 4th November 1996 1).

There was no further news about Indonesia until September 1997 when the *Circular* reported that in Thailand the currency had been devalued against the U.S. Dollar by a further 10 per cent, and the resulting fall in prices had sent shock waves throughout the world market. Fear of another fall in the exchange rate was making buyers wary of making commitments. Other Asian currencies had also suffered substantial devaluations in their currencies, reducing their purchasing power for buying imports. Countries affected included Indonesia, the Philippines and Malaysia. There was speculation that the Philippines would enter the market, but Indonesia still had substantial rice stocks estimated at over 3,000,000 tons, and was unlikely to need to import rice in the short term. The *Circular* also declared that *El Nino* was a danger in many areas of the world, with effects perhaps worse than in 1982/83. The weather abnormalities would be the same but more severe droughts would potentially affect Central and Southern Africa, Australia, Indonesia, Thailand, India and Pakistan, and in contrast, there would be abnormally cold and wet weather with possible flooding in Peru, Argentina, Uruguay and Southern Brazil (*LRBAC* lst September 1997 1). In November, there had been a sharp increase in prices in the Far East, particularly Thailand, due to the early entrance of Indonesia into the market as a buyer. The quantities they had covered were thought to be close to 500,000 tons or more. There was drought in Indonesia leading to a substantially smaller crop than in recent years, possibly 10–15 per cent less. Indonesia would probably need imports of over 2,000,000 tons, but it was not clear when they would decide to buy the remaining 1,500,000 tons they might need (*LRBAC* 4th December 1997 1). There was excitement in Pakistan because of approaches by Indonesian buyers, and the realisation that Indonesia would buy Pakistan rice. Some bids were in the market already and it was rumoured that Indonesia would need over 2,000,000 tons in 1998 (*LRBAC* 4th December 1997 2). From Thailand, it was reported that prices were firmer and that in the middle of November Indonesian buyers had entered the market covering over 400,000 tons of 25 per cent. This seemed to have included both old and new import licences, and many private buyers, rather than the usual government buyer. The situation was clouded by traders covering substantial quantities of 25 per cent on their commitments to the Philippines. The Indonesian shipments were for December/January, with the main emphasis on December, whereas the Philippines shipments were for arrival January/February/March (*LRBAC* 4th December 1997 2–3). There were further purchases by Indonesia and the Philippines. Indonesia bought 1,000,000 tons, and then sanctioned another 500,000 tons bringing the total to 1,500,000 tons. Although letters of credit were opened swiftly, most of the purchases were made in the local currency, with Singapore traders taking the risk of the exchange rate against the U.S. Dollar. But the Singapore banks involved had decided enough was enough and were refusing to open any more letters of credit. It was thought letters of credit were open for about 800,000 tons, and that as shipments took place the letters of credit would be rolled over to cover later positions. Indonesia had to have the rice, and funds would therefore be made available (*LRBAC* 6th January 1998 1).

From Pakistan, it was reported that after problems with supply from Sindh due to the rains in November and early December things were sorting themselves out. There was drier weather now in Sindh and rice was arriving daily in Karachi. Most exporters were fully covered for vessels in port, of which there were many. They were mainly loading for West Africa, but a few were now declared for Indonesia (*LRBAC* 6th January 1998 2–3). It was reported from Thailand that the largest proportion of the Indonesian business would be supplied by Thailand with much of the business concluded without the involvement of the international merchants (*LRBAC* 6th January 1998 3). From Vietnam, it was reported that the Government had recently sold rice to Indonesia and the Philippines, and these commitments together with those to Iran, Iraq and Malaysia would take most of the exportable quantities during January and the first half of February (*LRBAC* 6th January 1998 4). In January, currencies were again of concern, in particular the Indonesian Rupiah. A concerted effort to support it had little effect. The Thai Baht also fell, but was less volatile. Demand for rice was still strong and most exporting countries had very high commitments driven by demand from Indonesia and the Philippines (*LRBAC* 2nd February 1998 1). The Indonesian Rupiah continued to fall, hitting a low of U.S. Dollar $1 to 10,500 in the middle of the month, just before a combined visit by the IMF and a high-profile delegation from the United States. The Indonesian government agreed to make changes to tackle their failing economy, and with promises of help from the United States, this was enough to bolster the market. One of the main changes was the breaking of BULOG's monopoly on all commodities except rice, increasing speculation that BULOG's monopoly on rice would also be abolished in due course. Import tariffs on various commodities were reduced, in particular food items where tariffs were restricted to a maximum of 5 per cent. But the euphoria was short-lived because of new concerns about bank debts. The Rupiah fell to U.S. Dollar $1 to 15,000. Seeing the value of their currency erode again, the general public tried to stock up on essentials including rice. Local prices increased sharply and stocks ran down. Demonstrations took place as people took to the streets. Traders who had recently shipped to Indonesia were having problems negotiating their letters of credit, and if action was not taken soon, traders might not have confidence to ship further quantities, reducing shipments to Indonesia (*LRBAC* 2nd February 1998 2). From the United States, it was reported that it was thought by some that a new application for PL480 aid for Indonesia was likely. PL480 assistance had been available to Indonesia in the past, and then Indonesia bought California medium grain (*LRBAC* 2nd February 1998 3). From Vietnam, it was reported in early January that offers for Vietnamese rice had started to come in, with prices slightly reduced from offers of old crop quoted. This was seen by many international merchants as a tremendous opportunity to cover their sales to Indonesia, and by mid-January, it was reported that commitments in the first quarter had already reached 1,400,000 tons (*LRBAC* 2nd February 1998 3–4). In March, it was reported that the market realised that demand was high, and there was speculation that Indonesia needed over 5,000,000 tons. It was also reported that the Philippines intended to buy another 600,000 tons from June (*LRBAC* 4th March 1998 1). In 1998, Indonesia was likely to be the largest single buyer of rice in the world. For *El Nino* to coincide with economic collapse in Indonesia was disastrous, and with new fires reported in Borneo, the situation was likely to get worse. Indonesia actually needed more rice than it was logistically possible for them to take within the year. The limitations were finance, ability to discharge and distribute and limitations of supply. But the main problem was finance. A number of country of origin suppliers shipping directly to Indonesia, and traders who had shipped rice to Indonesia, had had trouble receiving payment. Those affected had all accepted letters of credit from Indonesian banks without outside confirmation. At the beginning of February this caused significant lack of confidence, and shipments were cut. After re-negotiation, and although some companies had still not received payment, most had, and were making further shipments. It was originally reported that no shipments would be accepted it they arrived after the elections at the end of March, but in fact substantial purchases allowed shipment through March and April, when the Indonesian crop would start to be harvested. This crisis came about because of the serious instability of the Indonesian Rupiah in January. But the exchange rate had now stabilised at about U.S. Dollar $1–9000. In further steps to stabilise the Rupiah in mid-February, President Suharto sacked the Governor of the Indonesian Central Bank, due to his opposition to President Suharto's plan to set up a currency board. This would not be welcomed by the IMF who had already threatened to withdraw the U.S. Dollars $43 billion rescue package if Indonesia proceeded with the currency board. President Suharto quickly appointed a new Governor, Sjahril Sabirin, and it seemed that he would pursue a variation of the currency board idea to try to keep the IMF from withdrawing. The instability would likely continue to the elections at the end of March, and would affect other countries in the region (*LRBAC* 4th March 1998 2). From Thailand, it was reported that early in February some exporters who had made shipments directly to Indonesia and had accepted letters of credit opened by Indonesian banks found that after delivery payment was not forthcoming. A general agreement was reached between exporters that no further shipments would be made to Indonesia until these payments had been received

(*LRBAC* 4th March 1998 2–3). From the United States, it was reported that USDA was reviewing its GSM 102 credit arrangement with Indonesia for the current fiscal year which began on 1st October. Indonesia had been allocated U.S. Dollars $400,000,000 in GSM short term credits and this might be extended. It was strongly rumoured that part of some of these programmes could be used for rice, but further clarification was awaited (*LRBAC* 4th March 1998 3). From Vietnam, it was reported that the armada of vessels expected to arrive after Chinese New Year did not come, which was a shock to Vietnamese exporters who had been preparing their cargoes. The payment difficulties experienced by traders on shipments of rice to Indonesia led to a severe lack of confidence, and a sharp slowdown on shipments as traders stopped nominating new vessels to load until payment had been received on vessels already discharged in Indonesia. The delay was only about 15 days but felt longer. Instead of prices rising under a flood of vessels, prices eased as exporters found they had rice already prepared but no vessels on which to load. The situation was short lived and after renegotiations with Indonesia confidence returned and vessels started to arrive in large numbers. One purchase heralding a return of confidence was 150,000 tons for Indonesia, and 100,000 tons for the Philippines, all 5 per cent brokens (Ed. 25 per cent?) for shipment March/April. At the end of February, there were meetings between the government and exporters to discuss the large export commitments which had been made and to consider the general stock position and the possible effect on forthcoming crops if the highly disruptive weather patterns around the Pacific Rim were to cause a failure of rains which were so important for the second wet crop (*LRBAC* 4th March 1998 4). With weather patterns in the whole region in turmoil, Thailand could not be sure that the rains would appear as usually about the middle of May (*LRBAC* 6th April 1998 3). From Vietnam, it was reported that during March 70 vessels completed loading 753,828 tons, the largest quantity ever shipped in one month. More than half this quantity was for Indonesia, the next largest destination being the Philippines. This left 25 vessels in port under loading, 4 vessels waiting for a berth or cargo and 10 vessels to arrive shortly. These vessels were expected to load a further 441,000 tons (*LRBAC* 6th April 1998 4). At the end of April, it was reported that demand for rice in 1998 remained enormous, with the largest requirement coming from Indonesia. The Philippines were still a buyer, and there were suggestions that due to drought Malaysia would have to substantially increase its purchases. In the past, when there had been a sharp increase in world demand, it had always coincided with increased supply from one origin or another. For example, in 1995, when demand rose sharply due to Japanese requirements, India exported record quantities and kept the lower end of the market liquid. But this year there were concerns that world supply would tighten (*LRBAC* 30th April 1998 1). From China it was reported that from January to March 1998, inclusive exports totalled 364,501 tons, and with shipments already made, sales totalled 1,000,000 tons. The Chinese authorities had indicated their intention to ship up to 1,500,000 tons, and other reports suggested this might be increased to 2,000,000 tons. This was due to continued demand from Indonesia and the Philippines in addition to traditional buyers such as Cuba, which took 84,000 tons in 1997, Libya 65,000 tons and North Korea 91,000 tons. In 1998, there had already been sales of 124,000 tons to Iraq. Rumours of weather problems in China were as yet unsubstantiated. But the general disruption of weather patterns on the Pacific Rim was clearly of concern to any country heavily reliant on its own crops to feed its people (*LRBAC* 30th April 1998 1–2). From Pakistan, it was reported that in April, six vessels had already completed, loading 91,000 tons with another underloading for 21,000 tons. Of these, four were for Indonesia carrying very low-quality rice which was all that was available (*LRBAC* 30th April 1998 2–3). In May, it was reported that markets, in general, had tightened up considerably. The temporary halt in shipments to Indonesia and the cessation of further purchases by Indonesia had reduced the pressure slightly (*LRBAC* 29th May 1998 1). May was dominated by the terrible events in Indonesia. The frustration and anger, which had built up over many years under President Suharto, finally erupted, initially with huge demonstrations in many major cities. This evolved into widespread rioting and looting before restraint was shown by student leaders who had taken over and occupied the parliamentary building. Finally, President Suharto stepped down, leaving the new President Jusef Habibie to pick up the pieces. The President quickly appointed a new cabinet, promising radical reforms, elections before the end of his term in office, and the setting free of a number of political prisoners. But concerns had already been raised that the new cabinet contained only a few new members and was otherwise just a reshuffle, and that no new date had been set for elections. Until then, there were new and free elections; many would be suspicious that former President Suharto was still pulling the strings from behind the scenes. Purchases of rice had now been suspended for over two weeks, and many with outstanding sales to Indonesia had put shipments on hold until they could be sure that letters of credit were secure. As an example, the Thai Exporters' Association had confirmed that although they had a commitment for over 200,000 tons, no further shipments would be made until they had a chance to re-evaluate the risk and had letters of credit opened by first class banks from third countries (*LRBAC* 29th May 1998 3). From Vietnam, it was reported that during May, there had been an increase in vessels loading for destinations other than Indonesia and the Philippines, with 11 for Indonesia, 4 for the Philippines, 5 for Africa, 5 for Iraq, 1 for Iran, 1 for Malaysia, 1 for South America and 2 for Baltic ports (*LRBAC* 29th May 1998 4). Supplies of rice from Asian origins remained tight, although the market had some respite as a result of reduced demand from Indonesia caused by the political upheavals there (*LRBAC* 3rd July 1998 1). The situation in Indonesia was still far from peaceful and there were regular demonstrations, some calling for more political reforms and elections, and others demonstrating against the economic problems and the very high prices which the general public faced, particularly of food. After lengthy meetings between the new Government and the IMF, loans had resumed, initially with a U.S. Dollars $225,000,000 Poverty Loan from the World Bank. This and other substantial loans had broken the paralysis, enabling new letters of credit to be opened against the substantial backlog of purchase contracts for rice concluded before Suharto's departure. It was still not clear whether a new structure or format had been agreed for the purchase of rice in the future, but certainly various options were being looked at, from purchases from free trade to government-to-government contracts, or even tenders. The Director of BULOG was understood to have lost his position, but so far a replacement had not been announced. There were however reports that BULOG might have bought directly from Thailand although this could well have been a renegotiation of contracts as letters of credit were opened for old purchases, or the replacement of contracts refused by late sellers due to late opening of letters of credit and sharp increases in prices of origin. Although it was difficult to get a clearer picture, it was thought that close to 3,500,000 tons had been shipped and received by Indonesia and there were still outstanding commitments to ship a further 1,000,000 tons during July, August and September (*LRBAC* 3rd July 1998 3). From Thailand, it was reported that the resumption of lending by the World Bank to Indonesia had meant that after a lull in shipment, new letters of credit were being opened for business concluded a little while ago, and there had been a sharp increase in the number of vessels loading for Indonesia. There were rumours that new sales had been made of 250,000 – 350,000 tons of 25 per cent to Indonesia, but it was not clear whether this was new business or renegotiations of old business as letters of credit were opened (*LRBAC* 3rd July 1998 3–4). From Vietnam, it was reported that up to the 24th June 12 vessels completed loading a total of 98,167 tons of which 1 was destined for Indonesia, 5 for the Philippines, 1 to Brazil, 1 to Iraq, 1 to West Africa, and 3 smaller vessels to Malaysia. There were a further 6 vessels in port expected to load another 65,600 tons, including 3 for the Philippines, 1 for Iraq and 2 smaller vessels for Malaysia. Almost all shipments in the past month had been made by the Government through the Southern Food Company (*LRBAC* 3rd July 1998 4). Indonesia made a number of moves to purchase more rice, but no significant new contracts seem to have been concluded since the change in leadership. Finance seemed to be the main problem and approaches were made to several Governments to get a credit line or delayed payment terms. At the end of July there were rumours that the Japanese might have given a substantial credit line to the Indonesian Government to purchase rice, but so far nothing appeared to have been agreed. The Vietnamese Government confirmed they would offer 1 year's credit of 100,000 tons at a reduced rate, but the Vietnamese delegation which returned from Jakarta towards the end of July could not conclude a sale due to the high price they were charging. Some exporters had hoped Indonesia would buy up to 300,000 tons. Early in August an Indonesian delegation was to be sent to Thailand to try to negotiate a substantial purchase from the Thai Government, thought to be 500,000 tons. They had already tried to get preferential terms but the Thai Government had resisted. It was thought that the delegation would push for delayed payments, but if the Thai Government agreed it would only be for a small portion of Indonesian requirements. These negotiations could set the tone for the market for the rest of the year (*LRBAC* 31st July 1998 2–3). From Thailand, it was reported that expectations of further sales to Indonesia and the Philippines had kept prices firmer, particularly for lower quality 25 per cent. There was a World Food Programme tender for Indonesia for 2 cargoes of 16,000 tons of 25 per cent, one from Thailand and the other with the option of Thailand or Vietnam. The business was thought to have gone to Thailand for both cargoes, shipment August. This was the low point for 25 per cent prices in July. The

Indonesian delegation was expected to buy up to 500,000 tons government to government. There were several vessels in port in Thailand, including vessels for Indonesia (*LRBAC* 31st July 1998 3–4). From Vietnam, there were two recent examples that the Vietnamese were not aggressively trying to increase their exports. The first was in their allowing the World Food Programme tender for Indonesia to go to Thailand, and the second their uncompromisingly high prices which led to the Indonesians rejecting their offer for 100,000 tons and turning again to Thailand. During July there were 2 vessels for Indonesia, 7 for the Philippines, 4 for Malaysia, 1 for Iraq and 1 for South America. There were 3 vessels currently in port to load another 23,239 tons, 1 for Indonesia, 1 for the Philippines and 1 for Iraq (*LRBAC* 31st July 1998 4). Severe weather conditions continued in the Far East, with flooding in China. The Vietnamese, who were also suffering with the weather, had stopped selling and did not expect to re-enter the market as a seller until the New Year. Nonetheless Indonesia had bought some quantities from Vietnam and Thailand, and was expected to increase these purchases substantially, either by tender or government-to-government purchases. However, discussions had been put back due to the recent resignation of the President of BULOG, Beddu Amang (*LRBAC* 28th August 1998 1). In Indonesia internal wrangling meant few decisions to purchase rice were made in August. The Government was believed to have purchased 100,000 tons of Vietnamese 25 per cent, but discussions to raise this to 300,000 – 400,000 tons came to nothing. The Indonesian Government then turned to Thailand where the Government there offered 100,000 tons on 1 year's credit and a further 400,000 tons on cash basis. The 100,000 tons was definitely concluded shipped Bangkok, being Thai long grain white rice 25 per cent super. But the 400,000 tons were not concluded. Then the Government announced a tender for 600,000 tons with origins restricted to China, Vietnam and Thailand. The tender which was to be on the 26th August was postponed to the 27th. Then as noted above the Indonesian President insisted on the resignation of the Chairman of BULOG, and the tender was postponed again to 10th September. Meanwhile Indonesia asked for an extension on the offer from Thailand for 400,000 tons for a reply on 1st September. There was enough rice in the local market to satisfy demand, but stocks held by BULOG were very small as they had been unable to purchase a reasonable quantity of locally produced rice due to the high prices. So it was thought that BULOG would need to import rice so they had a stock they could use to control prices in the domestic market by releasing stocks when local prices rose. There were concerns that once again new crops would be affected by lack of rain and again be below target, and it was thought that Indonesia would have to continue importing in the coming year (*LRBAC* 28th August 1998 2–3). From Pakistan it was reported that the Islamic Commercial Bank of Jeddah had offered Indonesia a substantial credit line for purchasing rice limited to Pakistan origin. There was also a similar offer made by the Faisal Islamic Bank for U.S. Dollars $100,000,000 (Ed. U.S. Dollars $100 million). This raised hopes for substantial demand in the coming season from Indonesia. But the Indonesian Government were trying to negotiate to use this facility to purchase from any origin as they were unhappy with the quality of the rice shipped from Pakistan at the end of the 1997 crop, shipment March/April/May

1998 (*LRBAC* 28th August 1998 3). From Thailand, it was reported that the Indonesian delegation only purchased 100,000 tons on 1 year's credit. But the tender announced by the Indonesian Government had fuelled speculation, as the situation in China and the fact that Vietnam had withdrawn from the market, probably meant that the only viable option for Indonesia would be to buy from Thailand. Thailand's hopes of selling to Indonesia remained high but the postponement of the tender to the 10th September came as a surprise, as did the Indonesian request for an extension of the offer for 400,000 tons from the Thai Government to lst September. Prices for 25 per cent and broken rice remained firm on expectation of sales to Indonesia, with brokens likely to be in demand for mixing to create the low quality required for the Indonesian market (*LRBAC* 28th August 1998 3). In the middle of August the Vietnamese Government announced it would not allow any more sales of Vietnamese rice although contracts already in place and registered with the Government would be executed. The second crop had little effect on availability and the Government was not expected to allow further sales until January. Vietnamese commitments were mainly for Indonesia, the Philippines, Malaysia, and Iraq. In August 14 vessels had completed loading including 7 for Indonesia, 2 for Iraq, 3 for West Africa, 1 for Brazil and 1 for Cuba (*LRBAC* 28th August 1998 1). In Indonesia a number of tenders had been announced, but then most of them were postponed. When they did take place, results were published on 18th and 22nd September (*LRBAC* 2nd October 1998 1). A tender announced in Indonesia at the beginning of September was for 600,000 tons, with origins limited to Thailand, Vietnam, China and Burma. This was then postponed several times, and eventually held on 16th September with results confirmed on the 18th by the Chairman of the tender committee, Mohammad Ismet. China was awarded 20,000 tons for October, 138,000 tons for November, and 94,000 tons for December (Ed. 252,000 tons). Thailand was awarded 20,000 tons for September, 40,000 tons for October, 20,000 tons for November, and 140,000 tons for December (Ed. 220,000 tons). Myanmar (Burma) was awarded 10,000 tons for September and 10,000 tons for November (Ed. 20,000 tons). Vietnam was awarded 24,000 tons for November. Subsequently negotiations took place for additional lots and 60 offers were made from different origins. An additional 190,000 tons were concluded. 50,000 tons were to Myanmar September/October, and 20,000 tons for December (Ed. 70,000 tons). China had 50,000 tons September/October, 25,000 tons November, and 45,000 tons December (Ed. 120,000 tons). This brought the total concluded to 716,000 tons (Ed. 10,000 tons not accounted for). In addition a further offer was made from Thailand for 400,000 tons of Thai 25 per cent super stowed Bangkok. On 2nd October negotiations were concluded between Vietnam and Indonesia for a further 200,000 – 300,000 tons of 25 per cent. But the 100,000 tons sold in September by the Thai Government did not have a letter of credit, although it was reported there would be one soon. This all sounded like a lot of business, but there were concerns that a number of companies who made offers had been unable to open their performance bonds, or had withdrawn since the tender. There were also concerns that Indonesia would not be able to open letters of credit for the full quantity within a reasonable time. There was no question that Indonesia needed rice and it seemed they would continue to import right up to the harvest of their new crop in March. This would be about 500,000 tons a month or 2,500,000 tons in all. Because of the potential problems Indonesia faced in opening letters of credit, they needed to look at offers made by various countries, including the Islamic Commercial Bank in Jeddah, and the Faisal Islamic Bank. Both of these offers were restricted to purchases from Islamic countries. Discussions were already taking place with the Egyptian Government for purchases of 100,000 – 200,000 tons and there were plans to send a delegation to Pakistan, where preliminary discussions had already taken place for up to 400,000 tons (*LRBAC* 2nd October 1998 2–3). From Pakistan it was reported that the market was excited by the prospect of selling large quantities to Indonesia. An Indonesian delegation was to arrive in Pakistan on 4th October but might be postponed (*LRBAC* 2nd October 1998 3). From Thailand, it was reported that the only real point of interest had been Indonesia, and at a tender a quantity of 220,000 tons was confirmed as accepted. Subsequently another 400,000 tons was concluded outside the tender. But there were concerns whether Indonesia would be able to open letters of credit promptly for these contracts, and prices fell for 25 per cent and 100 per cent Grade B (*LRBAC* 2nd October 1998 3–4). From Vietnam, it was reported that the government might lift the ban on new sales of rice. The Vietnamese Government had continued to try to make government-to-government sales both to Indonesia and the Philippines at the end of September and it seemed they had come to an agreement with Indonesia for a further 300,000 tons. Any private sales to Indonesia, the Philippines, Iran, Iraq and Malaysia had to have price approval from the government and prices had to be higher than sales made government to government. During August the Vietnamese loaded 12 vessels with 118,635 tons, mostly for the Philippines. By the 25th September 15 vessels had completed loading 152,815 tons of which 6 were for Indonesia, 3 for the Philippines 3 for Iraq, 1 for Eastern Europe, 1 for East Africa and 1 for Brazil (*LRBAC* 2nd October 1998 4). After the excitement of October's Indonesian tenders there was disappointment as letters of credit were opened slowly or not at all, meaning demand was far less than originally shown. World export demand which was expected to reach a record of 26,750,000 tons in 1998 was expected to decline in 1999 by anything from 3,000,000 to 7,000,000 tons, the main reductions coming from Indonesia, the Philippines, Bangladesh and Brazil (*LRBAC* 6th November 1998 1). From Pakistan it was reported that various meetings had been arranged between Indonesia and Pakistan, but nothing materialised and it seemed Indonesian interest in Pakistan rice was on hold (*LRBAC* 6th November 1998 3). From Thailand, it was reported that in October exporters were plagued with uncertainty about the Indonesia business reported last month. Some of the shipment periods were very prompt, but without letters of credit nothing could be shipped. Letters of credit were then opened for some of the amounts sold, but for the 400,000 tons sold shortly after the tender there was still no letter of credit and few believed this business now stood (*LRBAC* 6th November 1998 3). From the United States, it was reported that the market was generally quiet, and only helped by shipments of paddy to Brazil, and various Government programmes, in particular to Indonesia. So far 26,000 tons had been concluded for shipment to Indonesia in November, and there was a balance of 40,000 tons, but no tender had yet been held. It was reported that the U.S. Government had come to an agreement with China to help Indonesia, whereby the U.S. Government would ship some 500,000 tons of wheat to China, and in return the Chinese would ship 250,000 tons of rice to Indonesia (*LRBAC* 6th November 1998 4). From Vietnam, it was reported that new sales of rice had indeed been sanctioned by the Vietnamese Government, but prices were carefully controlled. Their main drive was to sell high quality rice, as low grade 25 per cent was already in great demand for their shipments to Indonesia, for which they had recent commitments to ship 500,000 tons. 200,000 tons of this had already been shipped, leaving a balance of 300,000 tons to be shipped during November and December. Due to the high prices Vietnam was demanding there was little business other than Government contracts with Indonesia, Malaysia and Iraq. During October 22 vessels loaded 184,000 tons, 13 vessels being for Indonesia, 5 for Iraq, 2 for Malaysia, 1 for Algeria and 1 for Eastern Europe. 5 more vessels were loading a further 48,000 tons, of which 4 were for Indonesia and 1 for Iraq (*LRBAC* 6th November 1998 4). From Pakistan it was announced that the long talked about tenders for Indonesia and the Philippines had finally materialised, but not necessarily in the form expected. The largest of the two was for Indonesia. On 23rd November the Trade Corporation of Pakistan (TCP) invited offers from private exporters to be given on 26th November for 200,000 tons of IRRI 6 25 per cent with shipments in lots of 25,000 tons to be shipped over 4 months at a rate of 50,000 tons a month. But an enquiry came from a non-government organisation in the United States, who were hoping to do the business, offering their own financing package to the Indonesian Government. It remained to be seen if any business would materialise from this tender (*LRBAC* 7th December 1998 2–3). From Thailand, surprisingly there was still talk of the single sale of 400,000 tons to Indonesia done about 2 months previously. It was not thought the letter of credit had been opened, but it was still possible, and exporters were trying to resurrect this business now that markets were at a more favourable level (*LRBAC* 7th December 1998 3–4). From Vietnam, it was reported that during November 18 vessels were loaded of which 12 were for Indonesia, 3 for Iraq, 2 for Malaysia and 1 for Japan. On 7th December there were 10 vessels in port expected to load 100,000 tons. 3 were for Indonesia, 1 for the Philippines, 2 for Iraq, 1 for Malaysia, 1 for Japan and 2 for West Africa (*LRBAC* 7th December 1998 4). In December the long awaited tender for Indonesia was finally announced to utilise part of the financing offer by the Islamic Development Bank (IDB). The tender was held on 16th December for 200,000 tons with options for origin including India and Pakistan for 10 per cent, and Egypt, China, Thailand and Vietnam for 25 per cent, shipment January/February. The tender took place on time but India and Pakistan were allowed to offer 15 per cent-20 per cent although previously only asked for 10 per cent. All offers had to be for a minimum of 20,000 tons, and 68 companies put offers in, but only 38 had their documents and bid bonds in order. All prices were for delivery to one safe Indonesian port. The tender was awarded just for Pakistan origin for 277,000 tons, shipment January/February although many expected these shipments to be delayed into March. This seemed likely with all the holidays associated with Ramadan, Christmas and New Year. The award was not actually offered in lots of 20,000 tons as requested. Indonesia was not expected to tender again until after their new crop at the end of March. But they might take advantage of various offers of aid and financing such as 100,000 tons being offered by the United States and due to be tendered on 6th January (*LRBAC* 4th January 1999 2). From Pakistan the most important news was their success in the tender held by BULOG in which they sold the 277,000 tons of Pakistan IRRI 6 15 per cent-20 per cent at heavily discounted prices (*LRBAC* 4th January 1999 2–3). From Thailand, it was reported that shipments in December had been mainly made up of 300,000 tons to Indonesia and the Philippines, but business to Indonesia and the Philippines could easily go to elsewhere such as Vietnam where prices were substantially lower, and a tranche had already gone to Pakistan (*LRBAC* 4th January 1999 3). From Vietnam, it was reported that prices had drifted lower, but not enough to take business from Pakistan. One possible opportunity to sell had been the Indonesian tender, but the Government Steering Committee in charge of setting prices increased the price by U.S. Dollars $10 and announced it would not allow any business to be done below a set price. This was not low enough to compete with Pakistan and was unsuccessful. The main destinations during December were again Indonesia and the Philippines (*LRBAC* 4th January 1999 4).

From Pakistan the initial elation after the results of the tender with Indonesia was short lived as the wait for the letters of credit began. But then some arrived. Sales in the tender were originally basis January/February shipment, but with the letters of credit only just arriving, new shipment periods must have been agreed. Then prices rose, one reason being the recent visit of a delegation from Indonesia to discuss a substantial barter, by which Indonesia would supply Pakistan with crude oil, palm oil and tea, and Pakistan would send rice and sugar to Indonesia. Figures up to 1,000,000 tons had been mentioned, but it was unlikely this business would be concluded, and almost certainly not in time to have an impact on this year's crop. More vessels were expected to arrive shortly for Indonesia, as there were 177,000 tons to ship (*LRBAC* 2nd February 1999 2). From Thailand, it was reported that in the hunt for commitments, the old contract with Indonesia done by the Government of Thailand for 100,000 tons of 25 per cent on 3 year's credit was resurrected and a Thai delegation was expected to visit Indonesia to press for it to be executed (*LRBAC* 2nd February 1999 3). From the United States, it was reported that there had been no development yet of the P.L.480 Title 1 agreements with Indonesia and Russia which were both scheduled for 100,000 tons of U.S. milled rice (*LRBAC* 2nd February 1999 4). From Pakistan, it was reported that prices were being sustained by the expectation that shipments to Indonesia would start soon for the 277,000 tons sold in the tender covered by the Islamic Development Bank financing. Although the letters of credit that had been received were unworkable, hopes had been kept high by the arrival of vessels to load for Indonesia, initially thought to be under Islamic Development Bank contracts, but actually loading for shipments under other contracts which might have been outstanding for some time. Some now doubted whether shipments would ever take place for the quantities concluded under the BULOG tender using IDB financing. So either Pakistan had 100,000 tons uncommitted or 400,000 tons uncommitted (*LRBAC* 3rd March 1999

3). From Vietnam, it was reported that there were 8 vessels in port to load 102,891 tons for destinations including the Philippines, but not Indonesia (*LRBAC* 3rd March 1999 4). From Pakistan, it was reported that there had been a steady flow of vessels arriving to load for Indonesia, but not the rush many had expected. Some were now loading under letters of credit opened using the Islamic Development Bank's credit, but it was believed that several of the companies with commitments to ship Pakistan rice to Indonesia had been given the option of shipping from other origins, in particular Thailand and Vietnam, and there was evidence of purchasing which suggested this was true (*LRBAC* 6th April 1999 3). From the United States it was reported that negotiations with the Government of Indonesia for their 100,000 tons P.L.480 programme were not going well. Both the Indonesian and Russian businesses were very important to the U.S. rice industry (*LRBAC* 30th April 1999 3). The Asian markets were again hit by bad weather. With the memory of *El Nino* so fresh in people's minds, many thought the heavy rain in Vietnam and Thailand was the result of *La Nina*. There was no question that the weather was very strange. Intense rain in Thailand in August and September was only to be expected, but not in May. The same was true for Vietnam (*LRBAC* lst June 1999 1). From Indonesia, it was reported that it had been a while since the last purchases by BULOG, but outstanding contracts were being shipped. Firstly those utilising the IDB credit line, and secondly a business of 400,000 tons originally done by a company in Bangkok, but subsequently taken by a Singapore trading house. The result was regular shipments from Vietnam, Thailand and Pakistan. There were rumours that BULOG might hold a tender for 300,000 tons. But it was not thought any purchases would be made until after the elections on Monday 7th June, as it would take a little time for the new Government to settle in and for further funds to be released by the World Bank (*LRBAC* 1st June 1999 2). From Pakistan it was reported that some shipments were still taking place, but preparation of cargo seemed to be taking longer and longer. Many of the vessels arriving to load were destined for Indonesia against contracts signed much earlier in the year using the Islamic Bank credit line (*LRBAC* 1st June 1999 3). From Thailand, it was reported that most demand was for low quality, particularly 25 per cent and broken rice for which there had been quite a heavy shipment programme which looked set to continue. Demand was strong for 25 per cent brokens to Indonesia covering old contracts which must have been close to completion (*LRBAC* 1st June 1999 3). The following month it was reported from Thailand that the market was a bit firmer as more vessels were nominated to load 100 per cent B for Iran, and 25 per cent for Indonesia. The amount of private business concluded with Indonesia had taken the market by surprise as this was now amounting to 100,000 tons a month. This, together with shipments of brokens to Africa, would keep the price of low quality 25 per cent brokens stable to firm (*LRBAC* 9th July 1999 3). From the United States, it was reported that USDA had at last issued purchase authorisation for Indonesia's P.L.480 Title 1 for 115,000 tons of U.S. No.5 or better, delivery July 20th through to 31st December 1999. Before any tenders went out, Indonesia would have to appoint a shipping agent. Out of a total P.L.480 allocation of 277,200 tons this year only 63,150 tons had been sold (*LRBAC* 9th July 1999 3). From Vietnam, it was reported there were many rumours of potential purchases by Indonesia and the Philippines, but so far nothing had materialised. But there was a regular flow of business from private buyers to Indonesia for small quantities of 2,000 – 5,000 tons. These buyers were paying reasonable prices compared to those offered by international merchants for larger quantities, and keeping prices up (*LRBAC* 9th July 1999 4). Asian markets remained stable in July due to the arrival of the second crop in Thailand and Vietnam, and heavy demand from Iran and especially Indonesia where demand from the private trade had led to shipments from different origins of 250,000 tons. On 2nd August BULOG announced a tender to take place on 10th August for 75,000 tons of 25 per cent, all origins acceptable except Myanmar. An Indonesian Government delegation was expected in Washington to organise a tender under the P.L.480 programme for 6 to 7 shipments of 15,000 tons each of U.S. No.5, 20 per cent brokens well milled, for shipments to the end of the year (*LRBAC* 3rd August 1999 1). From Thailand, it was reported that heavy shipments to Indonesia and Iran had led to heavy exports. July exports reached over 612,236 tons, even greater than June's 535.000 tons, which was the previous record for the year (*LRBAC* 3rd August 1999 3). From the United States, it was reported that P.L.480 allocations had been reviewed with a doubling of the quantity to the Philippines to 40,000 tons. There had been few tenders for these allocations, and of the total 300,000 tons only 63,000 tons had been taken up. Upcoming tenders included 13,750 tons to Indonesia, North Korea, Sri Lanka, Guatemala and Honduras (*LRBAC* 3rd August 3–4). From Vietnam, it was reported that the continued and very active trade to Indonesia for 25 per cent brokens had been the stabilising feature. Most of the enquiries were for small quantities of 2,000 – 3,000 tons and exporters had tended to get a slight premium for selling in these small lots. With the recent announcement of the BULOG tender, there had been a rush by private traders for Indonesia to get their shipments as quickly as possible. This caused a sharp increase in the nomination of vessels and a slight squeeze in supply which was holding prices firmer (*LRBAC* 3rd August 1999 4). The Indonesian tender held in early August was disappointing and many were taken by surprise by the very low offer made for Chinese rice. The purchase by BULOG was smaller than expected, and the price was also lower, weakening prices generally. Many believed that Indonesia would need to buy a substantial quantity of rice before the end of the year, which would dictate prices in the Far East in the run up to the new crop (*LRBAC* 26th August 1999 1). After being quiet for two months, Indonesia finally returned to the market and held a tender on 10th August for 75,000 tons of 25 per cent brokens for shipment September/October. Offers accepted were Thailand, Vietnam, China, Pakistan and Egypt. Many offers were received, the cheapest of which was for Chinese rice where 3 lots of 25,000 tons were offered by the same company. Many offers were received including from Pakistan, Thailand and Vietnam. But BULOG only confirmed 75,000 tons of Chinese rice. The price was very low and may have been based on Chinese old crop, which was not acceptable under the tender terms, or a mistake had been made. As the Indonesian authorities were under intense scrutiny by the IMF and the national and international media, great care was taken to ensure there was no hint of foul play. BULOG was now believed to have three contracts in hand, two of 400,000 tons of Thai rice 25 per cent super including two year's credit, and one lot of 75,000 tons bought in this tender. But there were concerns these contracts would not be delivered. The performance bond for the Thai contract had not been opened, and it was thought these contracts would be cancelled as they did not seem commercially viable. But Indonesia needed to buy and receive a substantial quantity of rice before the end of the year. However, the U.S. tender under the P.L.480 Title 1 for Indonesia went off smoothly. 99,335 tons were awarded for shipment September/October 1999. Private imports to Indonesia had been an important factor over recent months, and had increased to about 350,000 tons per month. Much of this rice was being sold on arrival to BULOG, who normally bought substantial quantities of locally grown rice at this time of year. There were reports in the press towards the end of August that BULOG had stopped buying locally, and many exporters in Thailand and Vietnam were wondering if contracts in hand would be lifted by the private sector (*LRBAC* 26th August 1999 2–3). From Thailand, it was reported there was a lack of enquiries causing the market to ease. This was not helped by the low price for Chinese rice in the Indonesian tender, and reports that BULOG had stopped buying from the private sector in Indonesia. A very substantial portion of exports over the past few months had been 25 per cent to the Indonesian private sector (*LRBAC* 26th August 1999 3). From the United States, it was reported that the Government Food Aid Programme was critical to the U.S. export picture, and activity in August had centred on a number of tenders that had added needed support to the U.S. milled rice export situation. Indonesia's Director of Foreign Aid Procurement and his team conducted a tender for 115,000 tons of U.S. 5/20 (Ed. No.5 20 per cent) on 12th August. This was awarded shipped Gulf (Ed. of Mexico) Port, shipment 1st September/31st October. Further tenders were announced towards the end of August under P.L.480, and the Philippines were allocated 40,000 tons of long grain 2/4 for shipment no later than the second half of December (*LRBAC* 26th August 1999 4). From Vietnam, it was reported that the lack of new demand from Indonesia had caused many exporters to lower their prices. Shipments to Indonesia had made up a very substantial proportion of recent exports from Vietnam (*LRBAC* 26th August 1999 4). In Asia, prices had fallen as the realities of the market became plain. Demand had fallen off considerably, and there was still a lot of rice available in Thailand and Vietnam. The new crop had started in Pakistan, was short of starting in India and would be available in Thailand from the end of November. Many had expected Indonesia to be importing substantial quantities, but due to the cancellation of the 75,000 tons concluded in the tender (Ed. from China, see above *LRBAC* 26th August 1999 2–3) and the political situation since purchases seemed to be on hold until after a new President was elected early in November (*LRBAC* 1st October 1999 1). There was very little news from China, although the ports had been busy with vessels loading against contracts concluded earlier. Some vessels were destined for Indonesia, but in main Africa (*LRBAC* 1st October 1999 1). For many, Indonesia was still seen as the key to the direction of the market during the new crop and the first part of 2000. As for the tender awarded in Indonesia in August (Ed. for China rice), it was eventually cancelled. The two other contracts of 400,000 tons each of Thai rice were also cancelled. Since then there had been no further purchases, except for the odd private business, and even private business was now restricted as the Government had brought in new regulations restricting private imports only to high quality 5 per cent and better. So the most important single buyer of Asian rice, Indonesia, had withdrawn from the market. Everyone was aware of developments in East Timor, and the humiliation that the withdrawal of Indonesian troops had caused. The political situation in Jakarta was very unstable, and President Habibie's authority was completely undermined. The People's Consultative Committee was due to elect a new President in November, and until then there was unlikely to be any improvement. The stocks of rice held by BULOG were being used up at the rate of about 400,000 – 500,000 tons per month and would need to be replenished by Government or private imports (*LRBAC* lst October 1999 3). From Thailand, it was reported that shipments to Indonesia fell very quickly in September as prices in Vietnam were cheaper. Prices continued to fall because of the new import regulations to Indonesia for private trade, and the lack of new purchases by BULOG (*LRBAC* 1st October 1999 3). From Vietnam, it was reported that Indonesia was to ban all private imports of rice except for high quality 5 per cent or better. This was received in Vietnam with concern due to the large quantities of outstanding contracts still unshipped. A grace period of a month was given, and it was thought this would cause a rush by Indonesian private buyers to get shipment as early as possible to meet the deadline. But the progressive weakening of the Indonesian Rupiah put paid to these hopes, and shipments were lower than expected. Without Indonesia as a buyer, supply far outstripped demand (*LRBAC* lst October 1999 4). In Indonesia, the election was won by Abdurrahman Wahid of the National Awakening Party. Megawati Sukarnoputri, who many thought of as a favourite, was elected Vice President. This result was generally welcomed by the international community, and it was hoped this would give greater stability to the whole region. After the election results the Indonesian Rupiah strengthened, giving an opportunity for a little more private business to Indonesia. But stocks in private hands kept the private business in check. There was a new sale of 250,000 tons of 25 per cent to BULOG (*LRBAC* 5th November 1999 2). From Pakistan, it was reported that the border with Afghanistan and Iran remained closed, but in a small way, this border trade was replaced by active shipments of containers of rice to Indonesia. These were carrying so called "5 per cent broken" rice to meet the import restrictions in Indonesia for private trade. But this would probably stop soon as it was thought Indonesia would impose an import duty on all imports of rice from 25 per cent to 35 per cent from 1st January 2000 (*LRBAC* 3rd December 1999 2–3). From Thailand, it was reported that the greatest demand was for high-quality Thai rice such as 100 per cent B for Iran, and 5 per cent for Indonesia. This was in sharp contrast to the last couple of years when shipments to Indonesia and the Philippines meant high demand for 25 per cent. Prices for high quality held their levels, but prices for low quality 25 per cent and broken rice fell sharply (*LRBAC* 3rd December 1999 3). From the United States, it was reported there were a few tenders early in November, including 4,500 tons for Indonesia. The P.L.480 Title 1 programme was of critical importance to the U.S. rice industry, and the U.S. Rice Federation had been lobbying hard to ensure inclusion in the 2000 programmes (*LRBAC* 3rd December 1999 3–4).

As regards the Philippines, in April 1990 it was reported from Vietnam that exports since January had been 500,000 – 600,000 tons with commitments for further shipments of 140,000 tons of 35 per cent to the Philippines via Indonesia, 500,000 tons to the U.S.S.R., 200,000 tons to China, 132,000 tons of 10 per cent brokens to Iran plus commitments to traders for lower quality to West Africa and other destinations (*LRBAC* 30th April 1990 3). Then in June, it was reported that Vietnam had export commitments of around 2,250,000 tons, of which a large part was 500,000 tons 35 per cent sold to the Philippines, and a balance of 100,000 tons of 5–10 per cent to be shipped to Iran all by the end of August. Vietnam was giving preference to these two commitments, which were both government-to-government contracts (*LRBAC* 30th June 1990 3). In Thailand, the Bangkok market thrived on rumours, and there were negotiations with the Philippines for 100,000–400,000 tons, and also with Iran and Russia. But in Vietnam, no more shipments were to be allowed in 1990 except to complete contracts with the Philippines and Iran. Even the balance of these, 100,000 tons for the Philippines and 30,000 tons for Iran had been put back for shipment in September (*LRBAC* 31st July 1990 1). From Thailand, it was reported that the government had sold 100,000 tons of 35 per cent to the Philippines, July shipment. There was an additional option for 300,000 tons at the same price which it was thought the Philippines would take up (*LRBAC* 31st July 1990 3). In Vietnam, all exports had been suspended until further notice and probably for the rest of 1990. The exception was the balance on government sales to the Philippines and Iran, but as noted previously even these had been put back to September (*LRBAC* 31st July 1990 3).

There was no more news about the Philippines until January 1991 when it was reported from China that 200,000 tons had been traded to various destinations, with more than 100,000 tons of this to the Philippines, quality 35 per cent (*LRBAC* 9th January 1991 1). There is then a gap until May 1992 when it was reported from the Philippines that drought was causing damage to all crops and would have some effect on rice production that year (*LRBAC* 31st May 1992 2). Then there was nothing in the Circular until June 1993 when it was reported from Thailand that 150,000 tons of 35 per cent brokens had been sold to the Philippines in exchange for fertiliser. These were already being moved, with some 65,000–70,000 tons of freight having been nominated (*LRBAC* 30th June 1993 3). Later in the year, it was reported from the Philippines that there had been in recent months a purchase from Thailand and another from Vietnam. The current crop shortfall was estimated at 450,000 tons, so there might be more purchases towards the end of the year, with Thailand and Vietnam expected to be leading suppliers (*LRBAC* 1st October 1993 3). By November, the main crop in the Philippines was estimated at 5,200,000 tons which was 330,000 tons down in 1992. This was the result of tropical storms that caused damage to standing crops in central Luzon and Cagayan. There was no news of possible imports (*LRBAC* 30th November 1993 3). (Ed. This coincided with bad weather in Japan and Korea). From Thailand, it was reported that its main buyers were the Philippines, Hong Kong, United Arab Emirates, Iran, Benin, South

America and Sudan, each of which took over 200,000 tons per annum, followed by Singapore, Malaysia and the United States, each of which took 150,000–200,000 tons per annum (*LRBAC* 31st December 1993 3).

In February 1994 hopes were high in Thailand that the Philippines would finalise a contract although these rumours had continued for weeks (*LRBAC* 28th February 1994 3). But then nothing was heard about the Philippines until May 1995 when it was reported from Thailand that there were rumours of sales to the Philippines of 75,000–80,000 tons of 35 per cent, some against fertiliser for payment, the rest being cash (*LRBAC* 31st May 1995 3). In Vietnam the government announced it would allow exports of 170,000 tons on government-to-government basis, including 30,000 tons to the Philippines (*LRBAC* 1st September 1993 4). In the United States there were rumours that the Philippines would soon be coming into the market to buy U.S. Dollars $10,000,000 (Ed. ten million) worth of rice under P.L.480 (*LRBAC* 1st December 1995 4). In Thailand, prices recovered due to the Philippines buying from the Thai government 150,000 tons of 25 per cent with an option for another 50,000 tons (*LRBAC* 2nd January 1996 4).

Then in February 199,6 the Philippines committed themselves to 884,000 tons for import, mainly made up of 25 per cent brokens divided between Vietnam 362,000 tons, China 225,000 tons, Thailand 150,000 tons, India 125,000 tons and the United States 20,000 tons (*LRBAC* 26th February 1996 1). (Ed. 20,000 tons unspecified). It was reported that there had been a steady increase in interest in rice from Pakistan, due partly to an increase in Indian prices, but particularly because of sales to the Philippines (*LRBAC* 26th February 1996 3). As previously noted, the Philippines had purchased 884,000 tons of 25 per cent (*LRBAC* 26th February 1996 3). From Thailand, it was reported that the major proportion of shipments so far in 1996 had been to the Philippines, Indonesia, Malaysia, China and Iran. There had been rumours of buying interest totalling 700,000 tons including a further 200,000 tons to the Philippines, but the *Circular* thought this unlikely in the near future (*LRBAC* 28th February 1996 3–4). From Vietnam, it was reported that it seemed most of their sales would be government to government, and also over the border into China. Their main sale was 262,000 tons to the Philippines (*LRBAC* 26th February 1996 4). Then it was noted that the Philippines would have received 450,000 tons by the end of April, and were not making new purchases (*LRBAC* 1st April 1996 3). This was supported by a report from Thailand that commitments were relatively small, mainly 150,000 tons for the Philippines expected to be shipped by the end of April (*LRBAC* 1st April 1996 3). However, although it had been thought the Philippines had finished purchasing for the year, it was reported they were in negotiation for another 100,000 tons of 25 per cent from Vietnam. Total rice purchased by the Philippines in 1996 was 884,500 tons of which 362,000 tons were from Vietnam, 225,000 tons from China, 150,000 tons from Thailand, 125,000 tons from India and 22,000 tons from the United States (Ed. 500 tons unspecified) (*LRBAC* 1st May 1996 2). In Vietnam, prices had dropped and Vietnam was now a very competitive supplier. There were rumours of negotiations for 100,000 tons with the Philippines (*LRBAC* 1st May 1996 3). From the Philippines, it was reported in June that new purchases from Vietnam had not been concluded, but it was thought they were in negotiation for 200,000 tons of 25 per cent (*LRBAC* 3rd June 1996 3). In Vietnam, prices were rising, but new offers were unavailable for brokens and 25 per cent, the unavailability of 25 per cent probably being due to the negotiations with the Philippines for this quality (*LRBAC* 3rd June 1994 4). From the Philippines, it was reported that new purchases from Vietnam had still not been concluded, although it seemed likely that they would be purchasing 200,000 tons in the near future (*LRBAC* 4th July 1996 3). In Vietnam, exports had been substantial in June and would continue on into July and August. There were unconfirmed reports of 150,000 tons of 25 per cent sold to the Philippines and 90,000 tons of 5 per cent sold to Iraq (*LRBAC* 4th July 1996 4). From the United States, it was reported there was a Philippines tender for 25,000 tons of U.S. No.2, 7 per cent brokens (Ed. *Sic*), shipment 7–27th August. Eventually, 21,000 tons were purchased. The price looked high compared to Far East prices, but was under a U.S. P.L.480 Title 1 allocation (*LRBAC* 5th August 1996 3–4). From Vietnam, there was still no confirmation of the sale of 25 per cent to the Philippines, or the 90,000 tons sale to Iraq, although Vietnam continued to be the cheapest origin (*LRBAC* 5th August 1996 4). At the beginning of September, there was still no sign of purchasing by the Philippines (*LRBAC* 3rd September 1996 3). In the United States, it was rumoured that new allocations of P.L.480 would be given to the Philippines allowing them to buy up to 26,000 tons of No.2, 7 per cent brokens (Ed. *Sic*) (*LRBAC* 3rd September 1996 3–4). But it did not seem that the Philippines would be purchasing any more rice before the New Year (*LRBAC* 3rd October 1996 1. *LRBAC* 3rd October 1996 3). At the beginning of November, neither the Philippines nor Indonesia were in the market (*LRBAC* 4th November 1996 1).

But in January 1997, the Philippines bought 50,000 tons from Thailand, and it was thought they would be buying up to 500,000 tons for shipment in the first half of the year (*LRBAC* 3rd February 1997 1). From Thailand, it was confirmed that the Philippines had bought 50,000 tons of 25–35 per cent for shipment in February/March, with a further 150,000 tons concluded subject to approval (*LRBAC* 3rd February 1997 3–4). At the beginning of March, the only sizeable new demand in the international rice trade was from the Philippines which had purchased 205,000 tons of 25 per cent from Thailand, and 100,000 tons from Vietnam with an option for a further 100,000 tons plus 100,000 tons of 25 per cent of optional origin, and yet another 100,000 tons at buyers' option. This was probably close to all they would need in the first half of 1997. In Vietnam, there had been little change in prices, although there were reports of considerable sales to the private trade in addition to those to the Philippines and possible demand from Iran (*LRBAC* 3rd March 1997 1). From Thailand, it was announced that the Philippines had indeed purchased 205,000 tons of 25 per cent for shipment from March to June (*LRBAC* 3rd March 1997 3). But at the start of April it was noted that the total the Philippines had purchased was up to 655,000 tons, and there were signs they still had more rice to buy (*LRBAC* 2nd April 1997 1). In Vietnam, it was reported that the Government had continued to protect their government-to-government relations, particularly to the Philippines, making it very difficult for private traders with commitments to these countries to cover them, and forcing them to pay higher prices or look for alternative origins. The ports had been busy mostly with shipments to the Philippines (*LRBAC* 2nd April 1997 4). Prices dropped in Vietnam as they came under pressure to sell from their large crop. This was not helped by them missing out on sales to the Philippines and Iran as a result of their policy of asking for higher prices to these destinations (*LRBAC* 2nd May 1997 1). From Pakistan, it was reported in May that there were only 4 vessels loading, with 3 due to start loading in the near future, 2 of which were for the Philippines (*LRBAC* 2nd May 1997 3). In Thailand, there were vessels loading 50,000 tons of 25 per cent for the Philippines (*LRBAC* 2nd May 1997 3). From Vietnam, it was reported that with the drop in prices there had been fairly high purchasing of 25 per cent and 35 per cent by traders for West Africa, and also quantities for the Philippines. Despite rumours of further enquiries from the Philippines, no further business appeared to have been done other than the covering of some old sales by traders. Of particular interest, there were large sales of broken rice at levels higher than the going rate of 25 per cent. This superficially looked attractive to sellers, but would pressure them to sell high quality rice resulting from the milling required to achieve the necessary quantity of brokens (*LRBAC* 2nd May 1997 4). In Thailand, activity during May included nine vessels loading 25 per cent for the Philippines (*LRBAC* 3rd June 1997 3). In June, the international market was very active, including heavy loading in Thailand for the Philippines, Iran and Niger, and large volumes shipped to West Africa from Vietnam (*LRBAC* 2nd July 1997 3). In Thailand, prices rose in June due to the continued heavy loading of 25 per cent for the Philippines, 100 per cent B for Iran and parboiled 100 per cent sortexed for Nigeria (*LRBAC* 2nd July 1997 3). Then the currency in Thailand was devalued by a further 10 per cent against the U.S. Dollar, causing export prices to fall and sending shock waves through the market. But fear of yet another fall made buyers nervous of making commitments. Other Asian economies also suffered big devaluations of their currencies and there were concerns this would reduce their purchasing power when imports were required. Countries affected included the Philippines, Indonesia and Malaysia. There was speculation that the Philippines would enter the market shortly, but Indonesia still had substantial stocks estimated at over 3,000,000 tons and was unlikely to import in the short term. Under the heading *El Nino* (in bold), the *Circular* went on to note that *El Nino* was a danger in many areas of the world, and could be worse than 1982/83, but the Philippines was not specifically mentioned (*LRBAC* 1st September 1997 1). In September, Thailand was the cheapest origin for nearly all grades. There had been a huge fall in prices because of the further fall in the value of the Baht against the U.S. Dollar. The Philippines, Indonesia and Malaysia were in the same predicament, and the effect on the rice market was falling prices and lack of confidence from buyers, meaning little business had been concluded. Prices in the local market quoted in Baht were firming up to take account of inflation, and the increased cost of imported material such as fertiliser and pesticides for the coming crop (*LRBAC* lst September 1997 3). A substantial purchase by the Philippines of about some 350,000 tons caused disappointment in Thailand as it received no direct business, and the same was true of Vietnam which did 100,000 tons but had hoped for more (*LRBAC* 3rd October 1997 1). The Philippines finally came into the market in the middle of September to buy 350,000 tons. It was thought the Vietnamese government had signed a contract for 100,000 tons, and the international trade through various government companies had a Memorandum of Understanding for a further 250,000 tons of 25 per cent for arrival in January/February 1998. Optional origins were thought to include Thailand, Vietnam, China and India. There were reports that a group of Pakistan exporters representing the Pakistan Government had concluded a further 45,000 tons, but this was surprising as earlier in the year Philippine inspectors had rejected Pakistan rice loading on 2 vessels due to poor quality (*LRBAC* 3rd October 1997 2). As noted, in this recent round of business by the Philippines, Thailand was unsuccessful in securing direct business (*LRBAC* 3rd October 1997 3). In Vietnam prices reached highs for 5 per cent double polished, and lower grades down to 25 per cent brokens. This was due to high water levels and high moisture rice in the second crop, and also indications that the Philippines were in the market to purchase a substantial quantity of rice. Vietnam had hoped to gain a large portion of this business but were only given 100,000 tons. It is not clear whether this contract had been signed and sealed or was just a Memorandum of Understanding (*LRBAC* 3rd October 1997 4). In November, there was a sharp jump in prices in the Far East, particularly Thailand, due to the entrance of Indonesia into the market as a buyer. There were real concerns the drought faced by Indonesia would lead to a substantially smaller crop than in recent years. It seemed certain Indonesia would need more than 2,000,000 tons but when they might buy the balance was not clear (*LRBAC* 4th December 1997 1) (Ed. The Philippines were not mentioned). In Thailand, prices were firmer and in mid-November Indonesian buyers entered the market covering over 400,000 tons. This seemed to include old and new import licences and many private buyers, instead of the usual government buyer. Traders were also covering substantial quantities to the Philippines of 25 per cent brokens concluded about 2 months previously. The Indonesian shipments were for December/January with emphasis on December, whereas the Philippines shipments were for arrival January/February/March (*LRBAC* 4th December 1997 2–3). Further purchases by Indonesia and the Philippines created excitement in December. Indonesia initially bought 1,000,000 tons, then sanctioned another 500,000 tons, bringing the total to 1,500,000 tons. The Philippines also purchased a further 200,000 tons with options for yet another 200,000 tons of which 100,000 tons plus 100,000 tons option was from the Vietnamese government. This brought the total purchased by the Philippines to 550,000–700,000 tons depending on whether all the options were included (*LRBAC* 6th January 1998 1). From the Philippines, it was reported that the Philippines government was discussing further purchases from Thailand of 150,000 tons of 25 per cent brokens (*LRBAC* 6th January 1998 3). In Vietnam, the government had recently sold unspecified amounts of rice to the Philippines and Indonesia (*LRBAC* 6th January 1998 4).

Demand continued strong in January 1998, and most exporting countries had high commitments, driven particularly by Indonesia and the Philippines (*LRBAC* 2nd February 1998 1). From Thailand, it was reported the Philippines, in negotiation with the Thai Government, had bought 100,000 tons of 5 per cent (Ed. Not the usual 25 per cent, but the price suggests it is correct). Shipment was March, April and May, with an option for a further 50,000 tons (*LRBAC* 2nd February 1998 2–3). The market was aware that demand this year was very high, with speculation that Indonesia needed upwards of 5,000,000 tons and recent reports from the Philippines indicated they intended to buy a further 600,000 tons from June onwards (*LRBAC* 4th March 1998 1). From Vietnam, it was reported that one substantial purchase was 100,000 tons for the Philippines, with 150,000 tons for Indonesia, all 5 per cent for shipment in March/April (*LRBAC* 4th March 1998 4) (Ed. Note 5 per cent, and again the price suggests it is correct). In Vietnam, the pressure on the market was immense as international traders pressed to get their vessels to load early to ensure they got their cargo. During March, approximately 70 vessels completed loading a total of 753,828 tons, the highest quantity shipped from Vietnam in 1 month. More than half was for Indonesia, the next largest destination being the Philippines. This left 25 vessels in port under loading, 4 vessels waiting for a berth or a cargo and 10 vessels to arrive shortly. These vessels were expected to load a further 441,000 tons (*LRBAC* 6th April 1998 4). International demand this year was enormous with the largest requirement coming from Indonesia. The Philippines was still a buyer and it was suggested that due to drought Malaysia would have to substantially increase its purchases (*LRBAC* 30th April 1998 1). In Vietnam, there had been an increase in May in vessels loading for destinations other than the Philippines and Indonesia, with 4 for the Philippines and 11 for Indonesia, plus 1 for Malaysia, 5 for Iraq, 1 for Iran, 5 for Africa, 1 for South America and 2 for Baltic ports (*LRBAC* 29th May 1998 4). But in June, up to 24th, only 12 vessels were completed in Vietnam, loading a total of 98,167 tons, including 5 for the Philippines, 1 for Indonesia, 1 for Brazil, 1 for Iraq, 1 for West Africa and 3 smaller vessels for Malaysia. There were a further 6 vessels in port expected to load another 65,600 tons, of which 3 were for the Philippines, 1 for Iraq, and 2 smaller vessels for Malaysia. Almost all shipments in the past month had been made by the Government through the Southern Food Company (*LRBAC* 3rd July 1998 4). From Cambodia, there were reports of a severe shortage of rice due to a poor harvest after recent drought conditions based on *El Nino* (*LRBAC* 31st July 1998 1). In Thailand, expectations of further sales to the Philippines and Indonesia kept prices firmer, particularly for 25 per cent. Negotiations were still taking place between the Thai government and the Philippines government on a possible sale of 100,000 tons, and an offer had been made which was valid for a reply on 15th August (*LRBAC* 31st July 1998 3–4). In Vietnam, during July, there were seven vessels for the Philippines, four for Malaysia, two for Indonesia, one for Iraq and one for South America. There were three vessels in port to load another 23,239 tons, 1 for the Philippines, 1 for Indonesia and 1 for Iraq (*LRBAC* 31st July 1998 4). The weather patterns in the Far East continued to be of great concern. Flooding in China was highlighted in the news in August, and fears had been voiced that the seasonal flooding in Bangladesh had lasted longer than usual causing severe economic problems and concerns for the rice crop. The flooding in China was expected to result in a substantial reduction in the size of the rice crop there, although reports that China would have to buy huge quantities of rice seemed overdone. Vietnam was also suffering from the weather, and had stopped selling and did not expect to re-enter the market as a seller until 1999 (*LRBAC* 28th

August 1998 1). From Vietnam, it was reported that the Government had continued to try to make government-to-government sales to both the Philippines and Indonesia at the end of September. Any private sales by Vietnamese companies to the Philippines, Indonesia, Malaysia, Iran and Iraq had to have prior approval, and the price had to be higher than sales on government-to-government business. In August, the Vietnamese had loaded 12 vessels with 118,635 tons, the biggest share destined for the Philippines. In September up to the 25th, a total of 15 vessels had completed loading 152,815 tons, 3 for the Philippines, 6 for Indonesia, 3 for Iraq, 1 for Eastern Europe, 1 for East Africa and 1 for Brazil (*LRBAC* 2nd October 1998 4). World rice import demand was forecast to reach a record 26,750,000 tons in 1998 but expected to decline in 1999 by 3,000,000–7,000,000 tons, the main reductions coming from the Philippines, Indonesia, Bangladesh and Brazil. This still indicated a substantial international trade in rice, but closer to the quantities traded in 1996 and 1997 (*LRBAC* 6th November 1998 1). In Vietnam, planting over most of the Mekong Delta was underway in November and weather conditions were favourable, as various tropical storms had missed Vietnam and tracked to the northeast over the Philippines and on into China (*LRBAC* 6th November 1998 4). From Pakistan, it was reported that to the surprise of many the long talked about tenders for the Philippines and Indonesia had finally materialised, but not quite as expected. The largest was for Indonesia. The second smaller one for the Philippines of 30,000–40,000 tons, came after an announcement that the Philippines would relax their requirements on paddy content in white rice. Offers were requested by the TCP (Trade Corporation of Pakistan) for shipment December/January in jute bags for 15 per cent and 25 per cent. The premium for jute bags over polypropylene bags was approximately U.S. Dollars $9 per ton. No results were announced for the tender. So the market remained confused, with two substantial tenders pending and no idea if either would materialise (*LRBAC* 7th December 1998 2–3). From Vietnam, it was reported that November shipments would total about 160,000 tons, bringing the total exported in 1998 to 3,180,000 tons. In November, 18 vessels were loaded of which 12 were destined for Indonesia, 2 for Malaysia, 3 for Iraq, and 1 for Japan, but none for the Philippines. In December, there were 10 vessels in port to load 100,000 tons. Destinations were more varied, with 1 for the Philippines, 3 for Indonesia, 1 for Malaysia, 1 for Japan, 2 for Iraq and 2 for West Africa (*LRBAC* 7th December 1998 4). In Thailand, shipments in December were mainly 300,000 tons to the Philippines and Indonesia and about 120,000 tons of parboiled to Nigeria. The Nigerian business could well continue, although Thai prices were now high compared to India, but business to the Philippines and Indonesia might easily go to Vietnam, where prices were substantially lower. Already a tranche had gone to Pakistan (*LRBAC* 4th January 1999 3). The main destinations from Vietnam in December were again the Philippines and Indonesia (*LRBAC* 4th January 1999 4).

There was no more news until the beginning of March, when it was reported that there were 8 vessels in port in Vietnam to load about 102,891 tons for destinations including the Philippines, Iraq, Syria, West Africa and Northern Europe (*LRBAC* 3rd March 1999 4). The largest buyer from Vietnam in March was the Philippines, but this contract was coming to an end (*LRBAC* 6th April 1999 4). Once again the

Asian markets were being affected by bad weather, and with the recent *El Nino* in people's minds, many were saying the heavy rain in Vietnam and Thailand was the result of *La Nina* (*LRBAC* lst June 1999 1). In Vietnam, there were rumours of potential purchases by the Philippines and Indonesia, but nothing had yet materialised (*LRBAC* 9th July 1999 4). In the United States, P.L.480 allocations had been reviewed with a doubling of the quantity for the Philippines to 40,000 tons. There had been very few tenders for these allocations and of the total 300,000 tons only 63,000 tons had been taken up (*LRBAC* 3rd August 1999 3–4). During the first half of August, heavy rains took their toll on many countries in the Far East. Flooding in the Philippines and Korea was very severe, and there was flooding in China and Vietnam, but that in China was probably overstated by the press (*LRBAC* 26th August 1999 1). In the United States, it was announced that the Government Food Aid Programme was critical to U.S. exports and activity in August centred on a number of tenders which added needed support to the U.S. milled rice export situation. Further tenders were announced towards the end of August under the P.L.480 programme, including one for the Philippines for 40.000 tons of long grain 2/4 (Ed. No.2 Grade 4) for shipment no later than the second half of December (*LRBAC* 26th August 1999 4). There was then no news until December when it was reported from Thailand that currently demand was for high-quality Thai rice such as 100 per cent B for Iran and 5 per cent for Indonesia. This was in sharp contrast to the last couple of years when shipments to the Philippines and Indonesia had meant high demand for 25 per cent brokens. As a result, the high qualities were holding their prices, whilst prices for low quality 25 per cent and broken rice had fallen sharply (*LRBAC* 3rd December 1999 3).

Reference

Andrews, John (2002) *Pocket Asia*, London: The Economist-Profile Books Ltd.

Conclusion

In the new millennium, the intra-Asian rice trade continued much as it had in the 1990s, mercifully with no *El Nino*/Southern Oscillation (*EN*SO) events for some years. Myanmar continued to be a minor contributor, but Vietnam increased its exports almost vying with Thailand, which itself expanded exports substantially. Meanwhile, Indonesia became increasingly self-sufficient in rice. But the Philippines in contrast became more import-dependent. Then disaster struck. In 2010, there was yet another *EN*SO event causing the usual havoc and substantially increasing imports to both Indonesia and the Philippines. But this is another story.

DOI: 10.4324/9781003492917-8

Index

Note: – Page references in **bold** for tables.

FSC
www.fsc.org
MIX
Papier | Fördert
gute Waldnutzung
FSC® C083411

Kolibri 360 GmbH
Ferdinand-Jühlke-Straße 7
99095 Erfurt, Deutschland
produktsicherheit@kolibri360.de